BLOOMING FLOWERS

Kasia Boddy is Professor of American Lite
Her other books include *Boxing: A Cultu
Since 1950* and *Geranium*.

T0021920

Further praise for *Blooming Flowers*:

'There is no doubt that anyone perusing the pages will view afresh the blooming flowers in their garden … A compelling, contextualising tapestry written with both vivacity and analytical rigour.' Chris Beardshaw, garden designer and broadcaster

'Dr Kasia Boddy, who lectures on American literature at Fitzwilliam College Cambridge, has written a book that not only displays her intricate knowledge of literature worldwide, politics and religion but also ecology, weather and above all botany. There is something of interest for everyone, and it is charmingly illustrated too.' Margaret Barrie, *Flora Magazine*

'A book to dip into little and often, which serves up a year's worth of intellectual stimulation, sensual pleasure and high-brow, pub-quiz trivia.' Jodie Jones, *Gardens Illustrated*

'Fresh and novel in its approach … Boddy's deeply individualistic assemblage will appeal to gardeners and literature lovers alike.' *Publishers Weekly*

'Unlike any book I have read on flowers. We get a superb range of cultural information and imagery from ancient times right through to the very modern, and from all parts of the world. Fascinating.' Margaret Willes, author of *The Gardens of the British Working Class*

'*Blooming Flowers* is a gorgeously lush evocation of twelve different flowers, each one steeped in its own stories, cultural associations and botanical wonder. It is not just a sunny celebration of everything floral – we learn how intimately flowers are entwined with global warming, transatlantic slavery, US imperialism

and nuclear radioactivity – but this is a beautifully written book, full of exquisite detail, startling facts and laced with just the right amount of poetry.'
Peter Fiennes, author of *Oak and Ash and Thorn*

'This illustrated guide unearths the history and influence of iconic flowers from across the globe, from spring daffodils to autumn chrysanthemums.'
Sophie Hannam and Caroline Wheater, *Home & Antiques*

BLOOMING
FLOWERS

A SEASONAL HISTORY OF
PLANTS AND PEOPLE

KASIA BODDY

YALE UNIVERSITY PRESS
NEW HAVEN AND LONDON

For information about this and other Yale University Press publications, please contact:
U.S. Office: sales.press@yale.edu   yalebooks.com
Europe Office: sales@yaleup.co.uk   yalebooks.co.uk

Set in Adobe Garamond Pro by IDSUK (DataConnection) Ltd
Printed in Slovenia by DZS-Grafik d.o.o.

Library of Congress Control Number: 2020932727

ISBN 978-0-300-24333-8 (hbk)
ISBN 978-0-300-26479-1 (pbk)

A catalogue record for this book is available from the British Library.

10 9 8 7 6 5 4 3 2 1

For Adele Wirszubska Boddy
and remembering Francis Andrew Boddy

This is a world where there are flowers.

Henry David Thoreau

Contents

Gathering Flowers

In 2012, the *North American Journal of Psychology* reported that male hitchhikers who carried flowers were more likely to be offered a lift. That makes sense to me. If a man has murder on his mind, he doesn't stop to pick up peonies first. But the researchers thought that something more was at stake, something more positive: we invite people bearing blooms into our cars, they said, because flowers are an 'inducer' of powerful emotions. This book is about those powerful emotions.

Sometimes it's a particular combination of colour and form that catches the eye: the dark blue of an agapanthus, the symmetry of a sunflower, the perfect globe of an allium, the elegant spike of a foxglove. Flowers provide us with a continuing aesthetic education, but we also look at them from the vantage point of the education we've already had. Daffodils made D.H. Lawrence think of 'ruffled birds on their perches'; yellow cabs reminded Frederick Seidel of daffodils. John Ruskin brought a fine-tuned sensibility to bear when declaring a bunch of anemones 'marvellous in their exquisitely nervous trembling and veining of colour – violin playing in scarlet on a white ground'. James Schuyler, a curator at New York's Museum of Modern Art as well as a poet, couldn't 'get over' the beauty that met him at five o'clock 'on the day before March first', 1954, when he saw the green leaves and pink flowers of the tulips on his desk against the backdrop of a setting Manhattan sun.

But it's not all looks. Sometimes, it's the fragrance: what Francis Bacon called the 'breath of flowers'. A fugitive whiff of jasmine creeping over a neighbour's fence; a sudden hit of thyme when we brush against the plant with bare summer feet; the heady inhalation of a musk rose. Sadly, an alluring fragrance is low down on most plant breeders' lists. Cultivated flowers are selected for size, colour, and, most of all, durability and suitability as freight. Nevertheless, florists report that the first thing customers do when they enter a store is bend over the blooms in search of scent.

Beyond the sensory hits, we also love flowers because of the density of associations that have grown up around them over the centuries, and that have been passed down to us in legends, histories, proverbs, poems, paintings, and wallpaper prints. Flowers live in our cultures as well as in nature. Girls are named for Lily, Saffron, Poppy, Rose and Daisy, but we also like to joke about a flower's botanical Latin nomenclature. The novelist Eudora Welty belonged to a club of night-blooming-cacti fanciers whose motto was 'Don't take it cereus, life's too mysterious'.

Flowering plants mark birth, death and almost every significant occasion in between. It's not surprising then that they inhabit our earliest and deepest memories: making daisy chains in the park; being told off for picking next door's tulips; planting sunflower seeds then watching them grow, it seemed, as high as the sky. And the flowers don't even have to be real. For Virginia Woolf, it was anemones, 'red and purple flowers on a black ground – my mother's dress; and she was sitting either in a train or in an omnibus, and I was on her lap. I therefore saw the flowers she was wearing very close; and can still see purple and red and blue, I think, against the black.'

Perfumes offer to recreate these kinds of moments, even if the flowers they evoke smell completely different. Creating a perfume called 'Daisy', Marc Jacobs wanted to evoke 'a friendly flower, not precious, not exotic' but, since daisies don't have much scent, he used jasmine. And jasmine is also an ingredient, along with bergamot and pink pepper, in Acqua di Parma's 'Sakura', designed to evoke the 'spectacle' (if not the scent) of 'blossoming cherry trees'.

Woman with a garland of flowers, *c.* **1910–20.**

One reason we love flowers is because they help us talk to each other about the big and small questions of life: about love, death, class, fashion, the weather, art, disease, an allegiance to a nation, religion or political cause, the challenges of space and the passage of time. Flowers are one of the most ancient of mediums through which we communicate. We send them, or their representations, to announce romantic intentions, convey condolences or proffer apologies.

Flowers play a part in public health campaigns and in the remembrance of, and opposition to, war. Laura Dowling recently wrote a memoir of conducting 'floral diplomacy' for the Obama administration. Beyond the White House, the carnation has spoken of revolution in Russia and Portugal, while saffron now tells the tale of Hindu nationalism in India. Protestants and Catholics in Ireland each have their own lily. In China, the sunflower generation is still coming to terms with Mao's legacy. All of these stories feature here.

A book about people and plants is also a book about greetings cards, badges, proverbs, lamps, songs, photographs, medicine, movies, politics, religion and food. It's about painting and plays, poetry and novels – for these are places where the myriad meanings of flowers are explored, challenged and reworked. And the metaphorical traffic is two-way. Almost since books were invented, they have been compared to walled gardens, garlands and bouquets, especially when they bring together disparate material. The word 'anthology', which originally meant a gathering (*legein*) of flowers (*anthos*), highlighted the fact that what was offered was a particular, even an artful, selection.

Blooming Flowers follows in this tradition, gathering together sixteen very different plants – garden and florists' favourites alongside agricultural crops. There are annuals and perennials, shrubs and trees. I have not tried to represent a different genus with each plant, in fact a quarter of the book explores members of the large Asteraceae (daisy) family, or even to highlight flowers of different colours – there's a lot of yellow in here! But variety enters in different ways. Some are wild flowers with ancient associations; other plants rose to prominence with the spread of empire, or are the products of recent industrial floriculture. The result is what the florists call a mixed bunch. My sixteen would struggle to inhabit the same vase – the saffron crocus is only inches high and almond blossom grows on trees – but in a book (and this is one of the great advantages of books), they can sit side by side. And while I can't promise that my prose will be as colourful and fragrant (as 'flowery') as the average bouquet, I hope it will last a little longer.

Jacques-Laurent Agasse, *Studies of Flowers*, 1848.

Some of the most fundamental floral associations concern enduring philosophical questions: appearance and reality, life and death, the nature of time. For many moralists, flowers exist primarily to instruct us that our eyes deceive us, and that beauty, in any case, won't last. The Old Testament lesson that 'the flower fadeth: but the word of our God shall stand forever' is insistently repeated. Poets remind us that 'this same flower that smiles today / Tomorrow will be dying' (Robert Herrick), and that the 'primrose way' leads to 'th'everlasting bonfire' (the Porter in Shakespeare's *Macbeth*). Hendrick Goltzius's sixteenth-century portrait of a young man holding two flowers – one of which looks like a dandelion 'clock' dispersing its seeds – hammers home the point by adding the Latin motto *sic transit Gloria mundi*. A recent reworking of the theme can be found in Anya Gallaccio's *Red on Green*

Detail of Hendrick Goltzius, *A Young Man with Flowers in His Hand*, 1582.

Detail of Anya Gallaccio, *Red on Green*, 2012.

which consists of a neat rectangle of 10,000 red roses whose stems have been cut off; the flower heads are laid on a bed of thorns and left to rot. Working more than four hundred years after Goltzius, Gallaccio is less interested in the transience of life than that of art, and of roses themselves, vast quantities of which are transported thousands of miles only to be thrown away after a few more days. In 2017, 4 billion flowers were airfreighted from Colombia to the United States.

The rose has considerable form in the discussion of ephemerality. Aesop even staged a debate between a rose and an amaranth (although it's unlikely that he meant the plant we know by this name). When the amaranth compliments the rose on its beauty, the rose reminds its neighbour that 'even if no one plucks me, I die, while you are able to blossom and bloom with eternal youth'. Aesop is on the side of the amaranth, whose flowers retain their colour after being cut and dried. Surely eternity is better than brief glory? Others are not so sure. I have included flowers from both sides of the argument – the short-lived roses and poppies that remind us that loss is inevitable, and the stalwart carnations and chrysanthemums that encourage us, nevertheless, to keep going.

The meaning of flowers in general, and of any particular flower, is always relative; that is, it only emerges through some kind of contrast. A violet is small (and 'shy') compared to a sunflower that's tall (and 'bold'); a field daisy is 'natural' compared to a hothouse orchid; an orchid is natural compared to a wire and silk rose; an imported plant is 'exotic' until (like the Mexican marigold in India or the South African pelargonium in Europe) it's been around for a while, and then it becomes an honorary native. In *Uncle Tom's Cabin* (1852), Harriet Beecher Stowe makes a clear distinction between the 'voluptuous' New Orleans courtyard of slave owner Augustine St Clare – filled with 'the choicest flowering plants of the tropics' including 'dark-leaved Arabian jessamines' – and the 'neat garden-patch' filled with 'brilliant annuals' that surrounds Uncle Tom's iconic slave cabin. While St Clare's 'luxuriant' (that is, imported and cultivated) roses strain 'beneath their heavy abundance of flowers', Tom's 'native multiflora rose' scrambles energetically over a pile of logs. Stowe's message couldn't be clearer.

While it's useful to understand what one rose rather than another signifies, or what it means to display a white rather than an orange lily – codes that the relevant chapters of this book will crack – the longer such conventions exist, the greater is the temptation to shake them up a little. Enough with the darling buds of May, we say, give us some of D.H. Lawrence's 'pure flowers of dark corruption'. Just seven years after *Uncle Tom's Cabin* became a global bestseller, Charles Baudelaire published *Les Fleurs du mal* as a direct challenge to nineteenth-century floral pieties. A typical poem in the collection begins with the speaker reminding his lover of a beautiful summer morning walk in the fields when she almost fainted. A familiar scenario, then . . . until we learn that the near-swoon was caused by the sun's exposure of a *carcasse superbe / Comme une fleur s'apanouir,* a magnificent rotten corpse blooming like a flower. 'You want a *memento mori*?' Baudelaire asks: the meadows have it.

Over the centuries, much of the accumulated burden of floral association has been placed on women: whether they are virgins in bud or whether, like Emily Dickinson's harebells, they have loosened their girdles to welcome 'the lover Bee'. Women's eyes are violets, their cheeks lilies, their lips roses, and their thighs lotus blossoms. During the eighteenth century 'botanising' in the wild came to be thought of as the perfect exercise for the minds and bodies of 'ladies', although digging and planting in the garden was best left to 'a stout, active girl'. In one of the earliest garden advice books, from 1839, Louisa Johnson suggested that those ladies who insisted on getting their fingers dirty should opt for a raised bed since 'many females are unequal to the fatigue of bending down to flowers'.

Told for centuries that they resemble flowers in their passive beauty and fragility, many women have adopted and adapted the floral medium to their own ends. We can find this defiance in the appropriation of the conventionally timid violet by the British Suffragettes, and in the poet Marianne Moore's instruction to a rose that her beauty is a 'liability rather than / an asset' and that she should acknowledge that her thorns are 'the best part'. At the height of the Black Arts Movement, Gwendolyn Brooks celebrated the 'furious flower' that lifted 'its face / All unashamed', while Alice Walker hailed 'revolutionary petunias'. More recently, Rita Dove has sung the praises of evening primroses that 'blaze / all night long / for no one', while Rupi Kaur recommends that women emulate sunflowers who 'choose to live / Their brightest lives'.

What constitutes a bright life is a question that flowers seem well placed to answer, for they are generally understood as ornaments rather than necessities. When Romantics like Ralph Waldo Emerson argue that 'a ray of beauty outvalues all the utilities in the world', utilitarians reply that we can't eat flowers. Franklin D. Roosevelt said exactly that during the 1936 Presidential campaign – mainly because his Republican opponent, Alf Landon, was Governor of Kansas, the sunflower state. Convinced that Roosevelt and the New Deal would keep them fed, American voters re-elected him with a landslide. Of course, the irony is that you *can* eat sunflowers. Indeed, we eat many things that derive from flowering plants. This book alone includes food stuffs that derive from a flower's seed (almond), fruit (rosehip, sunflower), stem and rhizome (lotus), and even its stigma (saffron).

Perhaps the real issue is access to luxury. It's certainly true that no culture ever planted a pleasure garden until its basic agricultural needs had been met. For thousands of years, growing flowers (rather than, say, picking them in the woods) was an extravagance of the rich, for only they could afford the necessary land and labour. As the anthropologist Jack Goody has shown, the modern 'culture of flowers' is largely a product of the development of urban, commercial culture and, with it, the growing power of the middle-class, and eventually working-class, consumer. Flowers gradually came to be associated with more or less affordable luxury. It was a revolutionary idea.

In 1910 Helen Todd, a Chicago factory inspector, made a case for women's suffrage by arguing that 'woman is the mothering element in the world, and her vote will go toward helping forward the time when life's Bread, which is home, shelter and security, and the Roses of life, music, education, nature and books, shall be the heritage of every child that is born in the country, in the government of which she has a voice.' The following year James Oppenheim published a poem which turned this argument into a rallying cry: 'Yes, it is bread we fight for – but we fight for roses, too!' That cry, in various musical settings and in the service of a variety of causes, has never really gone away. The point is clear: people shouldn't have to choose between bread and roses, or dumplings and cherry-blossoms (as a popular Japanese saying has it) or, in the language of Dickens's *Hard Times*, between facts and walking 'upon flowers in carpets'. Can't we have both? Don't we need both?

During the Second World War, when government instructed everyone to 'Dig for Victory' and plant vegetables, the British gardening press lobbied for flowers to stay. One seed catalogue reminded purchasers that flowers were important for 'brightening' both their homes and their 'mental outlook' – tending a few nasturtiums or marigolds wouldn't take up much space and tending them would be 'soothing on the nerves'.

The original version of this argument is ancient: it is sometimes attributed to the prophet Muhammad and sometimes to the Greek physician Galen. One of them is said to have declared that 'He who has two cakes of bread, let him dispose of one of them for some flowers of narcissus; for bread is the food of the body, and the narcissus is the food of the soul.' Other versions substitute a hyacinth or a lily but, by 1910, the rose, especially in its long-stemmed 'American Beauty' incarnation, was the ultimate luxury flower. The sociologist Thorstein Veblen, famous for coining phrases like 'conspicuous consumption' and 'trophy' wife, categorised such flowers (along with other examples of 'pecuniary beauty' like Angora cats and pristine lawns) as mere 'marks of expensiveness'. But the cultivation of this long-stemmed rose also provided a convenient metaphor for the workings of corporate capitalism more broadly. In 1904, John D. Rockefeller Jr, son of the founder of Standard Oil, famously drew an analogy between the 'growth of a large business' such as his own, and that of the American Beauty rose. The 'splendor' of both was 'merely a survival of the fittest', 'the working out of a law of nature and a law of God'. The comparison quickly became notorious and caricatures began to appear of Rockefeller pruning and 'sacrificing the early buds' (depicted as tiny skulls).

The cultivation and appreciation of flowers has long been cited as evidence that working people have feelings; that, as Claude McKay put it, 'a man-machine toil-tired / May crave beauty too – though he's hired'. D.H. Lawrence pointed out that many Nottinghamshire colliers looked at the flowers in their back gardens with 'that odd, remote sort of contemplation which shows a *real* awareness of the presence of beauty'. They were not admiring or delighting in the flowers, Lawrence insisted, but properly, disinterestedly, contemplating them which, he concluded, 'shows the incipient artist'.

Gardening as 'incipient' art was also Alice Walker's theme in a 1974 essay, 'In Search of Our Mothers' Gardens', about the limited outlets available for the 'creative black woman' of her great-grandmothers', grandmothers' and mother's generations. Walker celebrated the 'creativity' they brought to everyday activities: quilting, singing and, most of all, gardening. She writes movingly of her mother's garden 'so brilliant with colours, so original in its design, so magnificent with life and creativity' that strangers drove by 'to stand or walk among my mother's art'.

Guy Spencer's caricature of John D. Rockefeller Jr and an American Rose appeared in *The Commoner* in April 1905.

Walker grew up in Georgia, some years later than, but not too far from, another black Southern novelist, Richard Wright. The Mississippi Delta of Wright's youth was also a beautiful place, where the apple buds 'laugh[ed] into blossom' and the scent of magnolia filled the summer air. But, unlike Walker, McKay or Lawrence, Wright struggled to see how this elegantly varying seasonal scene could give rise to authentic art. He took the point of view of the Mississippi sharecroppers 'toiling from sun to sun', day on day, for whom the cycle of the year and its flowers meant nothing: 'Whether in spring or summer or autumn or winter, time slips past us remorselessly.'

Depending on where and how we live, we divide up the year in different ways. Seasons are most important to those whose livelihood depends on when they plant seeds, gather hay, and harvest corn. Which flowers were in bloom, as well as the weather, on a particular saint's day was often thought to provide an indication of the year to come. Snowdrops should be plentiful at Candlemas (2 February); crocuses on St Valentine's Day (14 February). Seasonal change is, fundamentally, a matter of light. Seasonal rhythm reflects the position of the earth in relation to the sun over the course of its year-long circumvention. The year is hinged by two solstices, the longest and shortest day, and two equinoxes, where daylight and night are equal. A meteorological calendar is simpler still: four seasons, each lasting exactly three months. Some degree of variability enters when we factor in regularly occurring natural phenomena such as monsoons or hurricanes – or if we measure the seasons ecologically, marking the start of spring, for example, by the appearance of the first snowdrop or cuckoo. But it does all, of course, depend on where you are in the world.

In many places the idea of four distinct seasons makes little sense. In India, for example, it is more useful to think of six seasons, each covering two lunar months, while in Egypt, there are three, based on the annual flooding of the Nile. John Muir pointed out that there were only two seasons in California's Central Valley, spring and summer: November marks the beginning of spring, a season of 'wonderful flowery vegetation', but by the end of May, 'it is dead and dry and crisp, as if every plant had been roasted in an oven'. The Caribbean also experiences two seasons, which the poet Derek Walcott thought represented the 'direct, dualistic force of drought and rain'. Walcott complained that Europeans, 'who see this climate as seasonless and without subtlety', consequently view West Indians as existing 'without the possibility of art'. But he also noted that West Indians themselves, 'brought up on Odes to the Seasons', and trained to believe that the best art emerges from a 'climate of evanescence' and 'dissolution', find it 'hard not to fear' that their 'hard-edged visions' are 'primal and basic and barbarous as ABC and the three primary colours'. I'll have more to say about these anxieties in the chapter on the daffodil, when I consider the response of Caribbean writers to spring and to Wordsworth.

This book is structured according to the four seasons, largely because that's the pattern that, growing up in Britain, I have always known. Many of the flowers included here represent the seasons in which they occur naturally and familiarly in the temperate northern hemisphere – the snowdrop in late winter, the sunflower in summer, and the chrysanthemum in autumn. But we have to acknowledge both that the long process of industrialisation and urban development has often been felt as a loss of connection with natural seasonal rhythms, and that modern floricultural practices have introduced a whole range of new rhythms, new ways of marking the passage of time. Since the late nineteenth century, glasshouse cultivation has resulted in the year-round availability of chrysanthemums, carnations, roses and many other flowers, and it's easy to forget that they once had a 'season'.

Moreover, new cultural traditions have emerged, even among modern city dwellers who can eat peaches and buy tulips every day of the year: traditions that encourage us to associate particular flowers with specific occasions rather than with the time of their blooming – roses for Valentine's Day, carnations for May Day, and so on. And there are other reasons why a flower might take on a new seasonal identity. The association of the First World War with the corn poppy, for example, has given the early summer bloom a second (artificial) flowering in November. Moreover, as climate change produces 'season creep' – nudging the northern climate towards a more southern pattern of two long seasons with short transitions – the four-part structure of this book may itself come to seem like an historical artefact.

DAISY

LILY

SPRING

DAFFODIL

CARNATION

Spring

It's a spring song!
I've been waiting long
For a spring song . . .

Langston Hughes, 'Earth Song'

Please Lord of Springtime,
Bring her and me together.
I'll bring you flowers.

'A Small Request', from *Indian Love Poems*

And so it begins again. The hint of a green leaf, the slow swell of a bud, the ever so gradually lengthening day, and then, suddenly, the tentativeness gives way to something more definite: the 'bustlings, strainings, united thrusts, and pulls-all-together' that Thomas Hardy described in *Far from the Madding Crowd*. The advance of the buds is underway, and it's all that the gardener, and the writer, can do to keep up. Snowdrop, aconite, crocus, omphalodes, primrose, anemone, tulip, hyacinth, violet, daffodil. The story of the spring is always the same – it's 'all in a rush / With richness,' said Gerard Manley Hopkins – but everywhere, and every year, it's a wonderful surprise.

The **daisy** is one of the true harbingers of the year's newness; it's only spring, the proverb says, when seven, twelve, nineteen (the exact number varies considerably) daisies emerge to 'kiss our feet'. If flowers are generally imagined as women, daisies are the sweet young girls of the year: except, that is, when they're not.

The sexual politics of spring's arrival are difficult. Ovid imagines it a kind of rape with a happy ending: the nymph Chloris is seized by Zephyr, god of the wind, and then, as she metamorphoses into the goddess Flora, flowers spill from her mouth. Zephyr 'made up' for the violation, says Flora, 'by giving me the name of bride, and I have no complaints in the marriage-bed'. He also gave her a dowry of perpetual spring ('always the year is full of bloom') and 'control of the flowers'. But control is perhaps not quite the right word. 'Often I've wanted to count the colours arranged there,' she explains, 'and not been able: the profusion was too great for the counting.'

In places like Britain and Japan, where the seasons are pronounced, poets, painters and song-writers have always welcomed spring flowers as heralds of what is not merely another season but the springing of their own imaginations into a whole new cycle of life. In Britain – and the English-speaking world more generally – no flower has prompted more imaginative reflection than the **daffodil**, largely in its role as Wordsworth's flower. It can be hard to comprehend what all the fuss is about if you live in Kingston, Jamaica or even Aberdeen, Scotland. 'People in these parts did not use the word "spring" ,' reflects Janet, the protagonist of Elspeth Barker's novel *O Caledonia*. 'They said "the end of winter" or "the beginning of summer" . . . winter ebbed into summer, there seemed no transitional period, none of the joyous awakening so welcomed by verse and song.'

Even in southern England itself, one might be sceptical about the burden of seasonal expectation. One sunny day, D.H. Lawrence's Lady Chatterley takes her husband Sir Clifford out in his bath-chair to see the woodland flowers. They've been arguing – Clifford insisting on the 'absolute' gulf between 'the ruling and the serving classes'; Connie, who's having an affair with the gamekeeper, disagreeing – when suddenly he notices the bluebells, hyacinths and forget-me-nots. 'What is *quite* so lovely as an English spring!' he exclaims. Does this point to a floral reconciliation? Not in the least, for Connie silently seethes, 'it sounded as if even spring bloomed by act of Parliament. An English spring! Why not an Irish one, or Jewish!'

Spring is not only the great transformer; it's also, notes Ali Smith, 'the great connective' – between times and places and people. ''S wonderful, 's marvellous', according to George and Ira Gershwin: a glamorous, amorous, 'four-leaf clover time'. In Connie's case, the connections are all with the gamekeeper (see **Summer**). For those left behind and unconnected, like Clifford, the only place to go – to quote another jazz standard – is up 'on the shelf with last year's Easter bonnets', 'praying for snow to hide the clover'. Of all the seasons in which to be broken-hearted, 'spring can really hang you up the most'.

The nineteenth-century sociologist Émile Durkheim observed that, contrary to what we might expect, spring is the time when the suicide rate rises – and precisely because 'everything begins to awake; activity is resumed, relations spring up, interchanges increase.' Ali Smith reminds us that the word 'April' comes 'from the Latin *aperire*, to open, to uncover, to make accessible, or to remove whatever stops something from being accessible.' But when there's nothing new to open up to, when we can't shake off the fetters of winter or access 'all this juice and all this joy', then a special kind of gloom sets in. Perhaps it has something to do with spring's peculiar combination of calendar regularity and absolute brand-newness. 'Will the world ever be so decayed that spring may not renew its greenness?' asked Nathaniel Hawthorne. Well, yes, sometimes irretrievably decayed is exactly how it feels.

'Winter is come and gone,' wrote Shelley, mourning Keats, 'But grief returns with the revolving year.' And for others, the mere passage of time is unwelcome. 'Perchance as we grow old,' wrote Thoreau a few months before his thirty-fifth birthday, 'we cease to spring with the spring'; perhaps 'our winters never break up.' Only the young can be such miserabilists. W.D. Snodgrass was also in his early thirties when spring blossoms landing in his hair prompted the sole thought that 'the trees and I will soon be bare.' Even at twenty, A.E. Housman's Shropshire Lad can't help counting the springs he has left. Assuming 'three scoreyears and ten', he realises 'that only leaves me fifty more.'

And since to look at things in bloom
Fifty springs are little room,
About the woodlands I will go
To see the cherry hung with snow.

Among the many young men who carried a copy of *A Shropshire Lad* to the front during the First World War was George Butterworth, who set this and several other Housman poems to music. Butterworth was thirty-one when he was shot by a sniper on 5 August 1916, one of a million young men to be wounded or killed in the Battle of the Somme.

Autumn is the time that floral festivals honour the dead; in spring, they rejoice in the living. This is an ancient and almost universal practice. Today, however, many spring festivals rely on commercially grown flowers that don't naturally belong to the season but have come to be associated with its celebrations. The marigold – a Mexican flower that is included in the Autumn section because of its centrality to that country's Day of the Dead – is also the flower of the Hindu spring festival of Holī. The flower that most Americans buy at Easter is a variety of **lily** from Japan; in other places, it's a calla or arum from South Africa (where its natural flowering season begins in August). Hopes for renewal can be social and political as well as personal or religious, and the final flower in this section is the emblem of May Day rallies all over the world – the red **carnation**, another summer flower that, due to glasshouse cultivation, is coaxed to flower early and so to join the spring song.

Daisy

Does Robert Burns's 'wee, modest crimson-tipped' daisy (*Bellis perennis*) really need an introduction? Its adjectives are sweet, homely, unassuming, humble, meek and plebeian. Elizabeth Kent thought it 'the *robin* of flowers'; John Clare welcomed it each year as his 'old Maytey'. The fact that the daisy grows in so many places – native to western, central and northern Europe, it has naturalised in most temperate regions including the Americas and Australasia – makes it either the most democratic of flowers or a common weed, depending on your point of view.

The daisy's far from solitary habit, meanwhile, seems to be the trait that earned it a place in the Victorian language of flowers, even though it had nothing to say but 'I share your sentiments'. Lewis Carroll satirised the sentimental moralising of this popular game – his flowers don't offer silent signals, they actually speak – but even he kept the familiar class associations. When daisies make an appearance in *Alice Through the Looking Glass*, it's not as Wordsworth's 'starry multitude' but as a noisy crowd. One 'shrill little' daisy voice is hard enough to bear, but it's their bad habit of all speaking at the same time that vexes the languid Tiger-lily (who only joins in 'when there's anybody worth talking to'). Eventually the imperious Alice stoops down and says threateningly, 'If you don't hold your tongues, I'll pick you!'

The daisy has everyday credentials in a different sense too, for its English name derives from the Old English *dægesege* or 'day's eye' – a reference to the fact that, as Leigh Hunt noticed, it closes its 'pinky lashes' at night and opens them again in the morning.

In the courtly 'marguerite' tradition of French medieval poetry, however, where daisies and women share virtues, the emphasis is less on light levels than on when it might be appropriate to be matey. 'That she opens and inclines towards the sun means that there is no pride in her, and that she is humble and courteously welcoming,' declared Guillaume de Machaut: 'Every time I gather her with my hand and can look at her at my will and lift her to my mouth, to my eye, and kiss, touch, smell, and feel, and gently enjoy her beauty and her sweetness, then I wish for nothing more.' But equally 'marvellous' is the beloved flower's ability to close up her petals 'so tight that nothing can enter in there' and 'that her golden centre should not be ravished or stolen away'. While Machaut's allegorical intention is not hard to discern, in talking of 'treasure' – and *marguerite* means pearl – he has inadvertently touched on botanical matters. In that context, however, the issue is not too much ravishment but too little. Since the right pollinators aren't about during the night, daisies close up to prevent their precious nectar from evaporating.

In 1900, as a way of marking the new century, Richard Kearton made a pre-dawn visit to a field near London to illustrate the daisy's circadian rhythms with more than poetry. Today considered one of the founders of natural history photography (his brother Cherry being the other), Kearton took two pictures, one before the sun had risen, and one immediately afterwards. When the images – 'Daisies Asleep' and 'Daisies Awake' – were projected onto a lantern screen, the audience, 'men and women who had lived in the country all their lives', responded with astonishment. This, Kearton said, proved the value of photography for everyone, for it was clear that rural as well as urban folk missed many of 'the interesting changes that are constantly going on around them'. But the pleasure we get from Kearton's photographs is more than simply documentary. His narrowly focused overhead shots of tightly packed flowers also bring to mind contemporary Voysey wallpaper designs or the two-dimensional panels painted by Gustave Caillebotte in the 1890s as an attempt to create a *Parterre des marguerites* in his dining room. Nature and culture, confused yet again. And that's before the added complication of artificial light enters into the equation. In one of his earliest poems, D.H. Lawrence imagines daisies which have 'waken all mistaken' in the yellow electric light of Piccadilly Circus, and compares them to the pale-faced prostitutes who have unhappily emerged at the same time. For Lawrence, it's never a good thing to interfere in natural rhythms, floral or human.

Although, in outline, the daisy's shape seems to be the simplest – it's what small children usually draw when they want to depict a flower – the structure is highly complex. The bright yellow central disc might, from a distance, look like a single flower, but it's made up of scores of tightly packed, tubular florets – each of which contains tiny pistils and stamens. The daisy's original family name *Compositae* refers to this 'composite' of small florets. The disc is surrounded not by petals but by another group of tiny flowers, known as 'ray florets'; Rousseau compared them to little white tongues. (While daisies and sunflowers have both disc and ray florets, some other members of the family have one or the other; the dandelion has only ray florets, the thistle only discs.) The structure of *Bellis perennis* is particularly appealing to flies, bees and butterflies, for the rays provide an excellent landing site from which to access the nectar and pollen on the disc. In the early spring, when other food is scarce, many insects rely for sustenance on the lawn daisies whose spreading rhizomes the bowling green or tennis court groundsman tries so hard to eradicate.

The plant provided treasure for people too. Apothecaries used both the flowers and leaves to create poultices for wounds and, especially, bruises (the daisy was sometimes known as bone or bruise wort). The shape and habit of the flower also meant that it was included among other 'ocular' flowers, like eyebright (*Euphrasia officianalis*), to treat diseases of the eye. This was according to the 'doctrine of signatures' employed by sixteenth- and seventeenth-century herbalists such as Giambattista della Porta and William Coles, who believed that God gave herbs 'particular Signatures, whereby a man may read . . . the use of them.' The daisy's low-growing habit was another signature for those who believed that contact with the flower stunted growth. Nursing mothers were instructed to keep their babies from touching daisies, while dog breeders

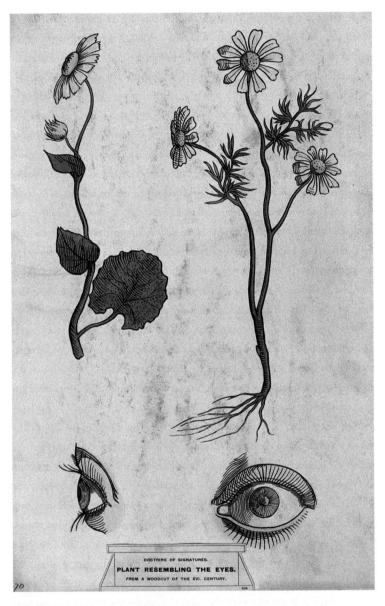

Eyebright and a human eye illustrating the 'doctrine of signatures', after a woodcut by Giambattista della Porta.

who wanted to keep their puppies small were told to put the flowers in their milk.

The daisy's size is one reason why it is so often associated with children: the flower's Yorkshire name is bairn wort. A more plausible explanation lies in the flower's abundance and ubiquity which makes it readily available for childhood games. Adults often look back nostalgically to the years when they roamed the 'daisied fields' (or the local park) and played those games; sometimes, though, they adapt them to more mature purposes.

Thinking first of the flower's white rays, we might remember how we used to pull them off one by one to find out if someone fancied us. Since the number of rays on a daisy varies, there is an element of suspense in the game although some claim that we're more likely to get an odd number and therefore a 'yes'. More sophisticated versions ask when, 'this year, next year, sometime, never'; who, 'rich man, poor man, beggar man, thief' or 'soldier brave, sailor blue, dashing airman'; and just how much, '*un peu, beaucoup, tendrement, passionément, à la folie*'.

Another game relies on the daisy's soft, pliant stem. Making a daisy chain requires a ready supply of flowers and a sharpish finger nail with which to create a small slit in the middle of the stem. Another stem can then be pushed through the slit, and on and on, until the chain is long enough to make a necklace, bracelet or crown. In *Flora Britannica*, Richard Mabey records several variations of this game, including Welsh 'caterpillars', where the head of a long-stemmed daisy is pushed through the yellow heads of several others, and the 'Irish' or 'Australian' daisy where the head is threaded through its own stalk so that it looks as if it's growing upside down.

Today, the phrase 'daisy chain' is widely used to describe the workings of both circular and linear sequences in all kinds of contexts, including: strings of airfields; commodity trading schemes; sexual activities involving three or more people; as well as all kinds of systems connecting electrical and electronic wiring, devices and data. And, carrying on a tradition that began more than a hundred years ago, every May a small group of Vassar College sophomores put on white dresses and carry an elaborate 150-foot rope of daisies and laurel to the graduation ceremony. The novelist Mary McCarthy attended Vassar in the

The Vassar College Daisy Chain, 1910.

early 1930s but was never 'on the Daisy Chain'; her classmates rather too gleefully recalled that, with her 'crooked' smile, 'limp' hair, and 'very Irish face', she 'wasn't Daisy Chain material'. Not very generous – but then they hadn't appreciated McCarthy's depiction of their friendships, sex lives and careers in *The Group*. The novel is much more than an exercise in delicious revenge, however. If the idea of the daisy chain provoked McCarthy into thinking about the intertwined lives of women, it's surely fitting that *The Group* itself initiated a long chain of similar stories, including the TV shows *Sex and the City* and *Girls*.

Another popular daisy game involves pretending the flowerheads are a flotilla of boats. What could be more fun than watching them float away? That's certainly the view of the monster (played by Boris Karloff) in the 1931 film adaptation of *Frankenstein*. He's delighted when a little girl called Maria invites him to join her in throwing daisies into a lake. It's a touching exchange

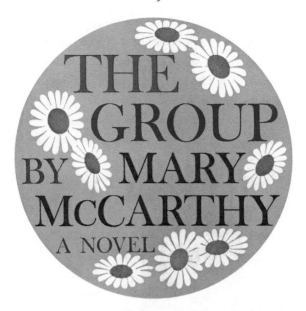

The first US edition of *The Group* by Mary McCarthy. The eight daisies represent the eight protagonists.

between two innocents until the monster runs out of flowers and, not knowing the difference between flowers and children, throws Maria into the water. Filled with remorse, he runs off into the woods. In the United States and elsewhere, censors reacted in horror, and the scene was eventually cut just before Frankenstein picks up the girl. But this only made the film more disturbing, for when her lifeless body appears later in the story, audiences were forced to speculate about just what might have happened. The original footage was only restored in the 1980s.

Tony Schwarz might have been thinking of Maria and the monster when he conceived 'Daisy Girl', the notorious advert that helped Lyndon B. Johnson defeat Barry Goldwater in the 1964 US presidential election, and changed the rules of political campaigning forever. It was the first commercial that made no attempt to provide information or establish an argument. The aim was clear and simple: to tap into, and direct, the audience's emotions. And to do so within 60 seconds. Needing to work fast, then, the director had to rely on images that were unambiguous and easily recognisable. A small girl pulling apart a daisy fit the bill perfectly: everyone knew what that meant.

The Cold War Daisy Girl faced a menace even more terrifying than a rampaging monster. The film begins as she counts each ray that she pulls off the flower, endearingly stumbling over her numbers – 1, 2, 3, 4, 5, 7, 6, 6, 8, 9, 10. We then segue to an all too efficient mission-control countdown. We close in on her (daisy) eye, and from its darkness emerges footage of a nuclear

mushroom cloud – the fate, it was implied, that Americans faced if they voted for the impulsive and bellicose Goldwater. But he's never named. Instead we hear Johnson's voice intoning, 'These are the stakes, to make a world in which all of God's children can live, or to go into the dark. We must either love each other, or we must die', the last line an echo of W.H. Auden's 'September 1, 1939'. Only then are we reminded, by another voice, what this has all been for: 'Vote for President Johnson on November 3'. Although the advert was officially screened only once, its shocking images meant that it was repeatedly aired on national news broadcasts. Johnson won the election with 61 per cent of

A girl and her daisy in Lyndon B. Johnson's 1964 Presidential Campaign advertisement 'Peace, Little Girl'.

the popular vote, and Monique Corzilius, the three year old plucking the daisy, went on to make commercials for SpaghettiOs and Kool Pops.

'Daisy Girl' is now a touchstone in the history of political advertising, and in recent years it has been repurposed by both Republicans (Rob Astorino and Mike Huckerbee) and Democrats (Hillary Clinton). In 2016 Clinton brought back Monique Corzilius to testify that the nuclear threat posed by the unpredictable and belligerent Donald Trump was as bad as it had ever been. 'This was me in 1964,' Corzilius says, as we watch her three-year-old self pick at the flower: 'The fear of nuclear war that we had as children, I never thought our children would ever have to deal with that again. And to see that coming forward in this election is really scary.'

Daisy girls are often in danger, but more often from 'deflowering' than from a monster or a bomb. This, of course, applies to all girls whose lives are imagined as flowers and thus follow an inexorable narrative from darling bud to reproductive bloom to extinction. But there are flowers and flowers. The trope was so well established by the late eighteenth century that when Robert Burns's plough runs over the 'slender stem' of the 'wee' flower, his mind immediately turns to the comparable 'fate of the artless Maid' – can her bloom escape 'Stern Ruin's ploughshare'? By the early twentieth century, that fate was often illustrated, and relished, rather than simply implied. The most explicit visual representation I've found is a rather lurid painting by Gari Melchers called *Red Hussar*. Thinking only of the dashing soldier who is caressing her breast, a naked woman knocks over a vase of daisies; while the water runs off the table, the fallen flowers – taller ox-eye daisies (*Leucanthemum vulgare*) – are still working hard to protect her modesty.

But the daisy's reputation for girlish innocence was under threat too, especially when confronted with the Jazz Age cynicism of *The Great Gatsby* (1925). Jay Gatsby's object of adoration seems to be a real daisy, a 'bright-eyed' vision in a white dress, the product of an impeccable 'white girlhood'. But after

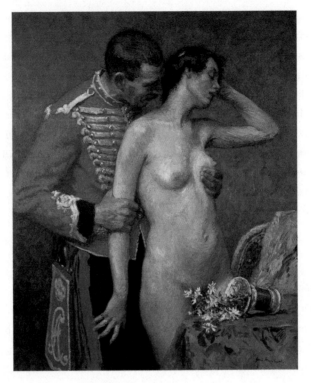

Gari Melchers, *Red Hussar*, c. 1912–15.

we've finished F. Scott Fitzgerald's story of sex, lies and deception, we realise that Daisy Buchanan's name is wholly ironic: she is not natural but 'artificial'; not fresh but 'sophisticated'; not humble and low-growing, but keen to sit 'safe and proud above the hot struggles of the poor'. Like all flowers, she speaks, but her voice is 'full of money'.

But once the stereotype had been overturned, what then? In the 1950s and 1960s, a new kind of daisy girl emerged: one that used the flower to reinvent childish innocence for a new era. The daisy became the bloom of choice for filmmakers keen to present the naturalness of the new sexual freedom, that is, of an infantilised sexuality. *Pull My Daisy* (1959), written by Jack Kerouac, and produced by 'G-String Enterprises', makes this apparent in its opening song,

'The Crazy Daisy'. Taken from a poem written by Kerouac, Allen Ginsberg and Neal Cassady, the lines are given a woman's perspective in Anita Ellis's airy cocktail-jazzy rendition: 'pull my daisy / tip my cup / all my doors are open'. The message was clear: the daisy was no longer trembling in fear of deflowerment but cheerfully in charge of its own sexual fate. We find another version of this in the amateur striptease performed by daisy-clad 'child-woman' Brigitte Bardot in Roger Vadim's 1956 comedy *En effeuillant la marguerite* (*Plucking the Daisy*), and yet another in *Sedmikrásky* (*Daisies*), by Czech New Wave director Věra Chytilová: the free-flowing story of Marie I and Marie II, two anarchistic girls who emerge from a field of daisies and take it from there. Over the course of little more than a hundred years, the cute wee robin of flowers had had quite a makeover. No longer modest or humble, it was now a sex kitten.

Brigitte Bardot promotes her 1956 comedy *Plucking the Daisy*.

Daffodil

Hoping to become a journalist, Mr Biswas, the eponymous hero of a 1969 novel by V.S. Naipaul, enrols in a correspondence course with the 'Ideal School of Journalism, Edgware Road, London'. The first exercise, to 'write four bright articles on the seasons', comes with a series of 'hints' and an instruction to look out the window. Since Mr Biswas lives in Trinidad, he manages to write about summer without any problem, but when it comes to writing about the other three British seasons, of which he has no experience, he is forced to abandon any pretence at reportage, instead inventing fictions full of blazing fires and Keats quotations. The Ideal School is impressed.

Naipaul is far from the only Caribbean writer for whom an insistence on four seasons is a potent sign of an all too distant and intrusive colonial culture. And of those seasons, none is more totemic than spring, and no flower more weighed down with its symbolism than the daffodil. The reason is simple. To study literature in colonial Trinidad (Naipaul), St Lucia (Derek Walcott), Antigua (Jamaica Kincaid), Haiti (Edwidge Danticat), or the Dominican Republic (Jean Rhys), was to study daffodils: Shakespeare's, which charm 'the winds of March with beauty'; Spenser's, called 'daffadowndillies' and scattered through April; and Herrick's, which 'haste away so soone' that he weeps. But most of all, schoolchildren in the Caribbean – and all over the British Empire – were 'made to memorize' Wordsworth's poem 'Daffodils', often known by its first line 'I Wandered Lonely as a Cloud'. As Naipaul put it, 'A pretty little flower, no doubt; but we had never seen it. Could the poem have any meaning for us?'

But if a feeling of being 'tired of learning and reciting poems about daffodils' runs through twentieth-century Caribbean writing, writers approach their own 'oddly charged relationship' with the Wordsworthian flower in very different ways.

Jean Rhys's 'The Day They Burned the Books' (1960) is almost an allegory of the ambiguities of the colonial experience. It tells the story of Eddie, a child torn between the values of his once-beautiful, 'coloured' Caribbean mother and his drunken, often-abusive, white British father. On the one hand, siding with his mother, Eddie declares that he doesn't like daffodils: 'Dad's always going on about them. He says they lick the flowers here into a cocked hat and I bet that's a lie.' On the other hand, when his father dies, and his mother gleefully sets fire to his library, Eddie is horrified (and rushes to save a copy of Kipling's *Kim*).

Daffodils also provoke ambivalence in Jamaica Kincaid. Her 1990 novel *Lucy* is about a nineteen-year-old girl who leaves a 'sunny, drought-ridden' Caribbean island to work as an au pair in an unnamed city in the United States, part of the four-seasons world where 'all the prosperous (and so, certainly, happy) people' lived. She arrives in January and does not encounter a daffodil until March; but somehow a daffodilish presence hangs over everything from the 'pale-yellow sun' that fails to warm the winter air to the family itself, with 'their six yellow-haired heads of various sizes [. . .] bunched as if they were a bouquet of flowers', and giving the impression that everything is 'unbearably wonderful'. What Lucy recoils against is not simply the colonialist assumptions that shaped her childhood, but the smugness with which they are maintained in a place that is supposed to offer a genuine alternative. When she finally sees some daffodils – presented by her employer as a great treat – she finds them 'beautiful' but 'simple, as if made to erase a complicated and unnecessary idea'. Daffodils, in other words, remind her both of 'brutes masquerading as angels and angels portrayed as brutes'.

While Kincaid's *Lucy* never stops thinking of herself as a 'weed' (in contrast to the angelic and brutal blond Americans), the characters in Edwidge Danticat's *Breath, Eyes, Memory* (1994) try to see themselves as daffodils. Martine's favourite flower is a variety that we learn was developed to withstand the heat of Haiti: 'they were the color of pumpkins and golden summer squash, as though they had acquired a bronze tinge from the skins of the natives who had adopted them.' She sees daffodils as adaptable immigrants who are able to hold their heads high and proud in 'a place that they were not supposed to'. When, after many years apart, Martine's twelve-year-old daughter Sophie goes to join her mother in the United States, she makes a card with the inscription 'My mother is a daffodil / but in the wind, iron strong'. And, in her yellow dress with its white collar, Sophie tries to look like a daffodil too. But it's not so simple, not least because Martine's story is rooted in trauma rather than triumph. The young girls in both novels – Sophie here and Lucy, in Kincaid's novel – have nightmares about floral aggression: Lucy of being chased through the streets and then buried alive by bunches of daffodils, Sophie of her mother wrapped in yellow sheets with long hooks for arms.

For both girls, growing up means finding other flowers. And for Caribbean writers, more generally, it means giving those flowers their own imaginative space. For too long, writes Derek Walcott, snow and daffodils were 'real, more real than the heat and oleander, perhaps', precisely because they lived 'on the page and in the imagination'. Writing from a postcolonial perspective means recognising the beauty of the oleander, hibiscus and poinciana; for Naipaul, the first step was learning that the white flower he had loved as a child is called jasmine.

Kincaid, meanwhile, eventually claimed to have made her peace with the daffodil, and with Wordsworth, whom she came to think she may have blamed unduly. In 2006, after twenty years living in Vermont – going 'back and forth with the daffodil' in her mind – she planted 5,500 bulbs of a variety called 'Rijnveld's Early Sensation', more than half of the 10,000 flowers Wordsworth claimed to have seen dancing in the breeze at Ullswater. Her ambition, she said, was not to compete with the poet, but rather to finally separate his verse and the flower from 'the tyrannical order of a people, the British people, in my child's life'. And yet the image that ends Kincaid's essay on bulb-planting is not a Wordsworthian one of floating free, like a cloud, above gleeful flowers, but rather a scene of further, if this time self-created, entrapment: 'I want to walk out into my yard,' she confesses, 'unable to move at all because my feet are snarled in the graceful long stems supporting bent yellow flowering heads of daffodils.'

The moment that inspired all this anguish – and two centuries of literary revisionism – took place on the 'threatening, misty morning' of 15 April 1802, when William Wordsworth took a walk around Glencoyne Bay, Ullswater, in the Lake District. He was not 'lonely as a cloud' that day but accompanied, as he often was, by his sister Dorothy. And, famously, it was her diary record of a 'busy highway' of daffodils along the shore that provoked his poem. It was Dorothy who first noted that the powerful effect was due to the mass or 'unity' of the flowers, and who observed how they 'tossed and reeled and danced & seemed as if they verily laughed with the wind that blew upon them over the Lake, they looked so gay ever dancing ever changing.'

Wordsworth's poem, published first in 1807 and then, with some revisions and additions, in 1815, was not highly regarded during his lifetime. The poet Anna Seward summed up what many thought at the time: 'if his worst foe had chosen to caricature this egotistic manufacturer of metaphysical importance upon trivial themes, he could not have done it more effectually.' It was only after both William and Dorothy had died, and after her journal was published, that 'Daffodils' began to attract attention – although not so much from other poets as from the tourist industry that followed the railway to the Lake District in the mid-nineteenth century. Wordsworth wrote poems about many local flowers – daisies, bluebells and his favourite, 'the little celandine'. What was it about the daffodil that so appealed to those who wanted to market his connection to the Lakes? Saeko Yoshikawa suggests that the daffodil's success might simply be due to the contrast between the golden flowers and the 'generally leaden' Cumbrian sky. (The celandine has golden flowers too, but they are tiny.) In any case, by the 1850s, guides to the Lakes regularly included Dorothy's account of her walk, along with what one writer called William's 'enfeebled paraphrase'. While initial interest centred on Ullswater, the precise location of the golden host gradually became less important and tourists were encouraged to look for 'Wordsworth's flower' all over the Lake District. Huge numbers of extra bulbs were planted to create a good show, although by no means all of them were the wild *N. pseudonarcissus* he and Dorothy had admired. In any case, there were, and still are, plenty of other daffodils to be had, in the woods, by the lake, along the roadside, and pictured on tea towels, biscuit tins, mugs, and dishes. In 2012, the Victorian hotel across the road from Wordsworth's house relaunched itself as The Daffodil Hotel and Spa.

A Royal Falcon Ware tray featuring the first verse of William Wordsworth's 'Daffodils'.

If I were a nineteenth-century tourist who had made a pilgrimage to Ullswater one April morning, and was lucky enough to find some daffodils 'dancing in the breeze', I might be tempted to think that I'd reached some kind of poetic source or origin, the point that would reveal just how the famous poem came into existence. It's a powerful idea, and one that's particularly tempting when reading a poet like Wordsworth. For, unlike his sister, William was less interested in describing what he saw and felt that day than in contemplating the way in which that kind of ordinary experience might produce a powerful imaginative aftershock. It was a full two years after his lakeside walk that he recalled both the 'laughing company' of flowers and himself looking on:

> I gazed - and gazed - but little thought
> What wealth the show to me had brought:
> For oft when on my Couch I lie
> In vacant, or in pensive mood,
> They flash upon that inward eye
> Which is the bliss of solitude,
> And then my heart with pleasure fills,
> And dances with the Daffodils.

What stimulated the pensiveness and pleasure, however, was more than the memory of a pleasant walk. Wordsworth may have found his golden daffodils not far from home but, when he recalled them, it was with an 'inward eye', an imagination, educated by a 'golden store of books': the standard Greek and Latin texts of his grammar school and Cambridge University education, but also a beloved 'little yellow canvas-covered copy' of *The Arabian Nights*, a book which, along with translations of Persian lyric poetry, had only recently become available to English readers. It was the combination of these two forms of 'gold' – the natural and the cultural – that brought him poetic 'wealth'.

In both the classical and Persian traditions, Wordsworth would have encountered many mentions of the narcissus, although the plant in question was not the yellow-trumpeted *N. pseudonarcissus* but *N. tazetta*, a native of Greece and Italy which spread along ancient eastern trade routes as far as China (where it's known as the Sacred Lily) and Japan. Since the plants were cultivated, and naturalised, all along the way, it is impossible to disentangle which are the true species. In any case, evidence of some kind of *tazetta* can be

Detail of Shaikh Zada's painting of 'Bahram Gur in the White Palace on Friday', Folio 235 in a sixteenth-century illustrated manuscript of the *Khamsa* by the twelfth-century Persian poet Nizami.

The eyes of *N. tazetta* look out in this detail from a mid-thirteenth-century Chinese handscroll by Zhao Mengjian.

found everywhere from the frescos of Pompeii to Persian miniature paintings to Chinese scrolls. The *tazetta* is the 'wondrous, radiant' plant that Persephone was reaching for when she herself was plucked by Hades and taken to the Underworld, and some even suggest it was the 'rose of Sharon' mentioned in the Old Testament.

N. tazetta looks very different from *N. pseudonarcissus* (they actually belong to distinct sub-genera). While the latter produces a single large flower at the end of the stem, each *tazetta* has multiple small flowers. Homer talks about a hundred heads, but that's rather an exaggeration; some, however, have as many as eight. More important, at least as far as poetry was concerned, was the fact that in the centre of each of these flowers, surrounded by white petals, was a distinctive yellow corona or 'eye'.

In both Greek and Persian traditions, the flower was associated with eyes and looking. The name 'narcissus' derives from the legend, made famous by Ovid, of a beautiful young man who, as punishment for his mockery of those who love him, is made to fall hopelessly in love with his own watery reflection. Although he can gaze endlessly into his own eyes, the moment he tries to get closer, the reflection disappears and eventually he withers away – only to be reborn as a flower with 'white petals clustered round a cup of gold'. That story crossed over into Persian and Arabic poetry, where it joined many other associations between the narcissus and the eye; at times, the two seem practically synonymous. 'Narcissus-eyes' can be wide-open (suggesting bewilderment or lovelorn insomnia), blurry (indicating intoxication), droopy (due to melancholy), or blind. They can suggest stars ('the narcissus of the night'), great wealth ('eyes of silver with pupils of molten gold united with an emerald stalk'), and 'enchanting' beauty – the perfect complement to 'rose-bud lips', 'cheeks like the tulip, and a bosom like the jasmine'. But if a lover comes to bed with 'narcissus-eyes all shining for the fray', her partner might first want to remove any real narcissi from the room; one story had it that they liked to watch people having sex. Taking another tack altogether, the fifteenth-century Persian poet Bushaq'i At'imma compared the flower to a fried egg surrounded by six slices of white bread.

Some, if not all, of these associations were surely known to Wordsworth and his wife, Mary – for it was Mary who suggested the image of the 'inward eye'. And that suggests a possible botanical confusion: a host of *pseudonarcissus* flashing on the eye of a *tazetta*. In any case, it's nice to think that it was only when Wordsworth took on the role of a foreign flower that he was able to see himself as a member of the golden Cumbrian crowd. Perhaps he recognised what so many Caribbean writers have since testified, that when you're thinking of daffodils, the experience of the imagination is just as important as a walk in the woods.

It's impossible to say if *N. pseudonarcissus* is a British native or whether it simply immigrated here a very long time ago. But the origins of another contender for the title of local hero, *N. obvallaris* or the Tenby Daffodil, are even more obscure. Smaller than *pseudonarcissus*, with a brighter flower and, as its name suggests, a corona that resembles a battlement wall, it was first observed growing in the fields near the Welsh seaside town of Tenby in the late eighteenth century. Since it resembled no other daffodil growing in Britain, rumours quickly proliferated about its origins. Richard Mabey sums them up: 'The bulbs had been traded by Phoenician sailors for a cargo of anthracite. They had been brought over by Flemish settlers in the early twelfth century, or to the physic gardens of French or Italian monks, perhaps in the monastery of Caldy Island, just off Tenby.' Convincingly local yet, once again, blessed with a host of exotic stories, the Tenby Daffodil became hugely popular for a brief period in the late nineteenth century. After that the flower and its stories were largely forgotten. It was only in the 1970s, after a chance request by a young boy looking for a present for his aunt caught the attention of the town's director of tourism, that Tenby fully began to exploit its distinctive flower. Mass planting (and the mass construction of holiday cottages called 'Daffodil') ensued, and today shows no sign of abating. Recently, however, the claim that the daffodil is 'unique to this corner of South West Wales' has been challenged.

Populations of very similar wild daffodils have been found growing in several places in the Spanish mountains, although further molecular analysis needs to be done before we can know if they are of the same species or just very close relations. This could turn out to be yet another story about the uncertainty of origins in a world shaped by migration.

Lily

Consider the lilies. Lilies of the field, valley, garden and water; of the bouquet, corsage, vase and coffin; Byzantium, Egypt, Peru, Bermuda and Guernsey lilies; tiger, cow, trout, spider and toad lilies. Some are 'lilywhite', but others are yellow, orange, red, and even blue. Very few of these, however, are 'true' lilies. Even the lily of the valley in the Song of Songs is probably something else.

This spring chapter is about just one kind, the modern, and sometimes modernist, Easter Lily. Actually, that's two: *Lilium longifolium*, and the arum or calla lily, *Zantedeschia aethiopica*. The first is a Japanese native, the second comes from South Africa. To understand how they both came to be associated with the Christian festival of resurrection means taking in some other lilies and festivals along way. For the names and meanings of flowers travel almost as much as they do.

The original white lily is *Lilium candidum*, known to us as the Madonna Lily. But that's a relatively recent idea. Long before it had any Christian associations, it was a food, medicine and ceremonial flower throughout the eastern Mediterranean. In Minoan frescos from 1600 BCE, it often appears alongside *L. chalcedonicum*, the scarlet Martagon or Turk's Cap Lily. Native to Turkey, Syria, Lebanon and Israel, where it is now considered an endangered species, the lily was first distributed along Phoenician trading routes and it was probably the Romans who brought it to Britain. Admired for its ornamental qualities, the lily was mainly valued as an ingredient in treatments for boils and dropsy.

Lilium candidum was also one of the many flowers connected to the Virgin in early Christian writings; the Venerable Bede said its white petals signalled her chastity and its golden anthers the divine light within. But many other flowers were also associated with Mary. For Saint Ambrose, the iris suggested her solitariness and the daisy her humility, while for Bernard of Clairvaux 'Mary is the violet of humility, the lily of chastity, the rose of charity, and the glory and splendour of the Heavens.' Numerous plant names that today begin with 'Lady's' – like *Alchemilla mollis*, lady's mantle, or *Cypripedium calceolus*, lady's slipper – were originally 'Our Lady's'. *Calendula officinalis*, 'Mary gold' and then marigold, flowered at the end of March and was therefore associated with the festival of the Annunciation. *L. candidum* came into bloom in July, its trumpet-like flowers announcing the Feast of the Visitation.

All of these seasonal associations were forgotten when the lily began to appear in Annunciation paintings during the late Medieval and Renaissance period. The miraculous, and allegorical, nature of the event when the Angel Gabriel appeared to the Virgin to announce her forthcoming pregnancy, could be emphasised by linking it to a flower then out of season. Furthermore, the lily spoke powerfully to Mary's unique combination of purity and fertility. That her pregnancy doesn't begin in her body is signalled by the flower's separation from her; it is shown either in a vase or in Gabriel's hand. The distribution of flowers on the stem could also be made meaningful. In many representations, where three blooms appear on a single stem, two open and one in bud, the lily reinforces the message that Christ's incarnation will complete the Holy Trinity.

It was only when other white lilies were introduced from China and Japan in the nineteenth century that *L. candidum* in particular came to be known as the Madonna Lily. Renewed interest in the flower, and the pictorial conventions linking it to the Annunciation, was largely due to the efforts of the Pre-Raphaelite Brotherhood; indeed, by the end of the century, the flowers even became known as Pre-Raphaelite lilies. Oscar Wilde's much-caricatured association with the flower in the 1880s is a legacy of this. (See **Carnation**.)

Lilies also began to feature more prominently in church decorations. While today flowers are a constant presence in almost every church building, for much of the nineteenth century their use was the subject of intense doctrinal debate. After the Reformation, Protestant churches rejected flowers, along with icons and incense, as agents in the ritualised devotion, and 'culture of luxury', of Catholicism. But gradually, the Victorian passion for flowers, and belief in their capacity to educate, began to change attitudes. The poet and priest Frederick William Faber summed up the argument: 'Lessons oft by them are brought / Deeper than mortal sage hath taught.' Moreover, insisted William Alexander Barrett in a widely circulated book on 'floral decorations of churches', the impulse to surround oneself with flowers was 'almost instinctive in human nature'. Blossoms did not only make homes and churches prettier; by 'pouring out in mute adoration their praises to the King of Kings', they also made them more holy. (See **Geranium** and **Snowdrop**.)

The new affordability of commercially grown flowers was also an important factor in these changes. If everyone agreed that lilies, and especially white lilies, were 'indispensable' for an Easter display, it was rarely the summer-flowering *L. candidum* that they meant. Instead commercial growers promoted flowers that could be made to come into bloom at just the right time.

One was *Lilium longifolium*, a Japanese lily from the coral Ryukya (Nansei) Islands that was brought to Europe by Dutch colonialists in the eighteenth century and then to Bermuda by British colonialists in the nineteenth. A tourist introduced it into the United States in the 1870s, where, marketed as *L. Harrisii* by a shrewd nurseryman called William Harris, it took off in a big way. This long-stemmed, long-trumpeted white flower resembled the Madonna Lily, but was much easier to force into bloom for Easter. Religious enthusiasts, however, tended to play down the skill necessary to time its maturity, preferring instead to imagine the flowers as pilgrims who 'encouraged themselves, though the darkness of their lives, in hours when they felt it was nothing but push, push' with the thought that 'light would come some time, and they would shine in all their glory'. The strong scent of these lilies was also an important factor in their success, and they were sometimes depicted as 'perfumed censers'. While the Communist poet Claude McKay had no interest in the lily as a 'sacred sign', he wrote nostalgically about its fragrance, recalling how 'I, a pagan, worshiped at its shrine / Yielding my heart unto its perfumed power'.

Today *L. longifolium* is the flower that everyone, in the United States at least, thinks of as the Easter Lily. And you don't need to go to church to see them. By 1900, the holiday was as much about fashion (the Easter bonnet) and gifts: coloured eggs, flowers and cards, many of which featured very un-Madonna-ish girls. When new shorter varieties were developed in the 1930s, *longifolium* was also sold as a potted plant. And this, today, is how

most people encounter it. After poinsettias, 'mums' and azaleas, the Easter Lily is the most popular potted plant in the United States, with most of the 10 million bulbs coming from just four farms in southern Oregon and northern California.

Before these elegant long flowers took over completely, there was another contender for the title of Easter Lily: the South African calla or arum (as it tended to be known in Britain). By the mid-nineteenth century, gardening magazines described it as 'so common as to be in the

Early twentieth-century Easter card.

A Happier Easter

Early twentieth-century Easter card.

collection of any person who cares the least for flowers'. But the demand was such (for Easter 1878, San Francisco's fashionable Grace Church required 4,000) that most callas were supplied by flower farms. In 1896, Charles Walter Stetson entitled his eerie depiction of fields near Pasadena *An Easter Offering*.

Charles Walter Stetson, *An Easter Offering*, 1896.

But while quantity was necessary, it was never sufficient. As the supply of flowers became more varied and affordable, floral decorations, at home and in church, became increasingly elaborate. And, as with every kind of trend-driven consumerism, it was important to keep coming up with something new. In 1887, for example, a New York florist called Peter Henderson offered a basket 'in the exact shape of a large calla' as an Easter novelty. Others began to talk about their Easter 'set designs', and it's hardly surprising that churches provided inspiration for window dressers in the new department stores. For Easter 1890, for instance, the window of one Chicago jeweller featured a large white cross, strewn white rose petals, and a series of calla lilies within which, 'like a drop of purest dew, sparkled a diamond'. The calla's early twentieth-century status as one of the most luxurious of luxury commodities is surely one reason it recurs so often in Diego Rivera's numerous paintings of weighed-down Mexican flower sellers.

Diego Rivera,
The Flower Seller (Girl with Lilies),
1941.

While the callas grown for Easter were white (they come in other colours too), they had little else in common with the Madonna Lily. The striking outer petal is actually a spathe, a modified leaf or leaf-like bract, inside of which is a thin column called a spadix, a fleshy stem covered with numerous tiny florets. Even before Freud pointed out the symbolism, the key to the flower's appeal to artists lay in its combination of a phallic spandix (which, for the Victorians, had presented upright integrity) and an enveloping spathe (previously seen as a cowl or shell-like form but, post-Freud, clearly a vulva). In a psychoanalytic era there has been no shortage of sexy callas, from Charles Demuth's much-reproduced *Calla Lilies*, 1926 – a coded homage to the cross-dressing vaudevillian Bert Savoy – to Salvador Dalí's *The Great Masturbator* (1929), and numerous photographs by Robert Mapplethorpe.

For others, however, the flower's appeal was primarily architectural. With its precise white contours, the calla seemed streamlined and modern, the antithesis of the wispy naturalistic flowers so popular in the Edwardian era. Styled by fashionable floral designers like Constance Spry, the calla became a cliché of Art Deco interior chic. But it was also the subject of a series of vast, radically cropped, close-up portraits by Georgia O'Keeffe. Although her husband Alfred Stieglitz successfully marketed the calla paintings as erotic, O'Keeffe herself insisted that her interests lay in structure, space, and making it new. The flowers

Georgia O'Keeffe, *Yellow Calla*, 1926.

were big, she said, so that people would 'be surprised into taking time to look' at them, rather than simply hanging all their own, tired associations upon them: 'you write about my flower as if I think and see what you think and see of the flower – and I *don't*.' (For more of this attitude, see **Rose**.)

There was still another way of seeing the Easter Lily. In 1925, the flower was chosen as the symbol of remembrance for the 1916 Dublin Easter Rising. The proposal came from Cumann na mBan, the Republican women's organisation, whose members wanted an alternative to the tricolour flag which, they felt, had been 'basely lowered' by its associations with the partitioned state established in 1921. Adopting the Easter Lily – itself a study in green (leaf), orange (spadix) and white (spathe) – they claimed the flag was 'raised again'. And there were more practical considerations too. Cumann na mBan had observed the huge success of the Royal British Legion's poppy appeal. The sale of Easter Lily badges would fund the National Graves Association's efforts in memorialising Republican dead.

The badges have been sold in Ireland ever since, despite attempts to curtail their distribution or offer alternative emblems of 1916. North of the border, the Easter Lily, with its tricoloured credentials further emphasised, became an increasingly important symbol during the 'Troubles', the intensified Protestant–Catholic conflict that began in the late 1960s and ended with the Good Friday Agreement in 1998. When the Republican movement split at the end of 1969, even the style of the paper lapel badge became significant. The following Easter, when the Official Irish Republican Army and the Provisional IRA set out on separate commemorative marches, the Officials wore self-adhesive badges while the Provisionals used the traditional pin. The Officials became known as the 'Stickies' or 'Sticks', but their attempt to label the Provisionals 'Pinheads' didn't catch on. As Belfast murals of Easter Lilies demonstrate, however, the pin became part of the symbol.

Acknowledging that it would hard to persuade either side to jettison such symbols, the Good Friday Agreement insisted that those creating the country's new institutions, in particular the devolved legislature of the Northern Ireland Assembly, should ensure that they would now be used 'in a manner which promotes mutual respect rather than division'. The Assembly even chose a new floral emblem – flax. If many struggled to remember its symbolism (six flowers for the counties of Northern Ireland and a nod to the country's linen trade) few disputed the need for a neutral symbol.

A mural featuring a lily pin, Béal Feirste, Belfast, 2010.

A reminder came in 2001, when the Democratic Unionist Party (DUP) recalled Parliament from its spring recess to debate a proposed display of Easter Lilies in the Assembly building. An earlier motion by Sinn Féin to place a notice advertising the work of the National Graves Association next to the lilies had already been rejected, but the DUP maintained that even the flowers were unacceptable. Insults flew about 'lily-white lilies of cowardice' and 'the Easter Lily-livered', and dire warnings were made about the flower's danger to cats ('kidney failure, vomiting, loss of appetite, depression and death'). 'Is that the sort of atmosphere we want to work in?' asked one Assembly member. Since cross-community approval was necessary, the motion was defeated and the lilies remained. The following year, the more moderate Ulster Unionists proposed a 'compromise' which would see the display of poppies in November, Easter Lilies in April, and, in July, orange lilies.

The orange lily was one of the symbols of William III, Prince of Oranje-Nassau and, after 1689, joint sovereign with his wife Mary of England, Ireland and Scotland. For Irish Protestants, however, its primary reference was to King Billy's defeat of the Catholic forces of James II at the Battle of the Boyne in 1690.

Jan Davidsz. de Heem, *Cartouche with a Portrait of Prince William III of Orange*, mid-1660s.

A native of much of southern and central Europe, *Lilium bulbiferum*, the orange or 'fire' lily, had been naturalised in the Netherlands by at least the fifteenth century, when it began to appear in Flemish paintings. Once known as the Herring-lily, because it flowered at the time of year when the big catches were made, its official Dutch name is now *roggelelie* or rye-lily, a reference to the fact that it is often found in the poor sand soil where rye is grown. The first evidence of the flower's association with William is in a ceremonial portrait by Jan Davidsz. de Heem. The adolescent prince is presented in a sumptuous cartouche that, along with sunflowers, peonies, morning glory, roses, cherries, melons, apricots and oranges, features two heraldic eagles and a rather unconvincing portrait of the Lion of the Netherlands, and, directly below the prince, an orange lily. De Heem was one of the masters of what the Dutch called *pronkstilleven* or ostentatious still life, and the painting is as much a display of wealth as it is an allegory of the power of the House of Orange. And *pronk* was also William and Mary's ambition in their gardens at Hampton Court. Rather than planting acres of orange lilies (as some now claim), they installed three state-of-the-Dutch-art heated glass cases to house what was the most extensive collection of tender exotics yet seen in England. There may have been some symbolic intention behind their orangeries, but the only lily that made it into the collection was *Agapanthus africanus*, the Blue Lily, from the Cape of Good Hope.

But that was of little interest to the Orange Order, established at the end of the eighteenth century, to celebrate the Battle of the Boyne with songs about the 'royal, loyal Lily, O', and banners decorated with sweet williams and orange lilies (as well as union jacks). And, like its more recent white Easter cousin, the orange July lily had proved hard to shift. In 2007, a company called Shaderoe (80 per cent of whose shareholders were Orange Lodges) bought 27 acres of fields of the Boyne battle site with the idea of growing lily bulbs to sell along with sods of 'genuine' battlefield soil. In the end, however, there has been more importing than exporting: in 2016, the Grand Lodge bought 180,000 Dutch bulbs to mark the centenary of the Battle of the Somme.

But perhaps things are beginning to change. In 2013, and again the following year, the Sinn Féin leader Gerry Adams tweeted a photo of orange lilies growing lustily in his garden, accompanied by the lyrics to the famous loyalist song 'Hey-ho the Lily-oh'. When his followers expressed surprise, Adams jokingly replied, 'the fact my garden is loaded with them is a testament to the changing times and demographics, we have a tolerationship . . .😊'.

Carnation

'I knew it was going to be terrible,' says Charlotte of 'the worst date' of her life: 'the man brought me carnations.' This is Manhattan, 2003 or, more precisely, the romantic minefield of HBO's *Sex and the City*. But Charlotte's dismissive reaction – 'they're filler flowers' – is one that many of us will recognise. Sprays of carnations are fine – cheap, long-lasting, always available at the supermarket (where, in Britain, we buy 60 per cent of our flowers), but they don't speak of a great deal of thought or effort. 'Would I present a hostess with a bunch of carnations?' asked *Vogue* editor Suzy Menkes: 'Never!'

How did *Dianthus caryophyllus*, the flower of Zeus, sink so low?

One of 300 species in the genus *Dianthus*, carnations are pinkish-purple natives of the Mediterranean; their long history of cultivation makes it difficult to pinpoint their origin precisely. By the fifteenth century, the flower was firmly established in northern European gardens, and since then there's been no looking back. The carnation's popularity largely rests on its amenability to hybridisation or, to put it less positively, its willingness to produce 'sports' or 'nature's bastards', with all manner of ruffles, streaks and stripes. Rarely, however, have 'monster-offspring' been so appreciated, first by the aristocrats who collected them, and then by the florists who bred and exhibited them. Today the word 'florist' is used to describe someone who sells flowers, but from the seventeenth to the late-nineteenth century it referred to amateur artisan flower lovers – for example, many weavers were florists – who cultivated

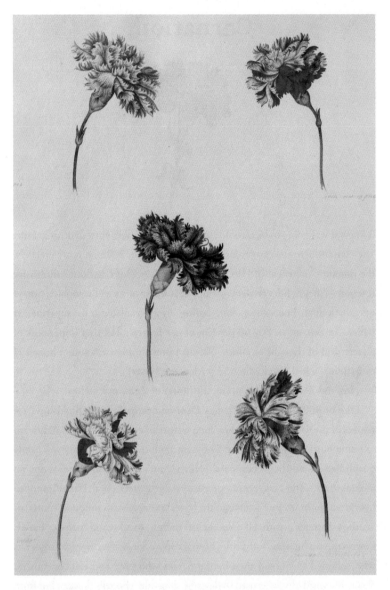

A page of carnations in Alexander Marshal's mid-seventeenth-century florilegium or flower book. On the reverse, Marshal names them as La Croix, Passe Manaque, Rondelle, General Cornelius, and General Beck. Sixty of the 284 flowers depicted in the book are carnations.

particular species for show and competition. Auriculas, tulips, and hyacinths were all popular, but only carnations could offer a menu of 'flakes' (flowers with stripes of a single colour on a white background), 'bizarres' (with stripes of two or more colours) and 'picotees' (whose margins were a darker colour than the rest of the flower).

All this began before the mechanism of plant reproduction was properly understood, and the difference between cultivars was usually attributed to an 'accidental coupling' or the skilful manipulation of environmental factors. To claim more would be to play God. The botanical revolution of the eighteenth century changed all that. Eventually it was acknowledged that – as Linnaeus baldly put it in 1735 – flowers are 'nothing else but the genitals of plants', and all manner of creations could be created by intervening in the 'marriage bed'. Carnations play a key role in this story too, for the first deliberately produced and documented hybrid of two distinct species involved *Dianthus*. The man playing God (or Cupid) was a Hoxton nurseryman called Thomas Fairchild. Fairchild transferred the male pollen of a Sweet William (*Dianthus barbatus*) onto the female pistil of a carnation to create 'a Plant differing from either'. This was in 1717, more than thirty years before Linnaeus's *Species Plantarum* established modern botanical nomenclature (genus followed by species) and a system of classification based on the number of a flower's (male) stamens and (female) pistils. Two specimens of 'Fairchild's Mule' (like the cross between a male donkey and a female horse, the hybrids were sterile) survive in the herbaria of Oxford University and the Natural History Museum in London.

Among the thousands of carnations that have been developed since then, I want to focus on the 'perpetual', a cross between a carnation and a pink (*D. chinensis*) which, taken up by American nurserymen, helped to establish large-scale commercial floriculture at the end of the nineteenth century. This then is partly the story of how a garden flower associated with high summer – signalled most strongly by its common name 'gilly' or 'July' flower – became a mass-produced year-rounder, as available for May Day and Mother's Day as it was for a night at the theatre in February.

Oscar Wilde thought the green carnation he 'invented' for his supporters to wear at the 1892 premiere of *Lady Windermere's Fan* was the ultimate monstrous offspring, less a plant than a 'work of art', and one that didn't require a visit to the potting shed.

It was not the first bloom in Wilde's repertoire. Ten years earlier, under the sway of the Arts and Crafts movement, he declared his two favourite flowers to be the sunflower and the lily – 'not for any vegetable fashion at all', but because they were 'the most perfect models of design, the most naturally adapted for decorative art'. (Both also featured in William Morris's textile and wallpaper designs.) Wilde's love of flowers was a gift to satirists unable to match his wit. In 1881, *Punch* depicted him with a sunflower for a head, and published a poem about his 'languid love of lilies', a flower which, it pointed out, might be 'long' and 'lithe' but was also 'fragile and thin / with dank leaves dangling'. Subtle.

By the 1890s, as aestheticism evolved into the 'new and beautiful and interesting disease' called Decadence, it was time to replace the lily and sunflower with something less natural, such as a vividly dyed carnation. Dye itself was admirably artificial, but not any colour would do. Along with yellow, green was the colour the Decadents prized most. That might be surprising since, as David Kastan notes, green is the 'colour of the vegetal'. Indeed, the shared root of the English words 'green' and 'grow' reminds us that photosynthesis (the process by which plants convert sunlight, carbon dioxide and water into food) depends on the pigment chlorophyll absorbing most of the electromagnetic energy in the blue and red parts of the spectrum. Nothing could be more natural than green – except when it comes to the petals of a carnation. Today, perhaps due to Wilde's influence, it is not hard to find greenish-yellow carnations ('Elsie Ketchen', say, or 'Julie Martin'), although Sweet Williams like 'Green Trick' or 'Green Magma' have more vivid hues. But the green that Wilde 'invented' (with the help of Edward Goodyear, his Burlington Arcade florist) was not due to breeding but to the aniline dye malachite green. Dying carnations was nothing new: before the nature of plant reproduction was understood, variation in flower colour was often attributed to the particular 'tint' of the water. Nevertheless, as more and more florists started to offer green buttonholes, rumours spread about the recipe for this 'shilling shocker, once a white carnation': was the secret ingredient ink or absinthe, or, as one sketch writer speculated, did 'they water them with arsenic'? *The Artist and Journal of Home Culture* revealed all in its April 1892 issue, instructing readers to plunge the carnations' stems into a solution of malachite green and then wait for the dye to rise up to the petals 'by capillary attraction': 'by the end of twelve hours they are well tinged. A longer immersion deepens the tint.'

It is sometimes suggested that Wilde did not invent the flower at all but simply borrowed an icon from Parisian gay culture. There is, however, little evidence for this theory, other than the fact that the French name for carnation, *oeillet*, meaning 'little-eye', was popular slang for anus. (See also **Rose**.) It's impossible to say, however, whether any of this was on Wilde's mind when he donned his *bouttonière* or quipped that 'a really well-made button-hole is the only link between Art and Nature'. The idea that the flower was a homosexual signal was largely established a couple of years later by *The Green Carnation*, Robert Hitchens's (anonymously published) *roman à clef* about Wilde's affair with Bosie, Lord Alfred Douglas. In fact, Wilde associated his lover with all kinds of flowers: Fleur-de-Lys and Jonquil were two of his nicknames. In 1895, as a tribute to Bosie, he choreographed a 'perfumed atmosphere' at the premiere of *The Importance of Being Earnest*, inviting his supporters to wear lily of the valley, while he himself again wore a green carnation. But by then, the flower that he had once claimed meant 'nothing whatsoever' had become a badge of many things: homosexuality, Decadent aestheticism, and, at the centre of it all, Wilde himself.

The legacy of Wilde's carnation can be located in many places – from a 1929 parody about 'haughty boys, naughty boys' by non-fan Noel Coward to the name of a Soho gay bar in the early 2000s. Less directly, its powerful clove scent can also be detected in two early twentieth-century school stories by women. In Katherine Mansfield's 'Carnation' (1917), we are told that Eve (a temptress, of course) always carries a flower to class – to twirl and tickle the neck of her friend Kate. The story is about the day that Eve brings in a 'deep, deep red' carnation, which has a nicely artificial look, 'as though it had been dipped in wine and left in the dark to dry'. Was Mansfield aware that, since carnation adds a clove flavour to infusions, one of its folk names is 'sops in wine'? In any case, as the teacher reads some (appropriately) French poetry, the scent of the flower floats across the room to Kate who is looking out the window at a bare-chested man pumping water: the intoxicating rhythms of scent, sound and sight build together and Kate experiences what can only be described as a kind of multi-sensory orgasm, a 'great rushing, rising, triumphant thing'. The moment passes, but Eve has noticed. '*Souvenir tendre,*' she whispers as she drops the carnation 'down the front of Katie's blouse'.

The teenage protagonist of Willa Cather's 'Paul's Case: A Study in Temperament' (1905) has a much less happy experience. Once again, the carnation in question is 'flippantly red' rather than green, but that probably speaks to what was available in Pittsburgh rather than its wearer's intent; otherwise, as his high school principal observes, Paul clearly has 'something of the dandy about him'. In this case, however, the consequences are tragic, for Cather is all too aware that Paul's is not a world in which it is possible to live as 'exactly the kind of boy he had always wanted to be'. One snowy night Paul runs away to New York to try to be that boy. Standing on the corner of Fifth Avenue, he is overwhelmed by the sight of the glass-covered florists' stands: 'whole flower stands blooming under glass cases, against the sides of which the snow flakes stuck and melted; violets, roses, carnations, lilies of the valley – somehow vastly more lovely and alluring that they blossomed thus unnaturally in the snow.' (See also **Violet**.) The next day, however, Paul notices that the carnations pinned to his coat are 'drooping' from the cold, 'their red glory all over'. The glorious flowers' 'brave mockery at the winter outside the glass' is ultimately a 'losing game'. He digs a small hole and carefully buries one of the blossoms. Then, in one final grand gesture, 'as though he were being watched', Paul throws himself in front of a train.

The carnation worn by Wilde, and perhaps by Paul too, was a Malmaison variety, a large rose-like, heavily scented flower that made for a blousy buttonhole. (This is the source of the apocryphal story that Wilde's favourite perfume was *Malmaison* by Floris when actually he preferred their *Canterbury Wood Violet*.) But it is unlikely that the flowers that Paul observed through the whirling snow were hard-to-grow Malmaisons; more likely, they were reliable glasshouse perpetuals. Paul's case, then, is not only a study of a particular adolescent temperament but of the possibilities for expressing that temperament that arose from more mundane factors – especially, floriculture's vastly improved production and distribution systems. The Fifth Avenue flowers probably came from a glasshouse in Tewksbury, Massachusetts – the self-described 'Carnation Capital of the World' – or from the 'forcing belt' of California or Colorado, where there was even talk of a 'Carnation gold rush'. Aesthetes like Paul tended to think of flowers as offering a beautiful alternative to the age of industrial infrastructure and mass-production, forgetting that their medium of protest was itself a product of that age. And the same can also be said of those revolutionaries who, for at least a century now, have been raising their carnations high like a mass of little red flags.

On 1 May 1886, thousands of workers in New York, Cincinnati, Chicago and many other American cities, went on strike to demand a shorter working day, and, as they marched, they sang:

> We want to feel the sunshine;
> We want to smell the flowers
> We're sure God has willed it.
> And we mean to have eight hours.

Two days later, at a harvesting machine plant in Chicago, the police opened fire on a group of strikers and, the day after that, a meeting held in protest in Haymarket Square ended in violence and mayhem. As the police again prepared to intervene, a bomb was thrown in their path, and, as a result of the explosion and the ensuing gunfire, seven policemen and four workers were killed. The event is remembered because of the conviction, and subsequent hanging, of a group of well-known, and mainly German-born, anarchists, none of whom had actually been present that day but whose ideas were said to have influenced the unidentified bomber. The novelist William Dean Howells was one of many who interpreted the trial as indictment of the nation itself: how could Americans boast of their 'free Republic', he asked, when it had killed five men simply 'for their opinions'?

One of the legacies of Haymarket was the enduring association of the campaign for workers' rights with rural 'Maying' customs. The link was consolidated in Paris in July 1889 when, among the issues discussed by the 400 delegates of the Marxist International Socialist Congress, was the proposal, made by the President of the American Federation of Labor, for a global day of demonstrations to fight for the eight-hour day and to remember the Haymarket dead. On 1 May 1890, the first International Workers' Day was celebrated in dozens of cities throughout western Europe, the United States and South America. Although, as Eric Hobsbawm has observed, May Day was 'about nothing but the future', its touchstones lay in the radical battles of the past, from the Haymarket martyrs right back to the French Revolution. And that's where the mass-produced red carnations come in, superseding the holiday's traditional reliance on country flowers like hawthorn and daisies.

It's hard to pinpoint just where and how red first acquired a radical (rather than royal) reputation, but during the seventeenth century it featured in protests as far apart as Japan and Italy. In England, the soldiers of Cromwell's New Model Army tied red ribbons round their arms, and in Brittany, protesters against the stamp tax came to be identified with their *bonnets rouges*. More than a hundred years later, during the French Revolution, the Jacobins revived those *bonnets*, in direct opposition to the red-heeled aristocrats, *les talons rouge*. And from then on, red was firmly established as the colour that signified both the blood of past martyrs and the fiery passion of future struggle. The commemoration of the Haymarket dead is said to have been the first time that red carnations were used for this purpose, perhaps because local market gardeners sold their wares nearby. In any case, to this day, the tall, red, flag-like perpetual carnation is allied with radicalism.

Arno Mohr's poster for the Socialist Unity Party of Germany advertises May Day, 1946.

The most iconic red carnations are those associated with the 1917 Russian revolution – Nadezhda Soboleva notes that 'red standards, red bows and ribbons, and red carnations were the hallmarks of the crowds on the streets of Petrograd and Moscow' – and therefore with its commemoration ever since. The flower's influence was felt everywhere on the Soviet parade ground, from the artificial flowers that decorated the lamp posts to the guns that trundled past (a 1974 howitzer was popularly known as the carnation or *Gvozdika*). And even the air was scented with the clove-like scent of carnations. In 1925,

С ПРАЗДНИКОМ ОКТЯБРЯ!

A Soviet postcard from the 1980s commemorating the October Revolution.

Brocard's 'Le Bouquet Préféré de l'Impératrice', a perfume created in 1913 for Czar Nicholas II's mother, was relaunched by its new state-owned manufacturer as 'Krasnya Moskva', *krasnya* meaning both 'red' and 'beautiful'.

Today, the revolutionary *Dianthus* can be found all over the world, and not only in May Day parades. In Greece, it is particularly connected to Nikos Beloyannis, a key figure in the Communist resistance to the Nazi occupation, who was executed on 30 March 1952 as part of a notorious right-wing political purge. On the way to be sentenced, Beloyannis was handed a carnation by an unknown young woman, and a photograph of him holding the flower and smiling was circulated widely. Pablo Picasso, one of many artists and intellectuals who petitioned for Beloyannis's release, used the image as the basis for a sketch that he named *L'Homme d'Oeillet*.

Another young woman who handed out carnations, and whose name did make it into the history books, was Celeste Martins Caeiro. On 25 April 1974,

A poster by Sergio
Guimarães celebrating
the Carnation
Revolution of
25 April 1974.

she was working as a waitress in downtown Lisbon. It was the restaurant's first anniversary and the manager had bought cigars and carnations to give out to customers. Plans changed, however, when the radio announced an imminent military coup and tanks began to roll through the city streets: the staff were told they could go home and that they could take the flowers with them. When Martins Caeiro went to see what was happening, a soldier approached her looking for a cigarette. Instead she offered him a flower which (perhaps thinking of the 1967 Pentagon protests – see **Chrysanthemum**) he dropped into the barrel of his rifle. Martins Caeiro carried on, handing out flowers to soldiers along the way. Thousands of locals took to the streets that day, and the military uprising against the forty-year Estado Novo dictatorship started to feel like a street party. The *Revolução dos Cravos*, the carnation revolution, was underway. Clearly Martins Caeiro could not have supplied the entire city with flowers, and other witnesses recall that most came from Lisbon's flower market. But although white carnations and lilies were also freely used – this was just ten days after Easter – they did not have the same significance; photographers invariably sought out the more glorious red, which duly became the lasting symbol of the revolution.

※

I end this chapter with one more instance in which carnations helped to invent a tradition: the American holiday of Mother's Day. The practice of reserving a day to offer maternal tributes dates back to antiquity, and was adapted by the early Christian church as Mothering Sunday (three weeks before Easter); gradually, it evolved into a day when household servants were given time off to visit their families, as well as the church of their baptism (their 'mother' church). The modern holiday is something different. Its origins lie in a particularly nineteenth-century view of the political value of motherhood, and in early twentieth-century anxieties about changes in women's roles and family life.

The story begins on Sunday 10 May 1908, when a woman in Grafton, West Virginia called Anna Jarvis donated 500 white carnations, one for each mother in the congregation of St Andrew's Methodist Episcopal Church. It was less a gesture of generosity than a declaration of intent. For the next six years, Jarvis tirelessly lobbied the US Congress until, in 1914, it voted to designate the second Sunday in May as a national holiday, 'a public expression of our love and reverence for the mothers of our country'.

Four years later, the Society of American Florists launched its first national publicity campaign with a slogan that remains in the vernacular a hundred years on. 'Say it with Flowers', we were told, and we continue to obey. The Society's aim was to embed the purchase of flowers into everyday routines, but (like greetings card manufacturers around the same time) it also realised the value of regular celebrations and rituals that would take advantage of modern dispersed families, and the technologies of telegraph and telephone, that would enable its members to send gifts to each other. By 1920, as *Florists' Review* pointed out, the Mother's Day holiday was firmly established as 'a splendid occasion for florists', not least because it was 'pre-eminently a day for long-distance messages'.

Jarvis was appalled. Mother's Day was meant to be a 'Home Day', a 'day of family reunions and homecomings', rather than one in which expensive gifts were delivered. In 1908, she had paid just half a cent for a flower, but by 1920 the florists (whom she had welcomed as allies while lobbying Congress) were selling carnations at a dollar apiece. Jarvis tried various strategies to undercut the trade. First, she suggested boycotting florists altogether and offering instead the gift of an American flag, or perhaps a 'modest and inexpensive' (surely free?) dandelion. Then, realising that something more distinctive was needed, the Mother's Day International Association started manufacturing its own authorised badge, featuring a white carnation. But it was too late, the genie was out of the bottle. 'Notwithstanding the high prices asked, as much as $4 a dozen in some cases,' reported the *New York Times* in 1922, 'florists did a thriving business in carnations.' Until that is, the demand for white carnations became uneconomical and then they tweaked Jarvis's formula to suit their own ends. Advertisements started to suggest that 'a wider selection of flowers' might provide 'a much more satisfactory means of celebrating', and a couplet was coined to nudge customers toward different species, and different colours:

For Mother at home, flowers bright;
In Mother's memory, flowers white.

In 1914, Mother's Day was the greatest gift the burgeoning flower industry could have wished for and, after more than a hundred years, it keeps on giving. In 2019 alone, Americans spent around $2.6 billion on Mother's Day flowers.

Why, though, did Jarvis choose the white carnation in the first place? The obvious reason is a traditional association with the Virgin Mary – some variety of *Dianthus* is said to have sprung up where her tears fell at the base of the cross – and therefore with motherly love. Jarvis offered an updated account of the flower's maternal virtues, freely adapting the Victorian language of flowers. 'Its whiteness,' she said, 'is to symbolize the truth, purity and broad charity of mother love; its fragrance, her memory and her prayers. The carnation does not drop its petals, but hugs them to its heart as it dies, and so, too, mothers hug their children to their hearts, their mother love never dying.'

Mother's Day Card, 1914.

But there were also more personal reasons for Jarvis's choice. White carnations had been the favourite flower of her own mother, Anna Reeves Jarvis, who had begun the campaign for a day commemorating motherhood. As much as the strikes at Haymarket Square, this desire was a legacy of the American Civil War. For Reeves Jarvis firmly believed that a day celebrating motherhood would serve the cause of national reconciliation, uniting families divided by the long conflict. White families, that is. Jarvis may have wanted to restrict the symbolism of white carnations to the conventional tropes of truth and purity but, in the United States of that period, other associations are inescapable. In the late 1860s, while Reeves Jarvis was urging Americans to put the war behind them, white vigilante groups were forming all over the South. In Alabama, two such groups styled themselves, florally, as the Knights of the White Camellia and the Knights of the White Carnation. This might seem mere coincidence until we recall that J. Thomas Heflin, the Congressman who proposed the resolution for Mother's Day, and who thought of himself as an unwavering supporter of 'our precious white women', was from Alabama. By many accounts, 'Cotton Tom' was 'the most shameless racist' ever to have served in the House.

SUNFLOWER

ROSE

SUMMER

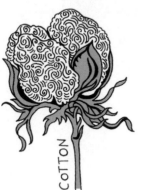

COTTON

LOTUS

Summer

Summer afternoon – summer afternoon; to me those have always been the two most beautiful words in the English language.

Henry James, in conversation with Edith Wharton

The pageant of summer! Almost too much of a good thing!

Head Gardener Bert Pinnegar
in *Old Herbaceous: A Novel of the Garden*
by Reginald Arkell

Henry James and Bert Pinnegar spent their summers very differently. Henry James was usually holed up in the 'garden room' of his Sussex home, from which vantage point, recalled his secretary Theodora Bosanquet, he 'never failed' to enjoy the sight of his 'English gardener digging the flower beds or mowing the lawn or sweeping fallen leaves'. Bert Pinnegar, meanwhile, *is* an English gardener – employed to do the digging, mowing, sweeping, edging, deadheading, watering and weeding. He doesn't have time to enjoy 'all the good things' and, although he doesn't like to find fault with the 'ways of nature', he can't help thinking 'if only the thing would stop for half a minute and let you look at it'.

If the flowering pleasures of spring come piecemeal, one by one, like a carefully curated tasting menu, summer's offerings are prodigious – the heaving table of an all-you-can-eat buffet. Colours and perfumes proliferate: red clashes with pink; the scent of jasmine with that of lavender. Our senses – like our gardeners – work overtime.

What to do with all the good things? Summer, said Henry David Thoreau, is the season when those who have time 'lay up a stock of experiences for the winter, as the squirrel of nut'. Many of Thoreau's experiences involved wild flowers, and he squirreled them systematically away in his memory and writing. 'I reckon that about nine-tenths of the flowers of the year have now blossomed,' he wrote in his journal on 26 July 1853 and, five days later, 'I calculate that less than forty species of flowers known to me remain to blossom this year.'

Arkell was describing summer in England, Thoreau in Massachusetts – places where 'floral days' are a long time coming and gone too soon. Flower growers in northern climates, whose main business lies between November and April, can't understand why the gift-giving holidays and celebrations don't take place in the summer when the temperature is warm, the days are long and the flowers are abundant and cheap. But that's precisely the point: we don't need florists in July. Summer is the season when we celebrate natural profusion. In the Northamptonshire village where John Clare grew up, the cottages displayed a 'Midsummer cushion' – a piece of grass 'full of field flowers'; in the Italian town of Genzano, an entire street is carpeted in flowers; in Brussels, the carpet fills the main square; on the island of Jersey, until recently, locals were encouraged to dismantle floral floats and throw great handfuls of blooms at each other in a joyous Battle of the Flowers. We can afford to be wasteful in the summer.

Time, too, becomes profuse, as long, hot days follow one another seemingly endlessly. Summer is the season of opened senses, of a luxuriance which satiation cannot dull: a paradise forever waiting to be regained. D.H. Lawrence imagined the June love-making of Lady Chatterley and her lover Oliver Mellors as an abundance of late spring and early summer flowers: columbines, campions, honeysuckle, bluebells, forget-me-nots, woodruff and hyacinths combine in 'wild obeisance' to the season.

For Lawrence, summer makes it possible for lovers to discover 'the flowers in each other', a reconciliation not only of modern man and woman but also of the sensual and the spiritual. That harmony is also at the heart of medieval Persian poetry, where it is primarily imagined through the figure of the **rose**, the earthly manifestation of divine beauty and an emblem of the transience of human pleasure. In the Persian tradition, the rose is associated with late spring but because it epitomises high summer in many other places, I include it here.

The rose takes its place in an unlikely posy with the **lotus**, the summer flower of Chinese and Japanese seasonal iconography. With its languorous leaves, heavy-scented flowers and watery home, the lotus evokes a cool world away from heat and dust. In India, however, when summer brings welcome rain, the lotus is a monsoon flower.

Neither lotus nor the rose grow above the Arctic circle – at least not yet. Summer means something very different in the very far north: celebrations focus on temperatures approaching 10°C and long, long days. When the American ethnographer Franz Boas visited Baffin Island, a Canadian territory in the Arctic Archipelago, in 1883, he noted that in the depths of winter the Inuit people would cheer themselves with songs of summer. They couldn't wait for the time when the gulls would cease crying and the reindeer return, when rivers would rush from the hills, meat and codfish become plentiful, and wildflowers reappear on the tundra:

Aya

Ayaya, it is beautiful, beautiful it is out-doors when the summer comes at last.

Less than a hundred and fifty years later, however, no one sings that song any more. Global warming is happening two or three times faster in the Arctic than elsewhere and, on Baffin, the ancient glaciers are retreating to reveal a landscape of plants that have been frozen for the last 40,000 years. Summer is now the time when the ice melts.

Further south, things are heating up too. Every year drought and heavy rains (often around harvest time) threaten this section's remaining two flowers, both of which are grown as agricultural crops. The large-scale cultivation and global distribution of **cotton** and **sunflower** plants have contributed to climate change, and its consequences now affect their future viability. In many parts of the world, the season's 'good things' are now under threat.

Knowing that more, and hotter, sunny days signal catastrophe rather than pleasure, those of us who live in the north need to readjust our thinking. Nevertheless, it's hard not to approach summer's end in a melancholic mood: defiantly, we try to 'extend' the season by planting flowers from the southern hemisphere like dahlias and salvias. John Keats observed that bees congregate on these late bloomers, mistakenly thinking that 'warm days will never cease'. But always, eventually, even now, they do. After Paradise, Fall.

And not to everyone's regret. In June, Thoreau worried that nature would 'get through her work too soon'; by September, he felt he had gorged long enough on 'Summer's sweets'. As the nights draw in, a new and less luxuriant season unfolds, bringing its own particular pleasures.

Rose

Must be respectful and must also bring 🌹
I only date men who shower me in roses.
I am looking for a cool Lady. Have a lot of roses if interested.
What's up with the roses? Every few posts are mentioning roses. I'm just
clueless over here. Lol.

About ten years ago, magazine articles began to warn online innocents that
requests like these did not refer to flowers but to cash: 'must bring roses' was not
an exacting demand from a hookup from hell but rather a way of circumventing
the dating website's ban on commercial solicitation. And once that was cleared
up, there was more advice for the hapless lothario regarding the flowers
themselves. While it was almost obligatory to give your girlfriend roses on
Valentine's Day – in the United States alone, 200 million were sold in 2018 –
and generous to add a bottle of Chanel No. 5, each 30ml bottle of which requires
a dozen *Rosa centifolia*, it was definitely not a good idea to bring either as a gift
on a (non-paying) first date. Roses were not only 'outdated', said the etiquette
guides, they screamed 'please like me', suggesting their bearers were 'needy and
supplicative'. Even worse, they created 'unrealistic' expectations. Give roses once
and they'll think 'you are some kind of superhuman "perfect guy"'. God forbid.

Was there ever a time when roses weren't implicated in human sexual
relations? There is virtually no lover's discourse in which they don't feature:

from the *Roman de la Rose*, a medieval allegory of sexual pursuit ('I longed, and it seemed good to me, to probe its very depths') to the Renaissance *carpe diem* injunction ('gather ye rosebuds while ye may,' instructed Robert Herrick); from Victorian innuendos about orgasmic flushing (Thomas Hardy observed the 'usually pale cheeks' of his character Sue Bridehead 'reflecting the pink of the tinted roses at which she gazed') to sculptures of many petalled vulvas (such as those created by Hannah Wilke in the 1970s).

Miniature of the lover tending the rose in a late fifteenth-century manuscript of *Le Roman de la Rose.*

Of course, the rose has plenty of other associations beyond the realm of love and sex. It has served as a royal emblem and a national flower. It represents Christian charity, the brevity of life, and hopes for happiness, a time when everything will come up roses. Secular and spiritual roses are often intertwined – for example, in Persian and Ottoman tales of the Nightingale and the Rose, or in Dante's epic of finding God while looking for Beatrice. In some versions of Islam, the prophet Muhammad communicates through roses; according to the Sufi poet Rumi, his fragrant perspiration falls to earth to produce its perfume. Stories of the mystical rose later spread east to India and west to Europe. Rainer Maria Rilke, for example, wrote endlessly about both the romance and the 'visionary power' of roses; the essayist William Gass describes the flowers scrambling through Rilke's life 'as if he were their trellis'. It was inevitable then that Rilke would rely on roses to woo his future wife, Clara Westhoff. And he also invented a 'new form of caress' for her: 'placing a rose gently on a closed eye until its coolness can no longer be felt'. It's a little mystical, sure, but also rather seductive.

In the Greek tradition, the rose's association with Dionysus as well as Eros and Aphrodite resulted in a lasting connection between romance, wine and roses – in short, the good life was to be had on a 'bed of a roses'. Since Aphrodite was the goddess of seduction, she was the protectress of courtesans and prostitutes, some of whom also sold flowers. 'You with the roses have a rosy charm,' declared Dionysus the Sophist, 'but what are you selling – yourself, the roses, or both?' Ovid, meanwhile, instructed 'girls of the street' to bring roses to the April festival of Vinalia for 'Venus is appropriate for the earnings of women who promise a lot.' Roses were associated with prostitutes in many cultures, and in Elizabethan England visiting a prostitute was commonly described as 'plucking a rose' – some towns allocated a Rose Street for this purpose. Somewhat confusingly, 'plucking a rose' also became a euphemism for female urination; Jonathan Swift describes a 'bashful maid' retreating behind a bush for this purpose.

There was considerable overlap between the metaphors used in pornography or bawdy humour and in medical reference books. In *The Midwives Book* (1671), the first account of the subject by a British woman, the author Jane Sharp relies heavily on flowers, and roses in particular, to explain female reproduction. Menstruation, for example, is called 'the Flowers' because 'Fruit follows', while 'Deflowerment' is explained by comparing the rupture of the hymen to 'a Rose half-blown when the bearded leaves are taken away'. What is fascinating about *The Midwives Book* is the way this kind of language sits alongside a more or less anatomically accurate account of the hymen's 'sinewy

A watercolour from West Bengal featuring two lovers, or a man with a courtesan, holding roses.

membrane'. A similar combination of science and symbolism occurs in Sharp's diagrams. In one, the uterus of a heavily pregnant women is opened up like a flower in full bloom, while her pudendum is depicted (or, rather, delicately concealed) by another flower.

Illustration of a
pregnant woman's
uterus from Jane
Sharp's *The Midwives
Book: or the Whole
Art of Midwifery
Discovered*, 1671.

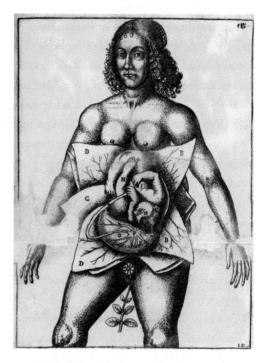

Every flower is a collection of sexual organs, and its beauty is the plant's method of attracting, in myriad, complex ways, the pollinators that enable it to reproduce. But the rose has particular physical qualities – colour, texture and form – that seem to evoke human sexuality. Some of these attributes can be found in the single-flowered (that is, five-petalled) species, but it is undoubtedly the case that thousands of years of rose breeding, creating complex 'double' flowers, has intensified the flower's resemblance to a woman's lips, cheeks or vulva. The result, as Michael Pollan points out, is that we can never be sure whether we are speaking of nature or culture 'when we speak of a rose (nature) that has been bred (culture) so that its blossoms (nature) make men imagine (culture) the sex of women (nature)'.

The stages in the rose's life cycle are also important in explaining its starring role in romance and erotica. In the imagination of Edmund Spenser (and many others), the dramatic action begins with the virginal promise of the closed rosebud, then develops into a full, fragrant blooming of passion – 'Lo see soone after, how more bold and free / Her bared bosome she doth broad display' – before ending up with the loss of petals, a sign of the fading of love or the loved one. The French surrealist Georges Bataille rather nastily compares decaying roses to 'old and overly made-up dowagers' who 'die ridiculously' on stems that had once 'seemed to carry them to the clouds'. Working in the tradition of Baudelaire's *Les Fleurs du Mal*, Bataille was determined to undermine the rose's rose-tinted reputation and to point out that the flower's 'angelic and lyrical purity' soon decays to reveal the 'sordid tuft' of the stamens. In Bataille's hands, the romance of the rose becomes a tragicomedy – 'from ordure to the ideal', and quickly back again.

The plant's thorns don't matter in Bataille's story of 'nauseating banality'. However, they play a big part in the Christian tradition, where the narrative is all one-way, leading toward Mary, the rose without thorns. Instruments of torture, thorns produce bloody wounds which are transfigured by divine grace into beautiful flowers. They represent the abjection from which faith rescues us rather than that which, from a materialist point of view, is all that awaits us. The rose is therefore the flower of martyrs and miracles – a theme that runs through Islamic and Christian writing and which, in modern secular form, lies behind its adoption as an emblem of Socialism. (For more on political martyrs, see the rose's rival, the red **Carnation**.)

As well as having thorns, roses are susceptible to a wide array of diseases, including mildew, black spot, rust and canker; the last is a fungal infection that shows up as black splotches on the plant's main stem and, without treatment, can eventually kill it. In the Middle Ages, 'canker' referred to a caterpillar or other insect larvae that destroys the plant from the inside. By the seventeenth century, it had come to refer to any destructive agent that operates in this way, particularly when it acts on something beautiful: 'loathsome canker lives in sweetest bud,' declared Shakespeare. The word shares a Latin root (*cancer,* meaning 'crab') with 'chancre', used to describe the red sore that appears as the first sign of syphilis. Because of its shape and colour, and because everyone knew syphilis was sexually transmitted, a chancre was often compared to a rose. The association emerged in the context of the syphilis epidemic that began in Naples in the late fifteenth century – and which many blamed on Columbus, newly returned from the Americas. A syphilitic chancre was also known as a red rose of Naples.

The association of sexually transmitted diseases and roses has proved enduring. In the eighteenth and nineteenth centuries, gonorrhoea was sometimes referred to as 'venereal rose'. We don't know if that's what William Blake had in mind in 'The Sick Rose', one of his *Songs of Experience*, but of the various meanings one might attach to the 'invisible worm' that crawls into the rose's bed of 'crimson joy', syphilis or gonorrhoea are certainly options. In the late 1960s, meanwhile, women in Vietnam and Taiwan worried about contracting 'Saigon Rose' (gonorrhoea) – the 'prickliest rose of all' – from American soldiers.

This long history has made the rose a readily available symbol in disease prevention campaigns, and never more so than at the height of the HIV/AIDS epidemic. In Hong Kong clinics, AIDS Concern displayed posters bluntly addressing its clients: 'You should be proud of yourself. You've got Vietnam Rose. Wear a condom, because next time you won't be so lucky.' In Germany, meanwhile, the national information *Mach Mit* (Join in) campaign promoted the same message with a rolled condom as the flower, and the opening phrase of Goethe's poem, 'Heidenröslein': *Sah ein Knab* ('Once a boy'). It was an apt choice, for the poem is all about the lure and dangers of sex. When the boy declares that he will pluck the little heath rose, the plant replies that she will prick him so that he will never forget her. But he doesn't listen, and there the analogy to HIV transmission seems to end. In the poem, it is the pricking rose who suffers while the plucking boy seems absolutely fine.

Sah ein Knab'...

mach's mit.

GIB AIDS KEINE CHANCE

Bundeszentrale für gesundheitliche Aufklärung, 51101 Köln. Gestaltung: M. Kolvenbach + G. Meyer. Bestell-Nr. 70805000, Serie Bestell-Nr. 70800000

A red condom replaces the rose in this 1990s poster by Marcel Kolvenbach and Guido Meyer for the German campaign to prevent the spread of HIV/AIDS through condom use.

At times, all this symbolism can become a little too much.

'The rose is obsolete,' declared the American poet William Carlos Williams in 1922; for too many years, he said, 'the rose carried weight of love', but now, finally, 'love is at an end – of roses'. It was time to throw out all the worn out words and ideas, and pay attention to the flower itself. Gertrude Stein thought that all one should say is that 'a rose is a rose is a rose'. In doing so, she reckoned that she had made the rose red 'for the first time in English poetry for a hundred years'. The rose is red – and *read* – again. Modernising the rose didn't mean giving up on poetic conceit, however, just refreshing it.

What really irritated modern (never mind modernist) sensibilities were the sentimental conventions of their Victorian forebears. The nineteenth century had been the great era of flowers: of flower shows and horticultural societies; of fresh-cut and dried flowers; of buttonholes and posies; of floral prints on clothes, curtains, wallpaper and dishes; of girls named Daisy, Lily, Iris, Violet – and Rose. It was the era of poems about men waiting for 'maidens' with rosy cheeks and rosy lips (like Tennyson's Maud) to 'yield', and of lengthy flower lexicons which laid out the subtle differences between a red rose, a deep red rose, a rosebud with or without leaves, with one bud or two buds open, held upright or upside down, and on and on and on. It all had to go. Like the chintz, the doilies, the antimacassar, and the dusty fern in the parlour, the symbolically overburdened rose was now an embarrassment, a liability.

Virginia Woolf was particularly determined to indicate that she was 'sharply cut off' from her Victorian 'predecessors', and part of what that entailed was acknowledging the rose's 'self-sufficient' nature. How strange it was, she reflected, that roses had come 'to symbolize passions, decorate festivals, and lie (as if *they* knew sorrow) upon the pillows of the dead'. She promised to really 'examine the rose', to observe 'how it stands, still and steady, throughout an entire afternoon on earth'. But it didn't take long before symbolism – modern rather than Victorian, but still symbolism – crept back in. Woolf's rose isn't allowed to be merely unmoving but rather, like a true member of the Bloomsbury set, it stands tall and faultless in its 'demeanour of perfect dignity and self-possession'.

There were, of course, many ways to be modern – for both women and roses. Ironically, the most modern of roses, the hybrid tea, was the most despised. Michael Pollan points out the nice coincidence that the first hybrid tea was produced in 1867, the year that the Second Reform Act gave the vote to middle-class men in Britain. In Bloomsbury eyes, a glossy-leafed, disease-free hybrid tea might be 'well-groomed, well-taught, compliant, and as tidy as a lady of fashion', but that just made it boringly bourgeois. Properly 'discerning' gardeners, like Woolf's lover Vita Sackville-West, found the hybrid tea 'tiresomely bright', the rose equivalent of the bedding geranium.

A superior kind of modernity was found in a return to Old Roses, the earliest garden Gallicas and Damasks, as well as the large, sprawling, once-flowering, highly scented varieties that had been cultivated in the eighteenth and early nineteenth centuries – the Centifolias, Bourbons and Moss Roses which were the stars of Empress Joséphine's garden at Malmaison. Sackville West adored these 'sumptuous and ravishing' flowers. Like her, they were aristocratic and Bohemian: they liked 'to express themselves in all their vigour freely as the fancy takes them'. It hardly needed saying that 'it isn't everybody who has room for them in a small garden'.

Woolf maps the difference between these two kinds of roses – less in terms of class than in temperament – onto two of her most famous characters, Mr (Richard) and Mrs (Clarissa) Dalloway. Because 'he could not bring himself to say he loved her; not in so many words', Richard presents Clarissa with a 'vast bunch' of red and white florist's roses (hybrid teas). While he succeeds in making a declaration, his choice of bloom, and mode of delivery, marks him out as dull and conventional. This is made painfully clear when his 'way with flowers' is compared to that of Clarissa's first love, Sally Seton. Sally doesn't go shopping for romantic tokens; she simply wanders through a walled country garden in the moonlight, plucking Old Roses with joyful 'abandonment'. Clarissa thinks that the 'most exquisite moment' of her life is the instant when 'Sally stopped; picked a flower; kissed her on the lips.'

The problem of modern life, at least as diagnosed by D.H. Lawrence, was how to shake off the discontent of an over-civilised life; how, in other words, to stop being a neurotic 'rose that could not quite come into blossom, but remained tense', and get back to the garden of primitive ecstasy. And that meant recognising, as Stein did, that one rose could 'caress' another – 'a cool red rose and a pink cut pink, a collapse and a sold hole, a little less hot'. Or it could even caress itself, as the strikingly androgynous Vaslav Nijinsky did when he performed *Le Spectre de la Rose*.

☦

Jean Cocteau's 1913 poster for the Ballets Russes, featuring Vaslav Nijinsky in the rose-petalled costume he wore in the title role of *Le Spectre de la Rose.*

THÉATRE DES
CHAMPS-ÉLYSEES
Direction GABRIEL ASTRUC

BALLETS RUSSES

So perhaps, love is not, after all, 'at an end of roses'. The flower might be prickly, cankerous, obsolete, and nauseatingly banal, and as a gift it might well come across as needy or desperate. But so what? Most people need all the help they can get in speaking of love – and if a florist's bouquet, a slab of rose-scented Turkish delight, or even an emoji helps, then surely that's all to the good. But I'll leave the final romantic gesture to Jean Genet.

Genet, a Catholic by upbringing, was a great believer in the 'miracle of the rose', the imaginative transfiguration of pain into beauty. He sees a crushed fingernail and is put 'in mind of a black flower'; a murderer walks by in handcuffs and suddenly the cuffs are transformed into a garland of white roses; the 'mingled odors' of farting prisoners transport him to 'a garden of saintliness where roses bloom'. Like much of his work, Genet's only film, *Un Chant d'Amour* (1950), is set in a prison and explores the efforts of solitary men to connect with each other. They do what they can; one finds a hole in the wall and inserts a straw through which he blows cigarette smoke for his neighbour to inhale. But the true medium of love, which the film returns to again and again, is a posy of flowers on a string which swings from left to right between two cells. We don't see the men, just their arms reaching out of the cell windows. The string seems too short, the task impossible, but finally, in the film's dying seconds, the arm on the right succeeds in grasping hold of the flowers. A song of love is complete.

Communicating with flowers in Jean Genet's *Un Chant d'Amour*, 1950.

Lotus

The lotus is a miracle. From muddy waters, an immaculate flower rises. Its scent is powerful enough to revive the dead. After eating its fruit, sailors forget to go home. A 'lotus' does all that, and more – but not the same lotus.

This chapter is mainly about three flowering plants that share the name: *Nymphaea caerulea*, the blue-flowered water lily that was venerated and eaten by the ancient Egyptians; *Nelumbo nucifera*, the sacred (and nutritious) lotus of India and much of south-eastern Asia; and, finally, *Ziziphus lotus*, whose date-like fruit fed Homer's 'lotus eaters' on an island off the coast of what is now Tunisia. The first two flourish in still or slow-moving water. The third is just one of many land-based plants the Greeks called *lotos*; others include a perennial clover, the Nettle or 'Lote' tree, and fenugreek. Across oceans and centuries, these three plants have got themselves into an almighty muddle.

The first confusion began around 500 BCE when the Persians introduced the pink-flowered Asian lotus, *Nelumbo nucifera*, into Egypt, where it gradually supplanted the local white and blue water lilies. By the time Herodotus visited in the fifth century BCE, *Nelumbo* was well enough established to be considered a native, and the two genera are freely mixed in Roman mosaics of the flora and fauna of the Nile. One of the most impressive of these mosaics was preserved at Pompeii and shows the pink *Nelumbo* in different stages of flowering and fruiting (a duck even carries a bud in its mouth); the frog in the foreground, however, is sitting on lily pads of a native blue *Nymphaea caerulea*.

A Roman mosaic featuring a Nile river scene, from the House of the Faun, Pompeii, 120 BCE.

Nymphaea caerula, known as the blue lotus, was fundamental to Egyptian cosmology, ritual and art. For a culture rooted in solar mythology – and therefore in the cycles of birth, death and rebirth – the most important feature of the plant was that its flower rises to the surface and opens in morning, then closes and sinks again at dusk. And the next day, it does it all again. There's a fair bit of poetic licence in this account, however. In fact, the flower buds rise to the surface over a period of two to three days and, when ready, open in the morning and close in the mid-afternoon; they don't submerge at night.

Nevertheless, the Egyptians held the lotus to be the primordial flower, out of which the sun (and therefore life) originally arose. In one creation story, the sun god Ra is imprisoned in a womb-like lotus bud and then emerges from its blossoming flower; in another, the flower opens to reveal a sacred scarab

A lotus inlay, Egypt, 1353–1336 BCE.

(dung beetle) which transforms itself into a weeping boy from whose tears emerges humankind. In the Ari papyrus (*The Book of the Dead*), the lotus god Nefertum arises each day carrying the essence of life to 'the nostrils of Ra'. Perfumes and unguents made with blue lotus were considered to contain this essence, and therefore aid in the reanimation of the dead. Lotus petals were included in the lavish floral collars that adorned Tutankhamun's mummy, and at the entrance to his tomb a small carving depicts the young king as a child rising from the flower.

It wasn't all symbolic. *Nymphaea caerulea* and the white, night-flowering *N. lotos* both contain the alkaloids nuciferine and apomorphine, which suggest that they may have been used as ritual emetics or mild hallucinogens – just as, across the Atlantic, *Nymphaea ampla* was used by the Mayans. (See also **Marigold**.) Certainly, these plants are often depicted alongside the opium poppy and mandrake, plants with known psychoactive properties. Blue lotuses also featured in erotic cartoons, suggesting an alternative use as an aphrodisiac, a theory supported by the fact that apomorphine is now prescribed for erectile dysfunction.

Another association was geographical: the lotus was the flower of Upper Egypt (the south of the country), just as papyrus was the flower of the Delta, and the union of the two kingdoms was represented by their entwined stalks. The lotus's emergence in the shallow waterways that feed into the Nile signalled the renewal of life made possible by the Delta's annual flooding. Seeds germinate in May when the inundation begins – it really is a question of 'just add water' – and the plant comes into flower in August, when the flood reaches its full height. The lotus was therefore also an attribute of Osiris and Isis, gods of fecundity and rebirth. But its arrival had practical advantages too. The seeds were ground into flour for bread and the rhizome eaten like a fruit – Herodotus thought it 'quite sweet'.

None of this prevented the Asian *Nelumbo nucifera* from taking over. Its large pink flowers, which rise over a metre above the water, are more spectacular than those of the white and blue water lilies, and its habits readily fitted the existing themes of fertility and rebirth. It is also more vigorous and even better to eat. Theophrastus called it the Egyptian bean. Today, *Nelumbo* is grown as a crop all over south-east Asia – with nearly half a million acres devoted to its cultivation in China alone. The seeds are ground into flour for noodles, porridge and pastes, roasted as a coffee substitute, or popped (like corn) for a snack; the stamens flavour tea; the young stems are eaten in salads or cooked as a vegetable; the leaves are made into tea, or used as a wrap for other food. Mostly, however, *Nelumbo* is grown for its large starchy rhizome. This too can be ground up, to form a kind of arrowroot, but most lotus root is sliced into discs that are pickled, fried, stuffed, or added to stews and soups. Its close relative *Nelumbo lutea* was used in much the same way by indigenous people in Central and North America. No one had a problem with using the same plant for worship and nourishment.

Nelumbo nucifera is the national flower of India, and its most ancient religious and cultural symbol – something acknowledged in the design of the modern multi-faith Bahá'í Lotus Temple in New Delhi. The Sacred Lotus even had a walk-on role in the country's political history. During the winter of

1857, a series of uprisings against colonial rule, known in Britain as the Indian Mutiny, was planned using messages concealed in chapatis and a silent signal of a lotus flower or leaf passed from hand to hand among sepoy regiments.

Hindu gods and goddesses, as well as the Buddha and his followers, are usually shown standing or seated on a lotus blossom, to suggest that they, like the flower, rise up from the mire of existence to encounter divine light. Vishnu, the supreme deity, is known as Padmanabha, or lotus-navelled, a reference to the emergence of Brahma, the god of creation, from the flower of his belly. The origins of life are also evoked in the oldest Sanskrit mantra, *Om mani padme hum*, usually interpreted as 'jewel in the lotus'. This seems to be a reference to the fully opened bloom which reveals a yellow pod (eventually the seed head) containing the female stigmas and which is surrounded by multiple rings of yellow-anthered male stamens.

The lotus was first associated with Lakshmi, the Hindu goddess of good fortune and beauty; one of her names is Padma, lotus, and many epithets connect her with the flower. In ancient love poetry, beautiful women emulate Lakshmi by wearing lotuses in their hair and they too are inevitably lotus-eyed, lotus-complexioned, and lotus-thighed. The poets sometimes extend the metaphor further to involve pollination: in one verse, as the woman blushes, her face resembles a lotus 'surrounded by a swarm of bees / Excited by its fragrance'; in another, the bees have become dark nipples sitting on her lotus breasts. A more unusual comparison pictures the beloved's breasts, powdered with the flour she's grinding, as 'two white geese sitting in the shade / Of the lotus of her face'. A deceived woman, meanwhile, grows 'lean / in loneliness' and compares herself to a water lily 'gnawed by a beetle'.

If the jewel in the lotus most directly evokes fertility and the birth of the gods, it also, by analogy, suggests the fruition of spiritual awakening. This theme became particularly important in Buddhism, which arose in eastern India in the sixth

A Northern Indian image of Vishnu and Lakshmi seated on a lotus blossom, early 1800s.

century BCE and then spread through China, Japan and other lotus-filled countries of south-east Asia. Two other aspects of the lotus now also became decisive. First, the fact that the prickly flower stalk rises over a metre above the water was thought to represent the way that spiritual understanding develops far beyond its mundane inception. But since all plants begin in the soil and grow toward the sky, any one of them could represent that theme. The lotus does something special, however – it remains 'unsoiled' by the mire. This idea, first discussed in the *Bhagavad Gita*, came to encapsulate the philosophy of non-attachment. The Buddha, Siddhārtha Gautama, explained it this way to his followers:

A wall painting of a Buddhist monk holding a lotus (and surrounded by lotuses) from the Kizil cliffs, China, sixth to seventh century CE.

Just as . . . a lotus, blue, red or white, though born in the water, where it reaches the surface stands there unsoiled by the water; just so, . . . though born in the world, having overcome the world, a *Tathāgata* [enlightened being] abides unsoiled by the world.

Over the years, this idea has travelled far and wide. In Concord, Massachusetts in 1854, Henry David Thoreau – a great reader of Hindu and Buddhist texts – applied it to the white-flowered water lily, *Nymphaea odorata*, he found in shallow waters near Walden Pond. It was a plant that he loved; every year, his journals delightedly record his first glimpse of the 'queen of the waters', 'our lotus'. What that meant became clear on 4 July 1854 when he took to the podium to address a meeting of the Massachusetts Anti-Slavery Society.

It was a day of fury and despair. One abolitionist, William Lloyd Garrison, burnt a copy of the Constitution while another, Sojourner Truth, warned that 'God would yet execute his judgment upon the white people for their oppression and cruelty.' Thoreau himself declared that his thoughts were 'murder to the State, and involuntarily go plotting against her'. Their words were not directed against the cruelties of slavery in general, however, but rather at the way those cruelties had been brought home to Massachusetts by the 1850 Fugitive Slave Act. Slave owners were now permitted to arrest suspected runaways without a warrant, and fugitive slaves were denied the right of trial by jury and the right even to give evidence on their own behalf. Anyone who helped a slave escape – as Thoreau had done – also faced heavy penalties. In June 1854, the implications of this became incontrovertible when a fugitive slave called Anthony Burns was escorted from a Boston courthouse in chains to be shipped back to slavery in Virginia.

Much of Thoreau's speech was bitter and angry – 'I cannot persuade myself that I do not dwell *wholly within* hell' – until close to the end, when he describes a walk to a local pond where he catches the scent of a single white water lily. Like the Indian lotus, the American water lily offers hope that 'purity and sweetness reside in, and can be extracted from, the slime and muck of the earth'. From the 'manure' of slavery and politics, Thoreau insisted, individuals might yet arise who 'recognise a higher law than the Constitution'.

Fifty years later, the same image was evoked, less hopefully, to characterise the mire of European colonialism in Africa. Marlow, the protagonist of Joseph Conrad's 1899 novella *Heart of Darkness*, has experienced the 'slime and muck' of humanity at its worst. His tale is told afloat, in a yacht anchored in the Thames estuary. He has an 'ascetic expression' and a 'yellow complexion' and, when he raises his palm outwards, he is directly compared to 'a Buddha preaching in European clothes and without a lotus-flower'. It's an intriguing image in many ways, but perhaps most striking is Conrad's insistence on the *absence* of the flower. He seems to be evoking Padmapani, the compassionate Bodhisattva with the lotus in his hand who helps others as he strives to achieve wisdom. Marlow, however, is one step further behind on the road to nirvana. Although he assumes the pose of the meditating Buddha (the lotus position), his voyage from the Congo to the Thames has been a journey out of one of the 'dark places of the earth' into another. Marlow is not 'unsoiled' by his experience of the world.

Exactly *how* the lotus cleans itself remained a mystery for thousands of years. Finally, in the 1970s, a German scientist called Wilhelm Barthlott got to the bottom of the 'Lotus Effect'. Barthlott compared the way that 340 different plant leaves managed to repel water, particles of dirt, and pathogens such as fungal spores. In many cases, particles stuck to the leaf's surface even when water washed over it but, in some, the water slid off the surface carrying the foreign particles with it. *Alchemilla mollis*, nasturtiums and prickly pear were all pretty good, but the lotus was the best self-cleaner of all – due, Barthlott surmised, to a combination of minute protuberances and a waxy finish on the leaf surface. In 1998 he patented the name Lotus-Effect® and began to work with manufacturers to develop paints, fabrics and glass that mimicked the plant's properties.

In looking to the Sacred Lotus of south-east Asia for a solution to European problems, Barthlott was in good company. The flower, and the cultures with which it was associated, had long been a source of fascination for Europeans and Americans. Indeed most modern lotus confusions result from a tendency to pick and mix between different cultures. A little Egyptian *Nymphaea* here, a little Japanese *Nelumbo* there, a touch of the classical *Ziziphus lotus*, plus various home-grown water lilies, made for an unholy but also productive mess.

European and American writers who were interested in any aspect of the 'Orient' – and in the eighteenth and nineteenth centuries that was most of them – thought of the lotus as entrancingly exotic and often erotic. Brought to public attention by stories of Napoleon's voyages to Egypt and, later, by the building of the Suez Canal, Egyptian lotus motifs became popular on everything from dinner services to brooches, and that was before the discovery of Tutankhamun's tomb in 1922 resulted in full-on Egyptomania. A fascination with Chinoiserie, and then Japonisme, further reinforced the lotus craze and, despite scholarly attempts to unpack the precise history and 'grammar' of the lotus, no one much cared if the plant in question was a *Nymphaea* or a *Nelumbo*. By the late nineteenth century, European conservatories and gardens began to fill up with hybrids of both. The most desirable were bred by Joseph Bory Latour-Marliac, who crossed brightly coloured tropical *Nymphaea* and *Nelumbo* with hardy European and North American varieties. His customers included Claude Monet, keen to stock his new water garden. Those with less interest in horticulture, meanwhile, found lotuses and water lilies to love in the Art Nouveau designs of Grasset wallpapers, Lalique pendants, and Tiffany lamps.

An early twentieth-century 'Pond Lily' leaded glass and bronze table lamp made by Tiffany Studios, New York.

The *fin de siècle* consumption of luxury goods had little to do with non-attachment or transcending the material world. Instead it chimed with another version of lotus: the 'sweet delicious fruit' that the *lotophagi*, the lotus-eaters, fed Odysseus's men in Homer's epic. Unlike Circe, who also drugs the sailors (see **Snowdrop**), the lotus-eaters are friendly and generous. But the net effect of this island visit is the same: the sailors become dopey and demoralised; 'they only wanted to stay there, feeding on lotus'. And so, like a drugs counsellor making an urgent intervention, Odysseus has to drag them back to the ship.

In the nineteenth century, when debates about work and idleness (or leisure) intensified, talk of lotus-eating began to extend beyond fruit consumption to those who, for all sorts of reasons, were content (as the Oxford English Dictionary defined it) to pass the time 'pleasantly doing nothing productive'. In 1832, Tennyson wrote disapprovingly of 'lotos-eaters' (they're really Romantic opium eaters) who 'falter life away' and in 1847, *Punch* picked up the trope to satirise 'The Lotus-Eaters of Downing Street' who are 'careless, if not entirely oblivious, of the wants and miseries of the country'.

It wasn't until James Joyce tackled lotus-eating in *Ulysses* that a more balanced view of the subject emerged. As he wanders through the streets of Dublin, Leopold Bloom is surrounded by lotus-equivalents: laudanum, 'lovephiltres', sleeping draughts, 'paregoric poppysyrup', cigarettes, liquor, tea, perfume, flowers, songs, the cinema, money, sunshine, betting on the horses, horses who don't 'care about anything with their long noses stuck in nose bags', Catholics who shut their eyes and open their mouths for the sacrament that 'stupefies them', or drink the 'waters of oblivion' at Lourdes, and red-coated soldiers on the recruitment poster, 'hypnotised like'.

Yet, unlike Odysseus, Bloom does not intend to intervene. He might think of himself as walking 'soberly' through Dublin, but it soon becomes apparent that the city is his own lotus, a welcome escape from his insistent thoughts of mortality and sexual betrayal. Musing about 'nymphs' and 'the far east' is particularly diverting. 'Lovely spot it must be: the garden of the world, big lazy leaves to float about on . . . Not doing a hand's turn all day . . . Waterlilies.' The episode ends as Bloom contemplates a trip to the local Turkish baths where he imagines himself reclining in warm water, while his penis becomes 'a languid floating flower'. If we've changed plant again, it is not to the expected Sacred Lotus – the upright plant of sexual as well as philosophical transcendence, whose essential quality, said T.S. Eliot, was that it 'rose, quietly, quietly'. Bloom may want the fluff washed out of his navel, but that's where the purification ends. For him, buoyancy is miracle enough.

Cotton

The Antiguan-American novelist Jamaica Kincaid was walking through the glasshouses in London's Kew Gardens one afternoon when she came upon 'the most beautiful hollyhock' she had ever seen. 'It had that large flared petal of the hollyhock and it was a most beautiful yellow, a clear yellow, as if it, the colour yellow, were just born, delicate, at the very beginning of its history as "yellow".' Kincaid grew hollyhocks in her garden and she wondered why she hadn't seen this particular variety before. So she looked at the label and realised her mistake: it wasn't a hollyhock at all, but a species of *Gossypium*, better known as cotton. The mix-up was understandable as both plants are members of the mallow family, Malvaceae. A passing horticultural student might have shrugged and moved on. But it was not that simple for Kincaid.

'My whole being was sent a-whir,' she wrote. Suddenly she found it impossible to look at a plant that 'exists in perfection, with malice toward none', without also seeing the 'tormented, malevolent role' it had played in global history, in the story of her ancestors, and even in her own life. As a child in Antigua, Kincaid once spent a summer helping a friend of her mother to detach the valuable fibres from the cotton seed: 'I remember my hands aching, particularly in the area at the base of my thumbs.'

Kincaid's story points in many directions: to Kew's role in developing one of the British Empire's essential commodities; to the experience of African slaves in the plantation economy of the Caribbean and United States;

Watercolour of *Gossypium hirsutum* from the Roxburgh collection, Royal Botanical Gardens, Kew.

and to the importance of cotton in household horticulture, long before industrialisation. I want to start, however, by returning to the plant itself in order to understand just how a beautiful flower turns into a commodity.

The genus *Gossypium* has been around for somewhere between 10 and 20 million years, and comprises about 50 species of plants. Thousands of years ago, four of these species – *G. arboreum* (on the Indian peninsula), *G. herbaceum* (Africa), *G. barbadense* (South America), *G. hirsutum* (Central

America) – were domesticated in order to extract the coarse hairs that cover the seeds. Raw cotton had some uses: for example, the Hopi of Arizona and New Mexico used it to cover the faces of the dead to signify their future existence as Cloud People. In most cultures, however, its value came when the hairs were teased apart and woven into fabric for clothing, furniture and even currency. Although cotton doesn't leave the most durable archaeological evidence, threads, fabrics and even fishing nets have been found in three continents; the oldest, dating back 5,000 years, was discovered in the Indus Valley of Pakistan.

Cotton germinates quickly and, about five to six weeks after the seedlings emerge, buds – called 'squares' – appear. After another three weeks, the flowers open. Flowering is quick and efficient. The flower only opens for a single day, during which pollination occurs. Sometimes bumblebees do the job, but cotton flowers are usually self-pollinated. Kincaid's description of pale-lemon blossoms suggests that she saw *Gossypium hirsutum*, the hairy cotton. By the next day, its petals would have turned pinkish red and, a day or two after that, they would be gone. The speed of this process inspired a children's riddle in the American South:

> First day white, next day red,
> Third day from my birth I'm dead;
> Though I'm of short duration,
> Yet withal I clothe the nation.

While the rhyme gives a sense of the accelerated flowering process, it mostly sacrifices accuracy for dramatic effect. It's only the petals that of are 'short duration'. On day three, the plant is far from dead but busy producing the next generation: the petals fall off to reveal the fruit, or boll, which ripens over the next 50 to 70 days, eventually opening to reveal 10 or so seeds covered in fuzz and lint (elongated cellulose cells). Left to their own devices, they help the seeds disperse in the wind.

As the lint dries, the cellulose gradually spirals and collapses into flat, hollow ribbons – something like miniature twisted fire hoses – which interlock with one another, making it easy to spin into a continuous thread. Its porous structure is what makes cotton such a breathable and fast-drying fabric. A lot also depends on the length of the fibre, known as its staple. The Asian and African species are short-staple varieties; the Americans long-staple. Cultivars of *G. barbadense* are also known as extra-long-staple (ELS) cotton; to qualify as such the fibres need to be at least 34mm in length. These are the most luxurious cottons. They were once called Sea Island cottons because they were grown off the coast of South Carolina and Georgia; we now know them, because of other places they've been cultivated, as soft and smooth Egyptian or Pima cottons.

Today, however, 90 per cent of the world's cotton crop comes from cultivars of another long-staple species, *G. hirsutum* or upland cotton. Its larger bolls are easier to pick, and it is less particular about where it's grown; it can, for example, tolerate some frost. On the downside, the seeds and fibres are very firmly attached. A desire to grow *hirsutum* on a large scale was what motivated Eli Whitney to develop a mechanical cotton gin that would detach seed from fibre.

Before American long-staple varieties took over, however, the types of cotton that the world knew best were the short-staple African, and particularly, the Asian species. Until well into the nineteenth century, India was the world's leading cotton manufacturer and its products were transported far and wide. Fine Indian muslins and cheap printed calicos reached Europe from the Middle East around 700 CE, but for a long time, all that anyone knew about cotton itself was that it came from some kind of Indian plant. Drawing perhaps on Herodotus's account of wild trees which produce 'a kind of wool better than sheep's wool in beauty and quality', the legend of the 'vegetable lamb' was widely circulated. In 1350, John Mandeville described a 'wonderful tree which bore tiny lambs on the endes of its branches. These branches were so pliable that they bent down to allow the lambs to feed when they are hungrie.' The idea lingers on in the German word for cotton – *baumwolle*, tree wool.

It wasn't until the seventeenth century, however, that, due to the efforts of the East India Company this exotic material became widely available and popular in Britain. Indian cotton came in a range of beautiful prints and colours; it was light, washable, and affordable. Wool manufacturers and their supporters were soon up in arms. Muslins and chintzes have 'crept into our

A woodcut of the Vegetable Lamb of Tartary from the 1725 edition of *The Voiage and Travaile of John Mandeville, Knight.*

houses', complained Daniel Defoe; 'our closets and bedchambers, curtains, cushions, chairs, and at last beds themselves were nothing but calicoes and Indian stuffs.' Defending the rights of male weavers often meant attacking the desire of women to gratify their 'Callico Fancy'. It was suggested that wearing light muslins ('thin painted old sheets') was akin to declaring oneself a prostitute. Even worse, the new fashions created class confusion: if both rich and poor dressed in the same 'tawdry Finery', who could tell the mistress and the maid apart? In short, a 'Callico Madam' was 'an Enemy to her Country'.

As a result of this agitation, imported calicos were banned in Britain and many other European countries, which only increased demand. And, not surprisingly, when Britain started manufacturing the stuff – production rose by 10 per cent every year between 1780 and 1800 – cotton suddenly didn't seem so bad after all. By 1802, British cotton exports surpassed wool for the first time, and even India (much of which was under the control of the East India Company) became a customer. Printed cotton was also much in demand in West Africa, and specially designed textiles known as Guinea cloth were a key commodity when trading for slaves. The slaves in turn were sent to British colonies in the Caribbean and to the United States to work on plantations producing sugar cane, tobacco and, eventually, the raw cotton that was required by the new factories around Manchester, a.k.a. Cottonopolis. It was a complicated commercial operation, to say the least.

Technological innovation was certainly an important factor in the development of the British textile industry. In the mid- to late eighteenth century, a series of inventions – from the flying shuttle to the steam-powered loom – revolutionised spinning and weaving. But production was only one part of the story. By solving the problem of how to separate the fibre from the seed, Whitney's cotton gin had made it possible to process large quantities of *G. hirsutum* quickly. Yet these devices didn't address the question of where the crop could be cultivated and who would pick it.

The question of where sufficient cotton could be grown was solved by the seemingly unlimited land that became available in the United States (its territory doubled in size after the 1803 Louisiana Purchase, which was then followed by the acquisition of Florida in 1819, and the 1845 annexation of Texas). To create the new plantations, Native Americans were dispossessed of their land and forests turned into farms. By 1850, 67 per cent of US cotton grew on land that fifty years earlier had not been part of the country.

Machines might have made it easier and quicker to process, spin and weave the cotton, but mechanised pickers weren't fully introduced into the fields in which it was grown until the mid-1960s. Until then, 600 hours of back-breaking human labour were required to harvest each bale (500 pounds). And that work was done by slaves. Some 200,000 were brought to the new American plantations from Africa before the international slave trade ended in 1808, and up to a million more were transported south from the older tobacco states of Virginia, Maryland and Kentucky.

There can be no doubt that Britain's textile industry, and the nation's industrialisation more generally, relied heavily on access to America's expropriated territories and enslaved labour.

Lamar Baker, *The Slave Plant*, 1939. **The image refers to cotton's association with African-American slavery but also to a sense that, by the early twentieth century, the land itself had been enslaved by the plant.**

The cotton flower only blooms for three days, but tending the plant is nearly a year-long business. One of the most vivid accounts of what was involved on a Southern plantation is that given by Solomon Northup, a free-born African American from New York who was kidnapped and sold into slavery in Louisiana. Northup wrote *Twelve Years a Slave* (1853) to persuade those who had 'never seen a cotton field' to support the abolitionist cause.

Work in the Louisiana cotton fields commenced in March when the ground was ploughed and the seeds sown. A week or so later, after germination, the intensive process of hoeing and 'scraping' began: weeding, shaping the ground between the rows, and thinning out the weaker plants. At all times, Northup notes, 'the overseer or driver follows the slaves on horseback with a whip':

> The faster hoer takes the lead row. He is usually about a rod in advance of his companions. If one of them passes him, he is whipped. If one falls behind or is a moment idle, he is whipped. In fact, the lash is flying from morning until night, the whole day long. The hoeing season thus continues from April until July, a field having no sooner been finished once, than it is commenced again.

Harvesting ran from mid-August to early December: there were three pickings. Slaves were equipped with long sacks and these were then emptied into baskets placed at the end of each row. Every evening, the baskets were weighed. 'A slave never approaches the gin-house with his basket of cotton but with fear,' Northup notes.

> If it falls short in weight – if he has not performed the full task appointed him, he knows that he must suffer. And if he has exceeded it by ten or twenty pounds, in all probability his master will measure the next day's task accordingly. So, whether he has too little or too much, his approach to the gin-house is always with fear and trembling.

The 'severest chastisement' was reserved for those who accidentally broke a branch from the plant.

Britain declared itself neutral during the American Civil War, despite the expectation of Southern planters that cotton interests would come to the aid of the Confederacy. Although they undoubtedly felt the brunt of the 'cotton famine', many mill owners as well as workers supported the Union cause and, in 1862, 'the citizens of Manchester' even wrote to Lincoln urging him to persevere in eradicating the 'foul blot' of slavery.

Emancipation and the end of the war had less of an effect on the cotton business than many had hoped (or feared). Keen to re-establish the bond between the Southern 'vales where cotton flowers' grow and their own 'hills of snow', Northern businessmen financed the resumption of large-scale cotton production. Freed slaves had been promised their own 'forty acres and a mule', but that ideal soon faded. Instead many became sharecroppers on former plantations. They paid rent for parcels of land on which they were required to grow cotton (rather than crops for food), and to hand over half the harvest. Slavery was technically over but, as writers like Richard Wright and Langston Hughes pointed out, African Americans in the South still existed in a world that was 'walled with cotton'; they were still 'plowing life away' for someone else's profit. And soon, many poor whites joined them.

By the end of the century, global prices were falling, the soil was depleted, and, in 1892, a cotton-loving long-snouted beetle crossed the Rio Grande into Brownsville, Texas. Travelling roughly 60 miles each year, the boll weevil slowly munched its way east, reaching Virginia by 1921. The weevil laid its eggs into the squares and boll, and hatching larvae ate them up. The leaves then also fell off – a denuded plant was a sure sign of infestation.

African-American attitudes to the boll weevil were complicated. On the one hand, by destroying the cotton, the beetle made life even harder; on the other, it became a kind of folk hero. In numerous blues songs, the boll weevil is presented as bold, tenacious and, crucially, free to go wherever it wants: 'Boll weevil left Texas Lord he bid me fare you well / I'm going down to Mississippi going to give Louisiana hell.'

As cotton became 'scarce as any southern snow', in Jean Toomer's phrase, and racial violence intensified, thousands of African Americans followed the weevil and took to the road, initiating decades of a Great Migration to the industrial cities of the North. The reign of King Cotton was ending, and not everyone mourned its passing. In 1919, the citizens of Enterprise, Alabama even erected a monument to the boll weevil, in 'profound appreciation' of its role in provoking economic diversification. The farming of peanuts around Enterprise not only returned vital nutrients to the soil, but also proved a successful cash crop for local farmers. Cotton production shifted westward to Arizona, California and New Mexico, with the weevil in hot pursuit.

The world's only monument to an agricultural pest. Enterprise, Alabama.

Cotton's continued importance to the world economy, and therefore to the lives of millions of people, cannot be overestimated. It's the same old story, with the same old characters. Only the location has changed. The threat of the boll weevil still looms large; although most of the southern United States is now free of the pest, 90 per cent of Brazilian farms are infested. Forced seasonal labour continues wherever mechanisation is considered uneconomical. In Uzbekistan and Turkestan, government employees (and often children) are required to take part in the harvest to help farmers meet their annual quotas. Textile workers from Bangladesh to Vietnam struggle to make a living wage.

The two main producers of cotton today are China and India. The industrialisation of cotton production in India began during the American Civil War and was initially subject to strict colonial control: to supply Lancashire's mills, Indian fields were planted with American *hirsutum* cultivars, and to protect their export business, Indian mills were only allowed to produce cheap grey cloth. Unsurprisingly, cotton became a focus of the independence

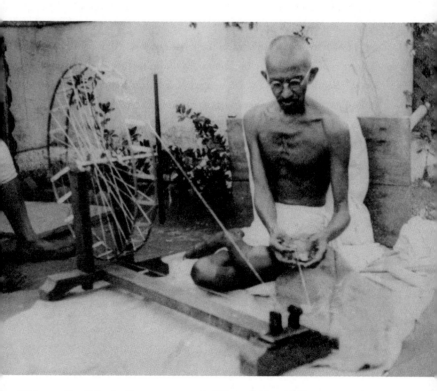

Mahatma Gandhi spinning cotton on a charkha in the late 1940s.

movement. In the 1920s Mahatma Gandhi urged Indians to boycott British fabrics, arguing that it was their 'patriotic duty' to spin and weave their own fabrics, as he did. The political symbolism of home-spun cotton was powerful but, after independence, India embarked on a major expansion of both cotton production and manufacture. Today, the vast majority of cotton grown in India (as elsewhere) is a bioengineered, insect-resistant cultivar of *hirsutum*. In 2018, 6.1 million metric tons of cotton were grown in India, with China just a little behind.

In 2014, Sven Beckert ended his history of the 'empire of cotton' by suggesting that only 'the spatial constraints of the planet' limited its continued expansion. Five years later, China – which devotes 3 million hectares to cotton production – sent a cotton seed to the far side of the moon. On 7 January 2019, it was announced that the seed had sprouted – 'the first green leaf' to grow, inside its sealed canister, on the moon's surface. Although the seedling couldn't cope with the freezing conditions of the lunar night and died within a day, scientists were not discouraged. Lunar agriculture does not seem impossible. It's a brave new world, but one thing is certain: whatever the future holds, we'll still be wearing cotton.

Sunflower

Sunflowers can sometimes seem too sunny, too guileless, too in your face, a little one-note.

That's what Michael Pollan thought when he contemplated his 'wholesome and cheerful' garden: the sunflowers were beautiful, but they needed a 'tinge of melancholy' to set them off. And so he planted some dark-leaved, spikey flowered, poisonous castor bean plants alongside. The effect was just as he had hoped: a 'heartbreakingly sunny' plant and its 'slightly evil twin', Jekyll and Hyde.

But the sunflower doesn't always need a companion to inject some gloom: it exists in its own melancholic shadow. Search for images of the flower online and pictures of green leaves and golden blooms are matched almost one for one by moody black-and-white photographs of decaying stalks and desiccated seedheads. The popularity of these latter images is largely due to the striking shape of the plant – it's what gardeners call 'architectural' – but structure only takes centre stage when the distractingly lovely colour is removed. The fascination of the sunflower's skeleton is surely more than formal, however. Like all ruins, it speaks poignantly of what's been lost – and sometimes that seems to include the death of the sun itself.

To Vincent van Gogh, a sunflower was not only yellow, it embodied and shouted out yellow, the colour of light, warmth and happiness. He completed his first paintings of 'nothing but large sunflowers' while living in Paris, but it was when he moved south that his life briefly became sunny. Van Gogh rented a yellow house in Arles and planned a studio filled with paintings of sunflowers, 'a decoration in which the raw or broken chrome yellows will blaze forth on various backgrounds – blue, from the palest malachite green to *royal blue*, framed in thin strips of wood painted with orange lead.' The effect, he hoped, would be something like that of 'stained-glass windows in a Gothic church'. But he also hoped that the paintings would launch a new art movement, a post-Impressionist 'Studio of the South'.

Vincent van Gogh, *Sunflowers*, 1887. One of two van Gogh paintings Gauguin owned and later sold to finance his trip to the South Pacific.

Van Gogh desperately wanted Paul Gauguin to join him in this endeavour and, eventually, Gauguin came to Arles. He painted a portrait of his friend at work on his sunflowers. Since this was December, the flowers couldn't have been painted from life; rather, Gauguin was acknowledging that van Gogh had become a 'painter of sunflowers' – he had found his motif, his style, his brand.

Paul Gauguin, *The Painter of Sunflowers (Portrait of Vincent van Gogh)*, 1888.

Gauguin warmly praised the paintings as a 'series of sun-effects over sun-effects in full sunshine', but privately he seemed to be thinking of yellow in quite a different way. In his sketchbook, opposite a study for the portrait of van Gogh, Gauguin wrote the words *crime* and *châtiment* in apparent allusion to Dostoevsky's *Crime and Punishment*, a novel in which yellow is the unambiguous colour of mental illness. Van Gogh's health was certainly in a fragile state, and Gauguin also recorded incidents in which his friend behaved erratically and sometimes violently. The ménage broke up soon after, with Gauguin returning to Paris, and van Gogh, a few months later, admitting himself to a psychiatric hospital. After his suicide in 1890, van Gogh's friends and followers honoured his memory with paintings of withered sunflowers, divested of their vibrant yellow.

Roland Holst, lithograph on the cover of *Tentoonstelling der nagelaten werken van Vincent van Gogh*, a memorial to the artist that was published in 1892, two years after his death.

Roland Holst's sunflower is the dead and colourless twin of van Gogh's sunlit bloom. Sometimes, though, a single plant could even act as its own foil, its own reminder of former glory. Consider the dusty specimen that Allen Ginsberg and

Jack Kerouac found lying on a pile of sawdust in a Berkeley railroad yard in 1955. To Ginsberg's eyes, its rays are a 'battered crown', its nearly seedless head a 'face' with a 'soon-to-be-toothless mouth'; there's even a dead fly in its 'ear'. The 'battered old thing' is 'big as a man', and so Ginsberg addresses it as if it were a man, and an *American* man at that, an inhabitant of a machine age. 'When did you forget you were a flower?' he demands of the plant; 'when did you look at your skin and decide you were an impotent dirty old locomotive?' Ginsberg's 'sermon', his 'sutra', is clear: 'You were never no locomotive, Sunflower, you were a sunflower!' But what's most important about the message is that it also applies to himself, to 'sad-eyed' Kerouac, and to 'anyone who'll listen': American men, he intones, 'we're not our skin of grime . . . we're golden sunflowers inside, blessed by our own seed'.

For Ginsberg, as for van Gogh, the sunflower at its sunniest does not merely represent the joy of a moment; it contains – in the many seeds that are the fruit of its decay – the promise of a radiant future. That idea, combined with the fact that in children's drawings most flowers look like sunflowers, makes it a popular emblem of childhood and hope. (See also **Daisy**.) Many late twentieth-century political posters combine sunflowers and a childlike graphic style to evoke the welfare of children, while Green parties and anti-war campaigns all over the world have taken the sunflower as their emblem.

Growing in a garden or a field, sunflowers can be even more emblematically hopeful. In 1996, to mark the final nuclear disarmament of the Ukraine, a group of US, Russian and Ukrainian politicians gathered on a former nuclear silo to plant sunflower seedlings because, they announced, 'sunflowers instead of missiles in the soil' would ensure 'peace for future generations'. They would also, of course, ensure food.

Today, sunflower oil is one the five largest oilseed crops in the world (although it lags far behind palm oil) and Ukraine and Russia are the world's largest producers. In 2018, for example, 15 million tonnes of sunflowers were

Poster for Die Grünen, the German Green Party, *c.* 1980.

harvested in the Ukraine. The plant was introduced in the seventeenth century by Peter the Great as part of his modernisation programme. By the mid-nineteenth century it was well established as a crop, providing seeds to eat and oil that was extracted from those seeds. In fact, what we call the seed is the sunflower's dry fruit or achene, an oily kernel surrounded by a dry hull, covered in a thin membrane.

Not all of Ukraine's sunflowers are edible, however: one group of plants was definitely to be avoided. These were planted in 1994 in the Chernobyl Exclusion Zone, an area of about 1,000 square miles around the former nuclear power plant, and they offered hope in a rather different way.

Following the explosion of reactor number 4 in April 1986, dust and rain carrying the radioactive isotopes caesium 137 and strontium 90 entered the soil for hundreds of miles around the Chernobyl plant. Scientists wondered whether sunflowers, which absorb nutrients such as potassium and calcium from the soil, could instead be used to extract these radioactive isotopes.

Various plants are used to soak up chemicals from contaminated land and ground water in other situations, a process known as phytoextraction. Arsenic has been removed by ferns, lead by brassicas, cadmium by willows, mercury by poplars. Sunflowers are good phytoextractors for several reasons: they are quick and easy to grow, have deep roots, and their large leaves and flower heads provide a substantial volume of tissue in which contaminants can accumulate. At Chernobyl, they were planted on Styrofoam rafts to float on a small pond just a kilometre away from the reactor and, within ten days, they removed 95 per cent of contaminants. For various reasons, they were less successful in the soil. The radioactivity had not been eradicated, but it was much easier to deal with in the concentrated form of plant material which could be stored in a single location.

Sunflowers were enlisted again in Japan in 2011, after an earthquake and tsunami damaged the Fukushima Daiichi power plant. The earthquake took place in March and by April government agencies, community groups and local farmers had joined forces to plant sunflower seeds: 8 million by one estimate. By July the plants were in bloom. The symbolic decontamination worked well; tourists arrived to see the flowers, and the phytoextraction had some success. Unfortunately, the main problem did not lie in the soil, but in the reactor's susceptibility to water, a problem which has yet to be fully resolved.

Sunflowers growing outside the nuclear power station at Saint Laurent des Eaux in central France, 2007.

The sunflower has such a global presence that it's difficult to remember where it originated – unless you're from the United States, that is. Wild annual sunflowers – branched and multi-headed – grew all over the American West and indigenous people traditionally sought them out for food and medicine, as well as using them for ceremonial purposes. Hopi women, for example, would honour the deity Kuwanlelenta, whose name means 'make beautiful surroundings', by painting their faces yellow with the ground-up petals and wearing flowers in their hair. It was in the east of North America, about five thousand years ago, that the plant seems to have been domesticated into the thick-stemmed single-headed plant we call *Helianthus annuus,* as Native Americans sought to increase the yield of seeds. It was never a primary crop, however: sunflowers were grown around the edges of fields or between rows of corn. In the early twentieth century, a Hidasta woman called Maxi'diwiac, or Buffalo Bird Woman, gave a visiting ethnographer a detailed description of the sunflower's cultivation and consumption, including a recipe for their 'very best dish', a kind of stew of sunflower meal, corn meal, squash and beans.

Archaeological records reveal great genetic diversity in the sunflowers grown by indigenous peoples. *H. annuus* readily hybridised with related species – such as the prairie sunflower, *H. petiolaris* – which meant it could survive in very different conditions, from the cold plains of North Dakota to the deserts of New Mexico. This adaptability is another hopeful sign. As global agriculture looks for ways of coping with climate change, that quality suggests that the sunflower is likely to play an important role in the future. Sunflower is also one of several oilseeds that are already being used for biodiesel and, compared to rape, for example, its cultivation produces significantly fewer greenhouse gases.

It is only relatively recently that modern Americans have been paying attention to sunflowers. Along with the indigenous peoples who grew them, an interest in sunflowers had gradually died out. For a long time, the colonists and their descendants considered the plant a weed, too 'rank and coarse' for the garden, quipped one poem, but 'a lovely bouquet for a horse'. The sunflower's reputation only revived in the nineteenth century when Mennonite and Jewish immigrants brought high-yielding Russian seeds. By the 1880s, seed companies like Burpee (see **Marigold**), which supplied American farmers with 'Mammoth Russian' sunflowers, also began to market ornamental varieties directly 'to the farmer's wife' who wanted to 'beautify' the farm. In other circles, the plant became fashionable through its association with the British Aesthetic Movement and Oscar Wilde, who frequently posed with the 'gaudy leonine' plant on his 1882 lecture tour of North America.

By 1918, Willa Cather was writing nostalgically of 'sunflower-bordered' roads on the Nebraska prairie and retelling the story of the Mormons who planted them on their way to Utah so that 'the next summer, when the long trains of wagons came through with all the women and children, they had the sunflower trail to follow.' It was an appealing story, even if it sidestepped the fact that sunflowers are native to Nebraska. A similar romantic attachment to 'frontier days, winding trails, pathless prairies' led Kansas to declare itself the 'Sunflower State' in 1903.

The sunflower was the most magnificent of the 'New World' plants that the Spanish shipped back across the Atlantic in the sixteenth century: the perfect trophy of imperial conquest. While apothecaries investigated its pharmacological properties and culinary uses (the curator of the botanical gardens in Padua thought the cooked stalks 'even more palatable' than asparagus) most discussion of the plant emphasised its size, its novelty and later, as the botanical revolution took off, what it revealed about the workings of the natural world.

Two aspects of the flower were particularly intriguing to Europeans: the arrangement of the thousands of tiny disc florets on the flower head; and the way that the flower head, whose wreath of yellow ray flowers makes it look *like* the sun, seems to *follow* the sun.

In 1597, the English herbalist John Gerard observed that the disc florets seemed 'set as though a cunning workman had of purpose placed them in a very good order'. That order is a spiral, produced because as each floret emerges from the centre of the sunflower it gets pushed outward by the next, in both clockwise and anti-clockwise directions. Mathematicians have calculated that this pattern (known as a Fibonacci sequence) is the most efficient method of packing the greatest number of florets (2,000 or more) into the minimal space. It's a pattern that's found everywhere in nature, but the sunflower provides a

An illustration of a sunflower clock, from Athanasius Kircher, *Magnes, sive De Arte Magnetica*, 1643 edition. A sunflower was attached to a cork and floated on water. As it rotated to face the sun, a pointer in the centre of the flower indicated the time on a suspended ring.

particularly clear and attractive example. Most of the time. In 2016, the Royal Society asked members of the public to grow sunflowers and check if their spirals formed Fibonacci patterns. It turned out that one in five demonstrated alternative mathematical patterns.

Of even greater interest to students of the sunflower is its heliotropism – the plant's habit of turning its head to follow the daily course of the sun (reflected in its French name, *tournesol*). Many flowers do this, but again, perhaps because of its size, the sunflower is the best known. Over the years, there have been many theories about how and why it does this, and, for some, profound philosophical questions were at stake. For philosophers in the Aristotelian tradition, the key distinction between plants and animals lies in the fact that the former respond 'passively' to their environment. Neoplatonists, however, did not believe that any distinction should be made, and that all things (plant, animal, human, God) are part of a single, hierarchical, system of being. For them, the sunflower's movement was not a passive reflex but the kind of behaviour an animal or a person might exhibit.

Scientists have observed that the flower faces the rising sun in the east, and then slowly follows its course to the west. During the night it turns back east to begin the cycle again. What seems to be turning, however, is in fact an elongation of different sides of the stem: during the day the east side elongates to turn the flower head west; during the night the process is reversed. Even on cloudy days, the plant's movements follow this pattern, suggesting that it operates according to a kind of internal clock or circadian rhythm; recently the growth hormone auxin has been identified as controlling the process. This makes sense because only young sunflowers are heliotropic. In order to grow big, the plant needs maximum light. When it reaches maturity, however, its priorities change. Then it settles down with its flower head to the east, where it gets the morning warmth that attracts pollinators, but doesn't overheat, which damages the pollen.

The poets may have to think again about heliotropism. Over the years, it has proved an all-purpose metaphor enabling writers to meditate on constancy or unrequited love, priests to preach on the soul's devotion to God or his Son (pun usually intended), artists to pay homage to their patrons, courtiers to do obeisance to their kings, and the masses to express unswerving loyalty to their political leaders.

The most enduring version is a love story, of sorts, first told by Ovid in the *Metamorphoses*. Clytie, a nymph transformed into a flower, pines for the love of the sun god Apollo and, although rooted in the ground, turns her head to follow him as he rides his chariot across the sky: to emphasise the difficulty of this, representations of Clytie usually show her twisting in the most uncomfortable way. The flower Ovid mentions is actually a purple heliotrope, but in the numerous retellings of the story, the plant itself underwent metamorphosis – first into a marigold and then, in the seventeenth century, into a sunflower, a plant that, even as it became a spectator, remained a wonderful spectacle.

These two roles are certainly at play in Byron's satire *Don Juan*. After her affair with the eponymous hero ends, Julia sends him a final letter which includes the often-quoted lines 'Man's love is of his life a thing apart, / 'Tis woman's whole existence'. Strong words. But Byron's view of Julia's 'misery' becomes clear when we learn that she's chosen a 'gilt-edged paper' and a new 'crow-quill' for the note, and a 'superfine' wax seal of a sunflower bearing the motto *elle vous suit partouti* (she follows you everywhere).

Julia may be in love, but she retains her poise and dignity. That wasn't always the case for sunflower Clyties; for many of them, sexual obsession tips into abjection. The poet Dora Greenwell, for example, writes in the voice of a woman who is not just a slave to love, but a 'willing slave':

> . . . I must droop
> Upon my stalk, I cannot reach his sphere;
> To mine he cannot stoop.

It's an image that lingers on, even into contemporary verse like Rupi Kaur's 'The Sun and Her Flowers': 'what the sun does to those flowers,' the speaker tells her lover, 'it's what you do to me'.

These were not the associations that the National American Woman Suffrage Association had in mind when they adopted the sunflower as their emblem in 1896. If the flower followed the sun, it was because it sought enlightenment. And more relevant still, and American, was the pioneer myth of the taming of the frontier: as the sunflower 'follows civilization, follows the wheel-tract and the plow, so woman suffrage inevitably follows civilized government'.

Was it the suffragists that the Victorian floral dictionaries were thinking of when they made the sunflower a symbol of 'pride' and 'haughtiness'? The association was much older, however. The sunflower depicted by the seventeenth-century poet Abraham Cowley is supremely haughty, and not

Wenceslaus Hollar, etching after Anthony van Dyck, *Self-Portrait with a Sunflower*, 1644.

coincidentally male. Indeed the plant does nothing but boast about his paternal 'Blood' to the 'Earth-born *Mushroom* brood' surrounding him. That's why his face is 'gold', not just the 'very picture' of his father, but 'his like and living coin'. Cowley's proud sunflower is not a lovelorn Clytie but a member of the Neoplatonic concatenated order of being. He looks up admiringly to his father, the sun, and down (with even greater relish) at the mushrooms below. It is tempting to imagine Cowley's speaker as the co-star, with Anthony van Dyck, in the latter's *Self-Portrait with a Sunflower* (1633) – their heads are even the same size. The painting marks van Dyck's early success as a court painter to Charles I, whose head appears on a medal at the end of the gold chain he is holding. The gesture of devotion is reinforced by his other hand, which points to the sunflower.

Devotion is also what is symbolised by the sunflowers that surround the 'red sun', Chairman Mao, in numerous posters, badges, textbooks and children's songs produced during China's Cultural Revolution (1966–1976). This is one:

> Chairman Mao!
> You are the red sun in our hearts!
> We are sunflowers.
> Sunflowers always face the red sun.
> We think of you day and night.
> We wish you a long, long life.

Today, artists of the so-called Sunflower Generation often employ the plant to reflect on life after Mao Zedong. Xu Jiang's sculptures and paintings of sunflowers always represent the flowers *en masse* – if they are usually parched and drooping, they are, nonetheless, still standing. Xu has said that they represent the 'collective memory' of a generation that used to 'wear the same

毛主席是我们心中最红最红的红太阳

A 1967 Chinese poster declares that 'Chairman Mao is the red sun in the hearts of the revolutionary people of the world'.

clothes, sing the same songs, to walk the same paths'. 'Like these sun-facing flowers,' he told an interviewer, 'we devoted our hearts to the sun when we were young and now we stand there like old soldiers with a sense of bitterness.'

Ai Weiwei, meanwhile, opted for sunflower seeds. A hundred million of them, weighing about 10 tonnes, were poured into the Turbine Hall at London's Tate Modern in 2010. In fact, they weren't actually sunflower seeds at all, but life-size porcelain replicas, each one of which had been intricately hand-crafted in small workshops. No two seeds were absolutely identical – a comment, perhaps, on the individuality that exists unnoticed within collective experience, but also on the relationship between China's history of fine porcelain manufacture and its current reputation for cheap mass production. Coincidentally, 2010 was the year in which China finally overtook the United States (the original home of the sunflower) as the world's leading manufacturing nation. For Chinese artists, it was necessary to do what sunflowers were most famous for: find a new orientation.

POPPY

SAFFRON

AUTUMN

CHRYSANTHEMUM

MARIGOLD

Autumn

The living light of summer gone too soon!
. . . all is bitterness to me.

Charles Baudelaire, 'Autumn Song'

Nay, cheer up, sister. Life is not quite over,
Even if the year has done with corn and clover.

Christina Rossetti, 'October'

Autumn is spring's alter ego, another hinge in the year. If spring is the time of 'not quite begun', autumn is 'not quite over'. The vernal offers hope for what is to come, the autumnal celebrates, and begins to mourn, what has already been.

Autumn flowers sometimes seem like echoes across six months of their spring precursors. The yellow witch hazels of October resemble the willows of May; the purple blooms of the September-flowering **saffron** remind us of the crocuses that emerged in February. Late-flowering feelings also recall, but are not identical to, those of spring – and the difference between them provides a poignant metaphor for much middle-aged reflection.

In 'The Autumnal', John Donne offered a tribute to ageing beauty (perhaps that of a widow called Magdalen Herbert) by comparing it to the comfortably temperate season. Some readers thought he was ungallant to discuss the lady's wrinkles, but who could object to being told that 'No spring, nor summer beauty hath such grace / As I have seen in one autumnal face'? Few embraced the season with such charm. John Ruskin thought that to live autumnally was to live altogether without hope, while for Ted Hughes, it was all about reconciling oneself to a 'slow goodbye'. As the dew settles, so too do melancholic poems about the 'last rose of summer' and the 'blight' that strikes down people as well as plants. Alexander Pushkin relished the 'splendid fading' of autumn; it had something of the quality of a 'consumptive girl' (she's 'condemned to die' but, meanwhile, her cheeks are a very attractive 'crimson'). Emily Dickinson went even further and decided that heaven itself must be autumnal.

In fact, Dickinson was thinking of that particular season within a season, the Indian summer – defined by the American Meteorological Society as 'a time interval, in mid- to late autumn, of unseasonably warm weather, generally clear skies, sunny but hazy days and cool nights.' This couldn't just be a continuation of regular summer, however; to be properly 'Indian', it had to follow a 'killing frost'. Similar weather patterns occur elsewhere: in many European countries, they're known as 'old women's' or St Martin's summer (St Martin's Day is 11 November). But it was in New England during the nineteenth century that this not particularly common phenomenon acquired its semi-mythical status. Some suggest that it refers to a spell of warm, hazy weather that enabled Native American peoples to resume hunting, but that may be apocryphal. Whatever the origin of the Indian Summer, the idea, and the phrase, became hugely popular in the late nineteenth century especially with a burgeoning tourist industry keen to promote trips to view the Fall foliage.

In numerous poems, Dickinson, who lived in Massachusetts, displayed a relish both for the destructive power of the frost – which she dubbed the 'blond Assassin' – and for the 'second sun' that sometimes followed. The assassination was so brutal,

> Apparently with no surprise
> To any happy Flower,
> The Frost beheads it at its play
> In accidental power.

that when the sun did come out again, and the gentians bloomed a heavenly purple, October in Massachusetts felt as if it must surely afford a vision of the afterlife.

William Blake preferred an earthier explanation. In his personification, the season is 'jolly Autumn', not a former lover turned wrinkly friend, but a vigorous Dionysian reveller who sings a 'lusty song of fruits and flowers' and who, when he reluctantly departs, leaves behind a 'golden load' to last all winter. Blake seems to have been thinking of a harvest festival, an annual celebration that occurs all over the world and that is mainly focused on food.

Flowers, however, take centre stage in other autumn festivals – mostly as emblems of remembrance. Three of the flowers included in this section feature in such ceremonies. In China and Japan, the **chrysanthemum** is the flower of the ancient Ninth Day Festival (9 September), a day on which longevity and the elderly are honoured. The chrysanthemum is a true autumn flower: its buds emerge when the nights begin to lengthen. After its global adoption as a garden plant, it earned especial praise for coming into bloom at a time when a bright yellow or orange flower is particularly welcome. Both its colours and what Louise Beebe Wilder called its 'nose twister' odour seem to complement the rotting leaves. Today, however, we've lost that association, for growers adjust the day-night balance in their greenhouses to produce chrysanthemums, of all colours, all year long for the cut-flower market.

Other festivals rely on flowers that are generally more abundant in other seasons but that are included here because we now think of them as autumnal. **Marigolds** flower from spring to the first frosts in Mexico, but growers make sure that particularly choice varieties come into flower for the Day of the Dead ceremonies that culminate on 2 November, All Souls' Day. The commemoration of the dead of the First World War, meanwhile, is marked in Britain, and some other countries, by the red corn **poppy**, a plant that flowered on European battlefields in early summer. Remembrance Day, however, is 11 November.

Autumn is undeniably a time of taking stock – in various ways – but it's not all about looking backward. For gardeners, there's lots to do: gathering the leaves that the trees flung about when they undressed for winter; pruning those trees; removing the dried-out skeletons of flower stems and heads. Some of that labour is a consequence of the implosion of the year that's been, but it's also a preparation for the year ahead. And then there's the job of sorting seeds and planting bulbs. Perhaps it is these seeds and bulbs – both 'kernels of memory' (Abū al-Qāsim al-Shābbī) and a 'bomb out of which a spring flower will burst' (Karl Čapek) – that are the true floral emblems of autumn, the season of destruction but also creation.

Saffron

It is not always easy to locate the geographical origin of a particular plant species, especially one that has spread all over the globe and whose name has changed many times in the process. But sometimes ancient sources can combine with contemporary genetics to provide an answer.

In 2019, a group of German and Iranian scientists published a paper that established the evolutionary origins of *Crocus sativus*, the small lilac flower whose dried orange stigma we call saffron. The first clue was Theophrastus's description of propagating the crocus through its 'large and fleshy root' (that is, its corm). This confirmed that *C. sativus* was around in the eighth century. For unlike its close relative *C. cartwrightianus*, the flower depicted in Bronze Age Aegean wall paintings, *sativus* is sterile. In other words, it doesn't produce seeds or fruits, but has to be reproduced vegetatively, by digging up the corms and separating off the baby corms or 'cormels' for replanting. This means two things: first, that every saffron bulb – whether growing in Spain or Iran, rural Essex or rural Pennsylvania – has been planted by a human hand; and second, that they are all more or less genetically identical.

The molecular tests proved what had long been suspected – that *C. sativus* is a mutation of *C. cartwrightianus* which the Cretans selected for its distinctively elongated crimson stigmas. When these threads are picked and dried, they constitute one of the world's most sought-after and expensive spices: saffron. Not for nothing is it known as red gold.

A woman picking wild *Crocus cartwrightianus* on a rocky hillside. A wall painting in Xestes 3, Akrotiri, Thera (Santorini), *c.* 3000–1100 BCE.

The cost alone is undoubtedly one reason why saffron has proved so enduringly desirable. But it's much more than a trophy plant. We now know it mainly as an ingredient of paella Valenciana, bouillabaisse Marseillaise, risotto alla Milanese, Jodhpuri lassi, Swedish buns, Iranian rice pudding, and Pennsylvania Dutch pot pie – but that's just the start. Saffron was a vital pigment in medieval European manuscripts and Persian rugs. The Egyptians used saffron in bindings for the dead, the Romans made it into an eye-shadow, and in India it is the sacred colour of robes worn by Hindu Sannyasis. Saffron is an ingredient in thousands of medicines. But it's also a verb: shirts are 'saffroned'; history textbooks 'saffronised'. In 1966, Donovan reached No. 2 in the pop charts when he confessed to being 'mad about Saffron', although the 'mellow yellow' of the song's title turned out to be a banana-shaped vibrator.

Harvesting the crop, in September or October depending where you are, has not changed much since ancient times. As each flower begins to open, and before the sun is fully up, it is handpicked and the three red stigmas severed

Illustration in *Taqwīm as-Siḥḥa (Maintenance of Health)*, an eleventh-century Arab medical treatise that was translated into Latin in the thirteenth century as *Tacuinum Sanitatis*.

Harvesting saffron in Iran, 2007.

with a fingernail – a finicky job usually delegated to women. The next day the process needs to be repeated for another flower will have opened. The crocus harvest is a short but intensive affair.

To avoid the colour and flavour fading, the stigmas then need to be dried very quickly (which reduces their weight by about 80 per cent). In Iran and Morocco, they are air-dried in the shade; in Spain, they're placed on mesh trays over charcoal; in England, at least in the sixteenth century, the 'chives' were pressed between weighted boards and made into a 'cake'.

It takes about 200,000 flowers, and more than 400 hours of labour, to produce a kilo of saffron. That's why the spice is, per gram, the most expensive farmed agricultural product, and a honeypot for criminals. Oddly enough, crime has sometimes been associated with the flower's least, as well as its most, valuable parts. After the stigmas have been removed, the rest of the crocus is considered a waste product, and thus ripe for fly (or rather flower) tipping. In 1574, after discarded purple petals clogged up the River Slade in the English town of Saffron Walden, a decree was issued announcing that further miscreants would be punished by two days and nights in the stocks.

That was nothing compared to the trouble caused by thieves. In 1374, a fourteen-week-long Saffron War kicked off when an 800-pound shipment of the spice was hijacked by a group of noblemen near Basel in Switzerland. When their demands were met, they returned the goods. As late as the nineteenth century, the proceedings of London's Old Bailey record numerous cases in which men were brought before the judge on charges of stealing the spice from druggists and warehouses; in 1835 two pounds of stolen saffron were valued at £21, while in 1871 two hundred pounds fetched £250.

The most profitable crime of all, however, as every drug dealer knows, is adulteration. This is easier to do when the spice is powdered. Then the saffron can easily be mixed with turmeric or ground-up petals of calendula marigold or safflower (a.k.a. 'bastard saffron'). Alternatively, the threads can be bulked out with other plant material such as pomegranate fibres, poppy petals, or, most often, with the saffron's own styles and stamen. But strips of paper, silk, horsehair and even fibres of smoked beef have all been used. An easier way to fool your buyer is to increase the saffron's weight by storing it in a damp place, or moistening it with honey, oil or glycerine. Many of these age-old methods are still in use today. In 2000, for example, British trading standards officers were alerted to the fact that, at a time when top grade Spanish saffron from La Mancha was selling at £3,750 per pound, a Bradford dealer was offering the spice for just £277. Tests revealed that a quarter of the product consisted of dyed stamens. In 1444, Jobst Finderlers was burnt at the stake in Nuremberg along with his adulterated saffron. In twenty-first-century Bradford, there was only a £5,000 fine.

But no one has ever doubted the scale of the problem, and the difficulty of identifying a fake. Back in the first century, Pliny the Elder recommended two tests: the first is to press the threads to see if they crackle (for moistened saffron 'makes no noise'); the second is to touch the spice and then your face – if it's genuine, you should feel a slight stinging. These are easy to do at home, but not really feasible on a larger scale. In Iran, which produces more than 80 per cent of the world's supply (around 220 tonnes annually), biosystems engineers have recently developed complex adulteration tests involving computer vision techniques and an electronic nose.

Saffron was common throughout the Roman empire, but then fell out of use in Europe until the Arab conquest of the Iberian Peninsula. Its use, and cultivation, spread gradually north and by the fourteenth century, it was widely used as an ingredient in food and medicine, and as a dye.

Spices in general were popular with medieval European cooks who drew on Arabic influences in order to add flavour and colour. But saffron also served another purpose: it offered an everyday way to display wealth (500g of the stuff cost the same as a horse). 'I must have saffron to colour the warden [pear] pies,' insists the clown in Shakespeare's *The Winter's Tale*. And he was not alone. European recipe books from this period often talk about 'colouring', 'yellowing', or 'endorring' (that is, gilding) dishes with saffron or saffron-laced egg washes. It is a key ingredient in the first English cookbook, *The Forme of Curye*

(1390) – 'curye' meaning 'cookery' – which compiled 196 of the best recipes from Richard II's 'master-cooks'. The grander the occasion, the greater amount of spice used, but even the simplest dishes feature saffron. 'Ryse of flesh', for example, is just rice cooked in broth, then finished off with salt, almond milk, and, 'to colour it', a pinch of saffron.

It wasn't only food that was gilded. Saffron was the key ingredient in compounds designed to imitate gold in paintings and book illumination, for example to add a flourish around the coloured initials that opened a chapter. Unlike most medieval pigments, it was easy to prepare – a pinch of stigmas simply needed to be infused with water or glair (egg white) – and, unlike other gold substitutes involving mercury and arsenic, it was not toxic. Master Peter from St Omer in northern France even claimed that Sicilian saffron was 'more beautiful than gold'.

Saffron was also employed as a disinfectant – the rich scattered it on their floors and sprinkled it into the fire – and as a medicinal ingredient that was thought to be effective against the plague. There was probably a placebo effect in all this; as today's wellness industry demonstrates, the more expensive the ingredient, the more likely the patient is to believe that it's doing some good. Many people were also guided by a conviction that the plant's appearance provided a clue to its medicinal uses (according to the 'doctrine of signatures' – see **Daisy**) or, here specifically, of colour analogy. Saffron was therefore prescribed for 'yellow' ailments such as jaundice and urinary tract disorders. It even came in handy for moulting canaries.

Saffron also seems to have been thought of as a stimulant and an anti-depressant. When Katerina Imhoff Lemmel became a Birgittine nun in 1516, she wrote often to her relatives asking for financial and other assistance. Her cousin, Hans, had an import business in Nuremberg – a centre for Mediterranean goods – and so Katerina asked him to send large quantities of saffron. The sisters needed it to colour their soup, she said, but it also made them feel 'much better'. Hans would have understood what she meant. Most herbalists prescribed saffron as a pick-me-up, useful for 'shaking off a heavy sleep' and even for making users a little 'merry'. Nicholas Culpeper thought it particularly useful for 'female obstructions and hysteric depressions'. Perhaps that's why, during particularly busy periods like Lent or Advent, each nun was provided with her own personal stash of the spice to fragrance her veils. Recent clinical trials into 'the Prozac of the Middle Ages' suggest that some of the claims made by the herbalists may have been justified. There is, however, no evidence to support Culpeper's anxiety about the dangers of saffron abuse: 'Some have fallen into an immoderate convulsive laughter,' he warned, 'which ended in death.' (It is more likely that they had imbibed 'meadow saffron', the highly toxic *Colichicum autumnale*.)

It's very unusual for a spice that flourishes in Kashmir, Iran and north Africa also to do well in Britain – even in rainy Cornwall (where saffron buns are still popular). Mostly, however, the bulbs were grown in the driest part of Britain: south Cambridgeshire and north Essex. Saffron was cultivated in the gardens of several Cambridge colleges, and taken to London by the Bishop of Ely, who established it in the extensive gardens of his London palace – an area that came to be known as Saffron Hill. But more modest gardens also devoted land to the profitable corms. Rowland Parker describes sixteenth-century smallholders in the village of Foxton growing crocuses in fields of anything from an eighth of an acre to two acres in size. An acre, he estimated, would have yielded about 6 pounds of saffron, worth about £6. It was therefore a highly profitable crop, but only if plenty of unpaid labour could be found. As Parker notes, 'unpaid labour was one of the basic features of farming then and for another two centuries'.

Cultivation on a much larger scale was centred a little further south, around the Essex market town of Saffron Walden, originally known as Chepyng Walden. The change of name, in the sixteenth century, was an acknowledgement of the crocus's contribution to the town's wealth. Its emblem of three plants growing within the castle's battlements was a heraldic pun: saffron walled-in. Why the trade flourished here in particular has been a matter of some conjecture. Local folklore favoured the romantic story of a Christian pilgrim who returned from the Crusades with a single corm hidden in his specially hollowed-out staff. Had he been caught, he would have been killed but, legend had it, he took the risk 'to do good to his countrey'. Perhaps so, but the exact same story was told about the introduction of silk-worm eggs. And there were more mundane, and convincing, explanations. The area had the right kind of chalky, free-draining soil necessary to grow crocuses successfully, and, most importantly, Chepying Walden was at the centre of the region's wool trade. And, of course, there must also have been a ready supply of labourers to pick the crocuses – 'crokers', as they came to be called. Observing the town's prosperity in 1598, Richard Hakluyt, best known for promoting the English colonisation of North America, suggested that other areas try the crop, if only 'for the benefit of the setting of the poore on worke'.

Another benefit that was often discussed, and which is also familiar in contemporary conversations about food, concerned the trustworthiness of a locally grown, rather than an imported, product. English saffron, acquired 'out of the hands of the growers pure and genuine', was surely more reliable than a foreign (and possibly adulterated) import. Saffron Walden's crop was 'the best of any foreign country', declared John Evelyn. But the local euphoria – 'God did shite saffron' – was not to last. By the mid-eighteenth century, the crocuses were all but gone: the soil was less productive than it had been, labour was harder to secure, culinary tastes had altered, and the wool trade was in decline. The fields were replanted with barley and the town settled into brewing.

In seventeenth-century Protestant England, where 'sad' colours were not only preferred but, in certain contexts, insisted on by sumptuary legislation, the use of yellow dyes in food and clothing came to be seen as inherently effeminate, foreign and, particularly, papist. Yellow had long been associated with continental Catholicism, but more immediate anxieties centred around the Scottish Highlands and colonial Ireland, where many refused to give up their 'saffroned' tunics or *léine croich*.

Ireland had a lengthy history of importing Spanish and Middle Eastern saffron – some claim from as early as the tenth century – and, later, in a limited way, for growing it (for example, at Saffron Hill, near Cork). What made the spice such a *cause célèbre* for the English Protestants was its oddly dual association with both outrageous extravagance and deplorable poverty or, worse, poor hygiene. For saffron did not only brighten clothes, it deodorised, disinfected and (especially if urine was added to the dye) de-loused them. It was widely accepted that, due 'to the beastliness of the people, and the want of cleanly women to wash them', Ireland 'swarm[ed] almost with lice'. Edmund Spenser argued that it was the Irish habit of 'much sweating and long wearing of linen' that led them to emulate the saffron-dyeing practice of (Catholic) 'old Spaniards', but the physician Thomas Muffet (famous for his study of insects) suggested, more plausibly, that things worked the other way round: that clothes remained unwashed precisely to preserve the expensive insecticide. Saffron was so costly that the Irish waited six months before laundering their shirts and applying a fresh 'size' (poultice). In any case, in the name of economy and cleanliness, but largely as a display of English colonial control, Henry VIII passed a series of laws forbidding typical Irish clothes, hairstyles, and anything 'coloured or dyed with Saffron'.

With all this cultural baggage, it is no surprise that seventeenth-century English satirists should have railed so vociferously when saffron briefly had a fashion moment in London itself, mainly as a dye for collars and ruffs. In 1616, Robert Anton declared that the 'yellow bands' (collars) 'now do staine the times' and even credited the crocus's stigmas with the power of transforming 'Gentilitie' into 'some painted whoore'.

In Ireland, however, the taste for yellow endured – the legislation was almost impossible to enforce – and perhaps even increased, as a sign of resistance to English rule. Although saffron probably was too expensive for general use, its hue could be approximated using local plants such as lichen (*Vulpicida juniperinus*), lady's bedstraw (*Gallium verum*), or dyer's rocket (*Reseda luteola*) – Ireland's own botanical treasures.

Even today, when green has become the official colour of the Emerald Isle, saffron retains a certain legendary status. That's largely due to the Celtic Revivalists of the nineteenth and early twentieth centuries who suggested that the dye was the product not of fifteenth-century European trade but rather of ancient Irish tradition. For example, one of William Butler Yeats's very early narrative poems 'The Wanderings of Oisin' evokes the 'saffron morning' of 'old Eri'. The idea of the saffron kilt as a form of national dress emerged a little later. James Joyce mentions the kilt both in *Ulysses* – where it is associated with debates about the yet unwritten 'national epic' – and in *Finnegans Wake* when, in epic style and pidgin English, he tells the story of the encounter of 'whiterobed' St Patrick with King Leary and his archdruids. Leary is a study in shades of green, so even his 'saffron pettikilt' looks a bit like boiled spinach. Joyce later described the scene as representing 'the conversion of St Patrick by Ireland'.

Nationalism is also at the heart of saffron's meaning in India today. The term 'saffronisation' was initially coined to refer to the practice of rewriting history textbooks from a narrowly Hindu perspective, but it is now used more widely to refer to nationalist attempts to impart a 'saffron hue' to every aspect of Indian society. A recent, very literal, example involved the team colours of the national cricket team. Saffron had long been associated with Hinduism, and especially the worship of the fire goddess, Agni. Purification by (saffron) fire would ensure that the (saffron) sun rose to dispel darkness and bring enlightenment. Saffron robes have long been worn by ascetics who renounce worldliness and embrace disinterestedness. Little about the current situation is disinterested, however. In 1947, saffron was chosen as one of the three colours of the Indian national flag, but today cartoonists often depict Hindu nationalists armed with large paintbrushes, determined to saffron-wash over the white and the green. No one, on either side of the debate, seems to remember the crocuses behind the controversial colour, or, more urgently, the recent collapse of the Kashmiri crocus industry.

Crocus sativus was introduced into Kashmir by the Persians sometime before the third century, where it was said to be grown as an offering to the

Buddha as well as to dye the robes of monks. Later the Moghul emperors, who had close ties to Persia, popularised it as a spice in biryani and other dishes. But Kashmiri saffron also became an important agricultural export. Workers in the fields near Pampore ('Saffron Town') used to sing songs celebrating the crocus's beauty while complaining that 'collecting it into heaps we are bathed in sweat'. Today, however, the singing has stopped. The combination of climate emergency and violent politics in this borderline territory has devastated the Kashmiri saffron fields. Now the serious lament is that 'the red-gold is turning to gray.'

Chrysanthemum

On 21 October 1967, the press photographer Marc Riboud was sent to cover the 100,000-strong march on the Pentagon in protest against the US role in the Vietnam war. As the soldiers of the National Guard lined up to defend the building from the converging demonstrators, Riboud's overwhelming impression was how young everyone was. 'I was taking photographs like mad,' he recollected and, in those pre-digital days, that meant he eventually found himself running out of film. But, as is often the case, Riboud said, 'the very last photo was the best': 'Framed in my viewfinder was the symbol of that American youth: a flower held before a row of Bayonets.'

Holding that flower, a chrysanthemum, was seventeen-year-old Jan Rose Kasmir. 'I was going back and forth, beckoning the soldiers to join us,' she recalled. 'None of them made eye contact. But the photographer later told me he noticed them shaking. I think they were afraid they were going to be told to fire at us. If you look at my face, I am extremely sad: at that moment I realised how young those boys were.'

Kasmir's gesture, immortalised by Riboud, was to become the iconic image of sixties flower power, but the idea of confronting guns with blooms did not begin there. Most accounts locate the origin of the strategy in a 1965 essay by the poet and activist Allen Ginsberg on 'How to Make a March/Spectacle'. Ginsberg's immediate concern was diffusing the threat of violence posed by a group of pro-war Hells Angels. Attempting to create a 'fun, gay, happy, *secure*'

Marc Riboud's photograph of Jan Rose Kasmir confronting the National Guard outside the Pentagon in 1967.

peace demonstration in Berkeley, Ginsberg suggested that the protesters be provided with 'masses of flowers', as well as toys, balloons and candy, to hand out to the bikers, police, politicians and journalists. 'Masses of marchers can be asked to bring their own flowers,' he advised. 'Front lines should be organized and provided with flowers in advance.' The event passed off peacefully and set a precedent for further demonstrations.

In May 1967, five months before the Pentagon protest, Abbie Hoffman, co-founder of the Youth International Party (the Yippies), led what he called a 'Flower Brigade' of anti-war campaigners in the Manhattan Armed Forces Day parade. Television coverage showed the protesters being punched, kicked and spat at, while their flowers and pink 'love' flags were angrily stamped upon. It was a frightening experience, but the publicity made it worthwhile. 'The Flower Brigade lost its first battle,' Hoffman wrote soon after, 'but watch out America. We were poorly equipped with flowers from uptown florists. Already there is talk of growing our own. Plans are being made to mine the East River with daffodils. Dandelion chains are being wrapped around induction centers. Holes are being dug in street pavements and seeds dropped and covered. The cry of "Flower Power" echoes through the land. We shall not wilt. Let a thousand flowers bloom.'

Events under the banner of flower power – defined by Hoffman as 'love plus courage' – carried on throughout the year, with commercial interests catching on fast. John Phillips wrote a promotional song for the Monterey Pop Festival urging visitors to San Francisco to 'be sure to wear some flowers' in their hair, and by the time the 'summer of love' arrived, garlands and floral prints were ubiquitous. But no one seemed to discriminate much between roses and lilies, daisies and daffodils. On 21 October 1967, 'armfuls of flowers' were available to hand to the soldiers at the Pentagon. Kasmir had taken a seasonal chrysanthemum, but a perpetual (all-year-round) carnation featured in the day's other iconic image – Bernie Boston's photograph of an eighteen-year-old boy carefully slotting a flower down the barrel of a National Guardsman's rifle. (The boy in question, George Harris, was en route from New York to San Francisco, where he would change his name to Hibiscus and move into a commune called Kaliflower.) The sunflower, meanwhile, was the choice of 'middle-class, middle-of-the road' protest group Another Mother for Peace (AMP). For although the AMP focused many of its activities around Mother's Day – traditionally a focus for anti-war initiatives – it had no interest in that holiday's founding symbol, the white carnation. While the campaigning women of the early twentieth century had focused on the purity and durability of mother love (symbolised by the carnation), the emphasis in the late sixties was on the rights and enduring innocence of adolescent children, which were better encapsulated in the childlike sunflower of Lorraine Schneider's poster 'War is not healthy for children and other living things'. Faced with the military-industrial complex, ideas of peace, love, childhood and flowers had formed an alliance.

But other alliances were also possible. The chrysanthemum carried by Kasmir was a descendant of a nineteenth-century import from Japan, a country with a long attachment to the flower, and a very different sense of what it might mean. In short: not so much peace, love and understanding as the consolidation of imperial power.

But first, we need to go to China, where most of the Japanese chrysanthemums, and ideas about chrysanthemums, originated. The Chinese began cultivating the flowers, for medical, culinary, decorative and ritual purposes, more than a thousand years ago. The earliest, and most famous, mention of the flower occurs in a poem by Tao Qian (Tao Yuanming), the fifth of his 'Twenty Poems on Drinking Wine'. At first sight, it seems an inconsequential reference: Tao simply describes going to pick some flowers by the eastern fence of his property and catching a glimpse in the distance of South Mountain (Mount Lu, in Jiangxi province). But the poem's significance is philosophical, hinting at the intimate relationship between here and there, between permanence and immensity (the holy mountain) and quotidian evanescence (the flower, the day, the season, a man's life). Much of the chrysanthemum's later significance in Chinese culture derives from these brief lines. In particular, they came to be associated with the ancient festival of Chong Yang, celebrated on 9 September, a doubly auspicious *yang* number. The mythical and the medical combine here, for the autumn dew that gathers on the chrysanthemum flower and leaf was thought to be an elixir of youth, or at least late-season vigour. (There are many stories, poems, plays and paintings about the search for that dew.) The Ninth Day festival is still celebrated today: families walk in the hills, carry dogwood leaves and berries (to ward off evil), and drink chrysanthemum wine or tea (rather than dew). In recent years, the festival has primarily become a day in which young people honour their elderly relatives.

By the tenth century, Chinese monks had established the chrysanthemum and its rituals in Japan. Emiko Ohnuki-Tierney describes how the Ninth Day was taken up with particular enthusiasm by the aristocracy, including the

A poster advertising the 2018 Chong Yang Festival. The date in the Chinese calendar is 9 September; in 2018, as the top righthand corner of the poster indicates, it fell on 17 October in the Gregorian calendar.

imperial family, which introduced a new ceremony designed to ensure its own longevity: 'while the emperor was viewing chrysanthemums, his body was wiped with "chrysanthemum cotton", the center part of the flower, wet with chrysanthemum dew'. These associations were revived during the Meiji restoration of the 1870s and 1880s, when Japan abandoned the feudal system and reinvented itself as a modern nation state with an emperor at its head. In 1889, a stylised, sixteen-petalled chrysanthemum was adopted as the crest and official seal of the imperial family, known as the Chrysanthemum Throne. The country's highest honour remains the Supreme Order of the Chrysanthemum, and the emblem features prominently on military insignia and weaponry. Collectors of Japanese rifles captured at the end of the Second World War have observed that the imperial emblem stamped on the breech is often scratched or scored through: some suggest that this was done at the order of General MacArthur, who commanded the army of occupation in 1945, but others believe the Japanese soldiers themselves made the mark to preserve the honour of the emperor (to whom each gun and each soldier 'belonged'). If the latter is true, it leads us to another traditional flower symbol that had been successfully militarised: the cherry blossom.

Since modern Japan defined itself as the land of cherry blossoms, falling flowers, the traditional spring symbol of life's brevity, came to be associated with patriotic martyrdom. In *The Book of Tea* – written in English in 1906 for a Western readership – Kakuzō Okakura explained the significance of 'the Flower Sacrifice' in terms of bravery and 'glory'. The cherry blossoms, he said, 'are not cowards, like men' and therefore 'freely surrender themselves to the winds'; 'then, as they sail away on the laughing waters, they seem to say "Farewell, Spring! We are on to Eternity".' Lecturing on the 'Japanese spirit' in the 1930s, Kiyoshi Hiraizumi was more explicit: 'in case of emergency, we need to fall like cherry blossoms for the emperor.' The simile reached its peak with the *tokkō-tai* (special forces kamikaze) operation at the end of the Second World War – a single pink cherry blossom was painted on the fuselage of each plane and teenaged girls waved cherry branches as the pilots set off to martyrdom.

Viewed in relation to this complex Japanese symbolism, Kasmir's gesture at the Pentagon in 1967 becomes even more resonant. At stake, as always in war, are the young men who fall from the sky like cherry blossoms or whose blood feeds the soil from which poppies emerge. If a Chrysanthemum Throne can order those deaths, then perhaps they could be prevented by a girl and her 'mum'.

The stakes were not always so high when it came to Japanese chrysanthemums. When, after two centuries of isolation, Japan opened its ports to world trade in the 1850s, many in the west went crazy for the country's porcelain, kimonos, folding screens, woodcuts and tales of geishas. The vogue for japonisme also fuelled a taste for peonies, cherry blossoms, maples and, of course, chrysanthemums, whose image was further boosted by *Madame Chrysanthème* (1887), Pierre Loti's bestselling novel, based on his affair with a woman called

Kiku (Chrysanthemum), and then by Puccini's adaptation *Madame Butterfly*. But it was the real thing that fascinated Gustave Caillebotte and Claude Monet, both as painters and as gardeners.

Chinese chrysanthemums had been introduced into Europe twice before the Japanese varieties arrived. In the late seventeenth century, a few hybrids were cultivated in Dutch gardens as well as the Chelsea Physic Garden but, perhaps because of their resemblance to native plants like feverfew, they were not particularly valued and soon lost. In 1789, however, three more attractive cultivars were brought back to France by a merchant who had been trading in Canton and Macau. Only one, 'Old Purple', survived, but by the end of the century, it had become a prized exhibit, whetting the European appetite. In 1843, when the Treaty of Nanking ended Britain's first Opium War with China (see **Poppy**), the plant collector Robert Fortune was sent by the Horticultural Society of London to find more – and preferably hardy – plants in the temperate parts of China. Among the hundreds of species and cultivars he brought back from his base on the floriferous islands of Zhoushan (Chusan) were the small-flowered parents of the pompom varieties. These became hugely popular with florists' societies and were, for many years, the only chrysanthemums that would flower early enough to be grown outdoors in northern Europe.

But it was the colourful, shaggy varieties that Fortune found in Japan in the 1860s that really made a stir; they quickly took on a starring role as both a cut flower and a conservatory stalwart. Dennis Miller Bunker memorialised Isabella Stewart Gardner's prize-winning Boston collection in an 1888 painting, while a few years earlier James Tissot depicted a young woman amidst a profusion of chrysanthemums in his own London conservatory. In Tissot's case, the profusion of white and yellow flowers both frame and echo the cosseted, luxurious sensuality of the woman herself; in a similar way, a 'blushing palette' of red, pink and white chrysanthemums enhance the 'strange, secret, splendour' of Odette and her salon in Marcel Proust's *À l'ombre des jeunes filles en fleur*.

With a growing reputation as one of the most hyper-cultivated of flowers, the Japanese chrysanthemum suited some tastes more than others. The novelist

James Tissot, *Chrysanthemums*, 1874–76.

H. Rider Haggard, for example, was not an enthusiast. While admiring the 'large and fine' cultivars with which a neighbour had won second prize in the famous Norwich chrysanthemum show, he forbade his own gardener from growing 'huge blooms' for competition. Walter Fish, the husband of garden writer Margery, went considerably further. Furious that their gardener 'used to stroke and fondle his chrysanthemums so much that he was neglecting the rest of the garden', Walter one day headed for the greenhouse with a knife, 'and slashed off all those pampered darlings at ground level'.

Caillebotte and Monet were more open-minded, making room in their gardens and paintings for both the large-flowered glasshouse chrysanthemums and the new hardy garden varieties that had begun to appear in sophisticated modern colours, including what the plantsman Charles Baltet promoted as 'Havana cigar, carob, otter-skin' and 'copper cauldron'. They collected the latest cultivars for their gardens and wrote letters to each other about which were the best and where to acquire them. Caillebotte managed to provide Monet with some of the special new cultivars that had been displayed in the 1891 Paris Horticultural Exhibition, while their mutual friend and fellow chrysanthophile, Octave Mirbeau, offered to send him cuttings, 'with crazy shapes and beautiful colours', from his own extensive collection. (A sign of Monet's dedication to his plants can be found in the anxious letters he sent home whenever he went south on painting trips. In April 1888, for example, he wrote from Antibes to remind his partner Alice Hoschedé about a new batch of chrysanthemums that she should immediately move to the vegetable patch, 'spaced well apart, so that they can grow, and on my return, we'll plant them out'.)

At the same time as Monet and Caillebotte tended their Japanese cultivars, they keenly studied Japanese floral painting. The flat, decorative effects of Hokusai's 'large flower' woodcuts in particular offered an exciting alternative to accepted European conventions of genre painting, still life and perspective. Adapting the style to French bourgeois surroundings, the canvas of Caillebotte's *Chrysanthemums in the Garden at Petit Gennevilliers* (1893) is filled, edge to edge, with blossoms and foliage – he's offering a detail from a scene rather than the scene itself – while Monet's 1897 series *Chrysanthemums*, painted after

Katsushika Hokusai, *Chrysanthemums and Horsefly, c.* 1833–34. Monet owned a copy of this print, which is displayed today in his house at Giverny.

Claude Monet, *Massif de chrysanthèmes*, 1897.

Caillebotte's death, perhaps as a tribute to his friend, removes any vestige of garden or greenhouse context. What's left is an abundantly packed surface that luxuriates in the pure painterly effects of colour and texture; one early critic compared it to a tapestry. The series represents an important step towards the almost-abstraction of Monet's later water lily paintings.

Happier with a tommy gun than a paint brush, 'short, limping, smiling' Dean O'Banion was, nonetheless, his biographers all note, an artist of the chrysanthemum. With 'a natural eye for design and color', he gained a reputation for 'artful floral pieces' and 'choice' funeral memorials during the bootlegger years of the early 1920s. O'Banion's main job was as the boss of Chicago's North Side Gang. In 1921, however, he bought a stake in the William F. Schofield Flower Shop, conveniently situated opposite the Holy Name Cathedral. The shop was partly a convenient front (Big Bill Schofield handled most of the day-to-day floristry, and the gang met upstairs to discuss the million-dollar trade in 'beer and blood'), but O'Banion took real pride in the lavish floral arrangements that gangster funerals required. They paid pretty well too.

For several years, the North Side Gang had a working arrangement with the Johnny Torrio/Al Capone Southside gang, and the 'terrible Gennas' of Little Italy. Things changed in November 1924, when O'Banion refused to write off one of Angelo Genna's gambling debts. 'To hell with the Sicilians' was his blithe if foolish attitude, for to hell with O'Banion was the Sicilian response. Genna persuaded Torrio and Capone to send their men to Schofield's, ostensibly to pick up flowers for the funeral of Mike Merlo. As president of the influential *Unione Siciliana,* Merlo deserved a lot of respect – and it was given in the form of $100,000 worth of floral tributes. Schofield and O'Banion created horseshoes, pyramids, pillars and quilts; Capone himself commissioned an $8,000 rose sculpture. Merlo's death was important for another reason, too. Keen to keep the peace, he had dissuaded Capone and Genna from going after O'Banion. But now Merlo was dead and soon afterwards, so too was O'Banion.

When the police arrived at the shop, he was found lying on the floor riddled with bullets (one also smashed a glass cabinet and lodged itself in a display of American Beauty roses). Inches from his left hand lay a pair of florists' scissors and some clipped and bloody chrysanthemums. So much for the flower's promise of longevity: O'Banion was only thirty-two. What was bad for him (and many other bootleggers) was, however, good for the store; in the six-year all-out gang war that ensued, business at Schofield's bloomed and boomed.

The incongruity of gang violence and floristry – like all the clashes and comings together of guns and roses (cherry blossoms or chrysanthemums) – gives the story an almost legendary appeal. Most recently, Schofield's featured in HBO's Prohibition-era drama *Boardwalk Empire*, and in 2018, a Glasgow florist, calling itself O'Banions, marked its launch and its determination to be 'the most badass florist in Scotland' by tastefully 'flower-bombing' the city.

Marigold

Which is the marigold's season? It depends who's asking. And which marigold.

In ancient Rome, the marigold was *Calendula officinalis* and it bloomed all year round: the Latin word *calends* refers to the first day of a Roman month, and *Calendulas* seemed to put in an appearance on every one of those days. In modern India, the flower is *Tagetes erecta* (the so-called African marigold that's actually from central America), and again, it's grown to bloom pretty much all year for use in spring and autumn festivals. In Mexico and Guatemala, where the species originated, *Tagetes* seeds are planted so that they reach their peak at the end of October in time for the Day of the Dead festivities. There, at least, the marigold is definitely an autumn flower.

When the Spanish conquered the Aztec capital of Tenochtitlan (now Mexico City) in 1522, they were overwhelmed by the extent and profusion of the gardens – the ornamental royal gardens, but also the garden farms they found in the *chinampas*, the 'floating' islands surrounding the city. Among the many plants cultivated there were several species of a flower they had never seen before – *Tagetes*. These were not only pretty to look at but, as they soon learnt, hugely important in Aztec medicine and religion. In fact, the two functions were closely related, with plants understood as intermediaries between humans and the gods, often working to restore balance in their relationship. *Tagetes* may have acquired its powerful reputation because of its strong musky scent, for highly fragranced plants were believed to be particularly effective in conveying prayers and messages to the gods. This idea was not specific to the Aztecs, of course. The native flowers of hot, dry countries tend to have stronger scents than those in the cool, damp north, so it's not surprising that these are the places where the use of aromatics and incense for religious purposes first flourished.

One of the most important species of *Tagetes* was *lucida*, known as *yauhtli* in the Aztec language of Nahuatl. It had some everyday uses – removing ticks, treating hiccups and easing rectal bleeding – but it was also (in combination with five other herbs) a treatment for those struck by lightning and a magical talisman against the dangers of crossing water. Most importantly, *yauhtli* was used as a ritual offering, either on its own or in combination with a blood sacrifice: petals of *yauhtli* were thrown in the faces of human victims to dull their senses. Contact with the supernatural was also achieved through trance-like states and *yauhtli*, while not effective on its own, enhanced the hallucinogenic power of other plants: it was sometimes smoked with *Nicotiana rustica* (a form of tobacco) or drunk in a cocktail of maize beer and cactus juice.

Tagetes erecta was known by the Aztecs as *cempoalxochitl* ('twenty flower'). Although it too had some medical uses, *cempoalxochitl* was mainly strung into garlands for rituals involving water, vegetation, fire, sun and sovereignty, and for ceremonies honouring the dead and Huitzilopochtli, god of the sun, warfare and sacrifice, who was said to have led the Aztecs from Aztlan, their mythical homeland, to Tenochtitlan in the fourteenth century. A stone relief in the great temple pyramids of Templo Mayor shows the flat ray flowers in a crown worn by Huitzilopochtli's sister, Coyolxauhqui, perhaps to signal her death.

Cempoalxochitl, or cempasúchil as it's known in Spanish, is still grown in great quantities today. For this marigold is the *flor de muertos*, used in the Day of the Dead ceremonies that combine Aztec rituals with the Christian festival that culminates on 2 November, All Souls' Day (the day after All Saints'). Offerings of marigolds are placed on both graves and home altars, with trails of yellow petals connecting the two: the colour is important, but once again it's the flower's pungent scent, combining with the smells of the cooked food and sweet *pan de muerto* offerings, that summon the spirits of the dead.

During the nineteenth century, as the newly independent Mexico sought to establish itself as a modern nation, these indigenous traditions and their associated flowers were often forgotten. Out went marigolds, zinnias, and dahlias in the parks and public gardens, and in came imported eucalyptus, chrysanthemums and violets. For the writer José Tomás de Cuéllar, the figure of the 'silent, taciturn Indian standing in front of a pile of *cempasúchil* flowers and sugared bread, in the light of two wax candles surrounded by smoking incense' represented how long the 'road to progress' was likely to be. He didn't care that those he called the 'ignorant *mestizos*' were devoted to 'the ugliest and foulest-smelling flowers of the land'; what worried him was the fact that the 'most refined element' of elite society also refused to give up these rituals.

Interest in the pre-Hispanic traditions only intensified during and after the 1910–1920 revolution, when 'indigenous sentiment' was championed as the basis of a distinctive national culture. An example of this is Saturnino Herrán's painting *La ofrenda* (1913), which depicts an indigenous family in flat-bottomed *trajinera* laden with marigolds from the floating islands to sell for Day of the Dead offerings. Mexican in subject matter, if still indebted to the European style, it is an important predecessor to both Diego Rivera's portraits of hard-working flower sellers (see **Lily**), and Frida Kahlo's flower-laden self-portraits and still lifes. Kahlo carefully introduced native plants into her garden in the suburbs of Mexico City, and lavishly employed them in her clothes, hair and paintings. Orange marigolds were colourful and decorative, but for her too, they provoked thoughts of death – thoughts which are never far from the surface in Kahlo's work.

Given the Mexican origins of *Tagetes*, it might seem odd that the two kinds we know best today are called African and French marigolds. This is entirely due

Saturnino Herrán, *La ofrenda*, 1913.

to the confused routes by which they entered Europe, or at least European consciousness.

The discovery of the African marigold was a by-product of another imperial conquest – Charles V's capture of the Ottoman city of Tunis in 1535. The soldiers collected what they thought were native plants but were really a naturalised population of escapees from Christian monasteries, introduced by

Spanish monks some years earlier. That intermediary step was forgotten, however, and seeds of the striking 'Flos. Africanus' were proudly sent back to Europe, earning a place in all the major gardens and herbal texts, alongside another geographically confused plant, the red and gold 'French marigold', *T. patula*. That flower's attributed nationality seems to have been due to its association with Huguenot refugees who brought it from France to England in the 1570s. (Suspicion about the scent, however, meant that most herbalists stuck to an older import – the pot marigold, *Calendula officinalis*, introduced by the Romans.)

A further journey, by Portuguese colonists, established both species of marigold in western India. Today specially adapted cultivars of *T. erecta* constitute some of the country's major floral crops, for the demand for garlands of marigolds – known as *genda, sayapatri* or *banthi* – is huge. Interlaced with mango leaves, jasmine or red hibiscus, marigold garlands play such an essential role in informal and formal celebrations, from welcoming visitors to marriage ceremonies to religious festivals, that many think that *Tagetes erecta*, like another widely used American plant, chilli, is a local. The state flower of Gujarat, the marigold has become an easily recognised shortcut for India itself – demonstrated in the titles of two recent films about Westerners falling in love with the country: *Marigold* (2007) and *The Best Exotic Marigold Hotel* (2012).

Despite difficulties in accessing quantities of fresh flowers, diasporic communities of Indians continue to celebrate with marigolds, often by resorting to paper and plastic garlands. In Trinidad, the spring festival of colours, Holī, is still welcomed with a song celebrating 'the season of the blooming of the marigold'. In New England, however, things are rather more muted – at least according to the novelist Jhumpa Lahiri. In *The Namesake* (2003), she describes how the American-born teenage children of Bengali parents have to be 'dragged' to a hired hall for the autumn festival of Durga. They complain that it's boring 'to throw marigold petals at some cardboard effigy of a goddess' and look forward to the 'fanfare' of Christmas.

Even in India, not everyone likes marigold garlands. Mahatma Gandhi thought they were wasteful – after political rallies great stacks are left to rot –

and encouraged garlanding with home-spun yarns. (See **Cotton**.) After Jawaharlal Nehru was hit in the eye by a heavy garland, he suggested a single flower might be offered instead. Indira Gandhi was allergic to marigolds and charged her staff with keeping them as far away from her as possible. When she was assassinated in 1984, however, this was forgotten and piles of marigolds were placed on her bullet-ridden body. Five years later, her son, Rajiv Gandhi was also assassinated – by a terrorist who approached with a group of garlanders.

While the colour of the marigold has religious connotations (see **Saffron**), its bright, dependable glow also makes it a popular garden plant in India, and in many other places.

Marigolds were not, however, included in the original nineteenth-century British bedding schemes made possible by, and designed to showcase, the new technologies of mass production (cheap greenhouses) and distribution (national railway networks). Although such schemes relied on emphatic colours for maximum impact – red geraniums and blue lobelia were staples – yellow was provided by another import, *Calceolaria rugosa*, the slipper flower. *Tagetes* was relegated to the vegetable patch, where its pungent scent warded off parasitic nematodes from tomatoes and potatoes.

A surprising advocate of both French and African marigolds was Gertrude Jekyll, the Edwardian gardener whose painterly emphasis on 'intelligent combination' still dominates planting styles today. Along with her mentor William Robinson, Jekyll applied an anti-industrial Arts and Crafts ethos to gardening. She published numerous articles in Robinson's weekly magazine, *The Garden,* and contributed a chapter on colour to his influential book, *The English Flower Garden* (1883). Like Robinson, she often described gardening as 'painting a picture' but, unlike him, she did not think strong colours were necessarily vulgar and 'showy'. 'Not once but many times,' Jekyll noted, visitors had 'expressed unbounded surprise' to find bedding plants in her garden, but she believed that, used correctly (and that was the haughty mantra), no plant nor colour need be excluded. While best known for her long borders which gradually progress through the colour spectrum to produce a 'river of colour', Jekyll did allow some annual bedding into her garden, including 'pale sulphur', 'lemon-coloured' and 'brilliant orange' marigolds that she bought from Messrs Barr and Sons. One scheme groups marigolds with half-hardy chrysanthemums and nasturtiums to demonstrate the virtues of 'restricted colouring' over the 'purposely contrasted, or wantonly jumbled'. Today, both wanton and subtle gardeners welcome marigolds into their beds – not least because there are so many more shapes and colours to choose from.

Much of modern plant breeding remains as it always was: one variety is crossed with another and the progeny that seem most promising (which depends of course on the goal – size, colour, disease-resistance) are then trialled and tested. But changes, or mutations, can also appear, sometimes spontaneously (producing the 'breaks' or 'sports' that so preoccupied sixteenth- and seventeenth-century gardeners) and, more often, with a little help from chemicals, or even electromagnetic irradiation. As Helen Anne Curry notes in her study of early twentieth-century attempts at 'evolution made to order', cotton, sugarcane, corn and marigolds were just a few of the crops whose seeds were sent to the University of California irradiation laboratory in the 1920s and 1930s, 'in the hope of inducing some variation that might permit some further improvement by selection'.

The inclusion of marigolds in this list was largely due to the efforts of their entrepreneurial champion David Burpee – a self-described combination of the legendary plantsman Luther Burbank (whose seed bank he purchased) and the great showman Phineas T. Barnum. Burpee took over his father's seed firm in 1915 and, realising that the market for ornamental flowers was growing, turned his hand to sweet peas, zinnias and chrysanthemums. He is, however, best known as America's leading breeder and booster of marigolds (many of which were bred to resemble other flowers – including buttercups, daffodils, carnations, chrysanthemums and peonies). Even during the Great Depression of the 1930s, Burpee knew that his customers would pay for something unusual, something that would 'shock Mother Nature'. Experiments with the chromosome-doubling compound colchicine (derived from the autumn crocus) resulted in the 'Giant Tetra Marigold' in 1939, and in 1942 Burpee launched 'Glowing Gold' and 'Orange Fluffy', which became famous as the 'X-Ray Twins'.

This was still, of course, the pre-Atomic Age. During the 1950s and 1960s, although marigold growers continued to delight in new cultivars such as Burpee's 1962 'Man in the Moon' (later relaunched as 'Man *on* the Moon'), science fiction became obsessed with 'ingenious biological meddlings', such as John Wyndham's triffids, or the carnivorous Audrey from *The Little Shop of Horrors*. Paul Zindel's prize-winning family melodrama *The Effect of Gamma Rays on Man-in-the-Moon Marigolds* (1964) centres around a school project to grow marigolds from seeds that have been exposed to Cobalt-60. Even when the teenaged daughter wins the science fair with a rousing speech about the 'strange and beautiful' possibilities of the new science, her mother refuses to give up her suspicion that these 'atomic flowers' will make the whole family sterile.

Pamela Payton-Wright as Tillie, a teenaged marigold breeder, in the 1970 Broadway production of Paul Zindel's *The Effect of Gamma Rays on Man-in-the-Moon Marigolds*.

But Burpee was immune to this kind of anxiety. Starting in 1959, he enlisted the help of Senator Everett Dirksen to lobby for the marigold to be designated the national flower of the United States. It was native to the Americas, easy to grow (therefore democratic) and, most importantly, it signalled the nation's (and his own) commitment to a prosperous future based on scientific and technological advance. Although Dirksen, a flamboyant speaker, couldn't have been more supportive in his advocacy of a flower that was 'as sprightly as the daffodil, as colorful as the rose, as resolute as the zinnia, as delicate as the carnation, as haughty as the chrysanthemum, as aggressive as the petunia, as ubiquitous as the violet, and as stately as the snapdragon', he was up against equally passionate sponsors of the dogwood, columbine, aster, corn tassel and rose. In the end – which was not until 1986 – the rose won out. (Just as it did in Bulgaria, Romania, Slovakia, Luxembourg, the Czech Republic, the Maldives and England.)

The Senate, however, was by no means Burpee's only target. In 1954, as another publicity stunt, he launched a competition offering $10,000 to the first gardener to send him seeds that would produce plants as big as 'Man in the Moon' marigolds – that is, having flowerheads with a diameter of at least two and a half inches – and as white as 'Snowstorm' petunias. As the years went on, Burpee regularly repeated the challenge and newspapers duly reported that he was 'still searching'. (In the meantime, Camel evoked his patience to sell slow-burning cigarettes.) Prizes of $100 were occasionally awarded to those who demonstrated 'significant progress' and along the way, Burpee sold great quantities of cream and ivory flower seeds. But it wasn't until 1975 that someone hit the snow white jackpot. The winner was an elderly farm worker from Iowa called Alice Vonk. 'I used to look in the seed catalogue for the largest yellow marigolds I could find,' she told *People* magazine. 'I would let the palest flowers go to seed, then collect the seeds' to send to Burpee's. When the plant scientists asked for the secret of her success, she assured them that God was 'still very much in charge'.

David Burpee and one of his marigolds advertising Camel cigarettes in 1940.

Poppy

There's something about the scarlet corn poppy, *Papaver rhoeas*, that eludes description. Why else would so many writers resort to comparison when trying to capture the colour, the texture, the mood of the flower?

John Ruskin described it as an 'intensely floral' flower (whatever that might mean), but then proceeded to liken it to all sorts of other things. The fineness of its petal reminded him of a scarlet cup, a flame, a ruby, 'a burning coal fallen from Heaven's altars', and painted glass – for 'it never glows so brightly as when the sun shines through it'. (This luminous, almost phosphorescent quality, is also what appealed to Impressionist painters like Monet.) Ruskin was greatly moved by the opening of the petal, which reminded him of the unravelling of a piece of silk that had been 'crushed into a million of shapeless wrinkles': 'the aggrieved corolla smooths itself in the sun, and comforts itself as it can,' he observed, 'but remains visibly crushed and hurt to the end of its days.' Gerard Manley Hopkins, who had also once hoped to become a painter, wrote vividly of 'crush-silk poppies aflash', but then wondered if the effect was not more 'blood-gush blade gash' or 'flame-rash rudred'. Blood and flames also appear in Sylvia Plath's images of 'little bloody skirts', 'a mouth just bloodied', and 'little hell flames'. For Anna Seward, however, the effect was more like a 'flaccid vest that, as the gale blows high, / Flaps, and alternate folds around thy head'. Fluttering clothes feature a lot in local British dialect terms; in Somerset and Kent, for example, poppies are red or old-women's petticoats. In Berwickshire, however, they are cocks' combs, and in Cornwall devils' tongues. 'A grounded sunset' is how Richard Mabey describes a field seen from a mile away.

Before the corn poppy became the object of such intense aesthetic scrutiny, it was a 'rank' weed, a 'canker rose'. George Crabbe wrote about its impact on the 'blighted rye' that grew near his home in the Suffolk village of Aldeburgh. After the farmers had disposed of the prickly-armed thistles, and the viper's bugloss (*Echium vulgare*), the gently 'nodding' poppies remained to 'mock the hope of toil'. John Clare, who worked in the fields of Northamptonshire, put the 'sickly' smelling corn poppy (a.k.a. the 'headache') at the top of his list of weeds that needed to be dealt with before the crops could be sown. Another old Northamptonshire name for the scarlet flower was 'pope', which meant that weeding was known as 'going a poping'.

The corn poppy has such a wide distribution that its precise origin is hard to pinpoint. It seems, however, to have been a product of the development of agriculture in the mountains running through Syria, southern Turkey and northern Iraq around 12,000 years ago, which, Andrew Lack points out, is 'not particularly long in the lifetime of a plant species'. While several closely related species stayed within in this area, the corn poppy turned out to be particularly vigorous and highly adaptable to different conditions. Unlike most agricultural weeds, which tend to be self-fertilising, the corn poppy relies on insects to do the job. And so, as the plant moved north, it developed something that few red flowers have – an ultra-violet-reflecting pigment which makes it visible to bees. Once fertilised, the plant maximises its reproductive chances still further by producing great quantities of seed. When the seedhead dries out, a series of tiny holes open up beneath the corona to release its fine black pepper of seeds, scattering them up to two metres away from the parent. (Colette so admired the design of the seedhead that she wondered why manufacturers of pepperpots hadn't picked up on it.) A single capsule can contain more than a thousand seeds, and a single plant more than 300,000 in one season. And so, however persistent the weeding might be, another generation of flames, silks, rubies, coals and dying suns is born.

Moreover, many seeds will settle into dormancy, waiting – sometimes for decades – for just the right moment to spring into life again. Their dogged drive to survive is partly why the poppy has become such a potent symbol of life after war. Since most battles in European history were fought on farm land in the summer, it was all too easy to connect the bloody bodies to the blood-red flowers of the fields. In Britain at least, this equation is so closely associated with the First World War that it's easy to forget how old and persistent it is. In the *Chanson de Roland* (*c.* 1100), when Charlemagne enters the Pyrenean meadows where his beloved nephew Roland had died fighting the 'pagans', he is startled to find so many flowers 'stained crimson'. Looking even further back, to the Trojan wars, Homer in the *Iliad* gives a wonderfully Peckinpahesque account of how King Priam's son Gorgythion, hit by an arrow meant for Hector, dies 'as a garden poppy, burst into red bloom, bends':

> drooping its head to one side, weighed down
> by its full seeds and a sudden spring shower,
> so Gorgythion's head fell limp over one shoulder
> weighed down by his helmet.

Of course, many cultures have associated flowers other than the poppy with death in battle. The Aztecs thought of warriors as 'dancing flowers' and their blood as 'flower-water'; spilling that water was rewarded by a new life as a butterfly or humming bird feeding upon the choicest blossoms. The sky rather than the soil, meanwhile, was evoked in the twentieth-century Japanese idea of the 'Flower Sacrifice', a practice shared by cherry blossoms and young pilots. These metaphors persist because it is reassuring to believe that there's something natural about war, that the brief life of the soldier is equivalent to the brief life of the flower and that both, in dying, generate new life. The follow-up question to 'where have all the flowers gone?', as the folk singer Pete Seeger sadly observed, is 'when will they ever learn?'

Going into the First World War, the poppy carried these but also other associations. First was the 'love that dare not speak its name', which, for Lord

Alfred Douglas, was personified in the figure of a beautiful youth whose 'wan' cheeks resembled 'pallid lilies' and whose lips were 'red / Like poppies'. Second was the vitalist belief that both personal and national reinvigoration required extreme (often to the point of fatal) experience, the kind of 'maximum of being' that D.H. Lawrence associated with the vivid, short-lived poppy. For Lawrence, the poppy's 'reckless, shameless scarlet' life was bold and manly. 'Better be a weed,' he thought, than a 'housewifely' lily, who carefully buries her bulbous 'storehouse', or worse, a cabbage, covering its heart in 'self-preserving' leaves. 'The world is a world because of the poppy's red,' Lawrence insisted. 'Otherwise it would be a lump of clay.'

Although largely forgotten now, both the vitalist and the homoerotic aspects of poppy lore fed into its First World War incarnations, including the poem that launched the flower as Britain's principal emblem of military commemoration. That story begins with death of a Canadian solider, Alexis Helmer, at the second battle of Ypres in May 1915, or rather with the poem his close friend John McCrae wrote immediately after his funeral. 'We Shall Not Sleep' appeared in *Punch* in December that year, and was then endlessly reprinted, becoming the most popular poem of the war. McCrae was writing about love, honour and remembrance, but his poem is also a piece of undisguised propaganda, written with the particular intention of persuading the United States to enter the conflict. McCrae's famous pastoral opening – 'In Flanders fields the poppies blow / Between the crosses, row on row' – is rapidly followed by a stern injunction to 'take up our quarrel with the foe'. The dead will only be able to 'sleep', he suggests, if they know that others are keeping 'faith' with the military aims of the war.

In November 1918, just two days before the Armistice, an American college professor called Moina Michael came across McCrae's poem in an advertisement for surgical supplies in the *Ladies' Home Journal*. Michael, who had visited France in 1914, was in New York training YWCA volunteers to go overseas. She already knew the poem well, but seeing it alongside Philip Lyford's startling picture of soldiers ascending from the poppy fields to heaven, she was moved beyond sentiment into action. She wrote some verses of her own, vowing to

We
Shall Not Sleep

"In Flanders fields
the poppies blow
Between the Crosses,
row on row,
That mark our place:
and in the sky
The larks still bravely
singing fly,
Scarce heard amidst
the guns below.

We are the dead.
Short days ago we lived,
felt dawn,
saw sunset glow,
Loved and were loved,
and now we lie
In Flanders fields.

Take up our quarrel
with the foe,
To you from falling hands
we throw the Torch;
be yours to hold it high;
If ye break faith
with us who die,
We shall not sleep,
though poppies grow
In Flanders fields."

*"If ye break
faith with
us who die,
We shall
not sleep"*

Philip Lyford's illustration for 'We Shall Not Sleep' first appeared as part of a Bauer and Black advertisement in the November 1918 issue of *The Ladies' Home Journal*. Here it is used, a month later, by E.E. Tanner, as the cover to his musical setting of John McCrae's poem.

remember the 'Poppy Red' and to wear it, and to persuade others to wear it, 'in honor of our dead'. She began by scouring New York for silk flowers – Wanamaker's department store had some – but soon the 'poppy movement' scaled up. The breakthrough came in 1920 when she persuaded the Georgia branch of the American Legion (the main veterans' organisation) to adopt the poppy as its remembrance symbol.

The idea arrived in Britain via France, or rather via another determined campaigner, Anna Guérin, who had encountered the poppy while fundraising in Atlanta for the American-French Children's League. She immediately saw its potential as a fundraiser and, in September 1921, visited London to discuss the matter with Field Marshal Douglas Haig, chairman of the Royal British Legion. Guérin persuaded Haig to take a million flowers made of cotton, and that

The original memorial poppy, made from cotton in France and sold for the British Legion in 1921.

November they raised £106,000 (£3 million today). The Legion never looked back, and the poppy symbol was adopted in many of the Commonwealth countries whose soldiers had fought in France: Canada, South Africa, New Zealand and Australia.

Despite its ubiquity, the red poppy has not been uncontroversial. For a start, the French veterans preferred another field weed – the cornflower or *bluet*, the nickname of the blue-uniformed conscripts. And then there was the question of what exactly the flowers were meant to be commemorating. In 1933, the British Women's Co-operative Guild, fearing remembrance ceremonies had become celebrations of militarism, started producing white poppies to signal that 'wars must never happen again'; the idea was then taken up, and is still promoted, by the Peace Pledge Union. More recently, other colours have emerged. A purple poppy badge is sold in recognition of 'animal victims of war', although another charity prefers a purple paw to signal that 'exploitation', not voluntary sacrifice, is being commemorated. Since 2010, the 'contributions made by the African/Black/Caribbean/Pacific Islands communities to various wars since the 16th century' have been recognised by a Black Poppy Rose.

As other poppies have been introduced, the red flower's frame of reference has also been queried. In 1966, the Ulster Volunteer Force, a Protestant paramilitary group styling itself after the Ulster Volunteer regiment which fought at the Somme, adopted the poppy, often flanked by orange lilies, as its emblem. (See **Lily**.) Almost inevitably, this made Remembrance Day an IRA target and, in 1987, twelve people were killed in what became known as the

Enniskillen 'poppy day massacre'. The result, wrote the Belfast poet Michael Longley, was simply that people 'added to their poppies more red poppies', bloody wounds to bloody wounds.

While much of the recent trend in memorialisation is toward greater specificity, the countermove can also be observed – with the poppy coming to represent not simply those who died in battle but the nation in whose name they died. This was certainly the case with 'The Red Poppies on Monte Cassino', written in 1944 by Feliks Konarski to commemorate the soldiers of the Polish Second Army Corps who died while capturing a German stronghold. The song begins with thoughts of poppies fed on 'Polish blood instead of dew' and ends, once again, with patriotic exhortation. Many of the men who died at Monte Cassino had previously been Soviet prisoners, as had their leader General Anders. The song's final insistence that 'freedom, by crosses, is measured' had as much to do with hopes for an independent Poland as for Nazi defeat.

In Britain, too, the poppy has recently been elevated into a national emblem for those who believe that Muslim women should use their hijabs to 'stand up to the extremists'. In 2014, after the *Sun* newspaper suggested that union jack flags be worn as headscarves, the *Daily Mail* raised the stakes with a poppy-themed motif. It seems impossible to keep flowers out of the symbolism of wars.

The poppy's connection with war does not end, or rather begin, with the symbolism of remembrance. The pain of wounded soldiers has for centuries been alleviated by the flower itself, or rather by the many effective, if addictive, pain-killers derived from its 'milk'. And the demand for those pain-killers has been so great that further wars have been fought over their supply.

I'm not, however, talking about the red *Papaver rhoeas* anymore, but *Papaver somniferum*, the large, robust, white or pink-coloured, notoriously 'sleep-making' opium poppy. The two are often conflated. John Keats gets them muddled up in his ode 'To Autumn' when he imagines a 'fume of poppies' in a 'half-reaped furrow'. And in *The Wizard of Oz* (1900), Frank Baum goes even further when he has Dorothy and her dog Toto fall asleep simply by inhaling the 'spicy scent' of a flowery meadow; when the cowardly Lion bravely tries to rescue Dorothy, the flowers are 'too strong' for him to resist either. After that, it's a race against the clock for the unaffected — Scarecrow and the Tin Woodman, since they are 'not made of flesh' – to get her out of there. But while corn poppies contain small quantities of a mild sedative, rhoeadine, no one has ever fallen asleep walking through a meadow.

One of W.W. Denslow's illustrations for L. Frank Baum's *The Wonderful Wizard of Oz*, 1900.

96 THE WONDERFUL WIZARD OF OZ.

"I'm sorry," said the Scarecrow; "the Lion was a very good comrade for one so cowardly. But let us go on."

They carried the sleeping girl to a pretty spot beside the river, far enough from the poppy field to prevent her breathing any more of the poison of the flowers, and here they laid her gently on the soft grass and waited for the fresh breeze to waken her.

A field of opium poppies is pretty harmless too, for considerable work needs to be done to get at the valuable sedative. The traditional method of extraction has been to score the immature seed pods (up to three or four times over the course of a few days) using a sharp, shallow blade. The milky 'tears' of latex oozing from the cuts congeal into a sticky residue which is then scraped off and dried. A hectare of poppies can yield up to 12kg of opium in a year. The world's primary producer is currently Afghanistan. In 2000, the Taliban banned poppy cultivation but the following year, after the invading American and British troops removed the Taliban, farming resumed. Some fields were targeted by air strikes, and photographs of US and allied forces slashing or spraying plants have often appeared in the press. But the allies relied too heavily on the farmers and their government sponsors to interfere much in this profitable crop. Before the invasion in 2001, 285 square miles of Afghanistan were devoted to poppy cultivation; in 2017, it was 1,266 square miles.

Raw opium contains three alkaloid drugs – morphine, codeine and thebaine – which can then be refined into more potent forms, known as opiates. The best known of these is the drug currently being produced in clandestine Afghan labs – heroin, named in 1897 for its 'heroic effects' and initially marketed as a non-addictive morphine substitute. Numerous semi-synthetic and synthetic opioids then followed, including methadone, pethidine and oxycodone – the drug at the heart of the current opioid epidemic. In 2017 alone, more than 47,000 Americans died from an overdose of opioids, 40 per cent of which were prescription drugs.

Opium has been a balm for the wretched for thousands of years: associated with the gods of sleep and death, and recommended – in vapours, suppositories, powders, poultices, syrups and tinctures – by every ancient medical text for every conceivable condition. By the sixteenth century, dissolved in alcohol and often sweetened with spices, it was known as laudanum ('worthy of praise') and then loddy. Alexander Hamilton was given some after being shot by Aaron Burr; Samuel Taylor Coleridge took it regularly after developing jaundice and rheumatic fever. Hamilton died, but Coleridge became addicted. Not much later came the first misery memoir, *Confessions of an English Opium-Eater* (1821), by recreational user Thomas De Quincey. The typical nineteenth-century addict, however, was a chronically ill middle-aged, middle-class white woman or, in the United States, a Civil War veteran who had been liberally injected with morphine for his injuries or camp-contracted dysentery. Nearly ten million opium pills and three million ounces of tinctures and powders were issued to the Union Army alone.

By the end of the nineteenth century, although opioids continued to be used medically, they were increasingly associated with other expressions of 'decadence' or 'degeneration', such as homosexual and interracial liaisons in the opium dens of Chinese immigrants. Although Arab traders had brought opium to China in the eighth century, nearly a thousand years passed before smoking the drug became popular. Eventually opium trading was banned, but the drug continued to enter the country, largely due to the desire of the British to trade opium grown in India for Chinese tea, silks and ceramics. The first Opium War broke out when the Chinese seized and destroyed huge quantities of the drug, and it ended with the British taking the island of Hong Kong and resuming trade, and plant-hunting, in China. (See **Chrysanthemum**.) By the 1860s, the national demand for opium was so great that the Chinese began to harvest their own poppies.

This history was not much discussed in the opium dens of London and San Francisco around which the *fin de siècle* moral panics centred. For the panics were often about other matters: race, sex, national standing. When Arthur Conan Doyle's Dr Watson goes looking for a friend in such a place, he feels like he's entering 'the forecastle of an emigrant ship'. The imaginative possibilities of pasty-faced men with pin-point pupils or, better still, heavy-lidded 'needle-dancers' were impossible to resist. Even later, as the typical opioid user was re-characterised as a working-class heroin 'junkie', something of the old glamour lingered on. We're still encouraged to feel it every time we open Yves Saint Laurent's lacquer-bottled 'Opium' and inhale the perfume's 'spicy oriental' blend of jasmine, rose, and carnation – but not, of course, poppy.

SNOWDROP

GERANIUM

WINTER

VIOLET

ALMOND

Winter

The cruel season

Thomas Sackville, 'Winter'

. . . all seasons shall be sweet to thee

Samuel Taylor Coleridge, 'Frost at Midnight'

Winter is a victim of climate change. In recent years, it has become apparent that the frosts come later, finish sooner, and appear less often through the winter months. The first buds and pollinators arrive earlier, and those who live in the north can grow, or overwinter, plants they had never previously considered. In 2016, the American Environmental Protection Agency reported that the length of the growing season in the United States had extended by two weeks since the beginning of the twentieth century, with a particularly sharp increase in the last 30 years. While all this might seem like great news to gardeners as well as farmers – in my own garden, January often finds last summer's salvias and roses blooming alongside next spring's primroses and crocuses – the actual effects are more complicated. Early blooming flowers can still sometimes be hit by frost; longer summers mean increased risk of drought; pests and diseases that were previously wiped out by the cold survive and thrive; different species that rely on each other respond differently to environmental cues, threatening fragile ecosystems.

Remembering 'proper' winters of the past, it's easy to become nostalgic about ice and snow. But the history of winter is filled with displeasure and downright resistance. One way in which people have tried to deny the season's arrival is by cultivating flowers that belong in other seasons. This book is full of unseasonal flowers – lilies and carnations in April, chrysanthemums in July – but winter was the original spur for changing a plant's flowering season. During the nineteenth century, the developments of rail networks made it possible to bring the early **violet** to customers further north, while today, large parts of the world rely on air freight from Kenya and Colombia to supply summer roses in February.

Perversity is the point, effort the intention. As the old song goes, we want 'a rose in the wintertime / When it's hard to find' – *because* it's hard to find.

A taste for unseasonal flowers dates back at least to the Romans, who imported thousands of roses and narcissi from Egypt during the winter months, and who developed heating systems to speed up their own blooms. The epigrammatist Martial paid tribute to Caesar Domitian by praising his 'forced garlands'. Ordinary roses were merely a 'sign of spring', but Caesar's winter roses demonstrated influence and 'power'. Even then, not everyone was convinced that such displays were worth the trouble. Interfering with nature in pursuit of luxurious display was roundly condemned, both by the early Christians, who thought it represented the worst kind of covetousness, and by the Stoic philosophers, who believed that happiness could only be found in accepting the world as it is. 'Is it not living unnaturally,' asked Seneca, 'to hanker after roses during the winter, and to force lilies in midwinter by taking the requisite steps to change their environment and keeping up their temperature with hot water heating?'

While few would accept all of Seneca's definitions of unnaturalness – for example, he condemned cross-dressing – floral stoics still make a virtue of embracing each season in turn. Like Berowne in Shakespeare's *Love's Labour's Lost*, they insist that at Christmas they 'no more desire a rose / Than wish a snow in May's new-fangled mirth; / But like of each thing that in season grows.'

But, pre-climate-change, not much did grow in a northern winter. And so *hiverophiles* (as they're known in France) mostly had to occupy themselves with thinking about flowers to come – while cleaning their gardening tools, perusing plant catalogues, and cherishing the 'little Snatches of Sunshine' that occasionally poked through the clouds. They were also warmed by the gratifying suspicion that an enjoyment of winter was rather sophisticated. Loving summer was rather obvious ('the whole country blooms' – yeah, yeah); finding a scrap of life amid the 'bleak and barren prospects' of winter was surely a sign of a refined sensibility. That, at least, was what the eighteenth-century essayist Joseph Addison argued.

Inspired by Francis Bacon's idea of continuous garden life – *ver perpetuum* – Addison suggested that gardeners make space for a dedicated 'winter garden', a 'natural' space filled with evergreen trees. The idea was to prove enormously influential. Even today, winter gardens remain popular, although modern tastes tend toward bright red stems of cornus against stark white birch trunks, and the heady scent of flowering shrubs like viburnum, wintersweet and daphne. Modern gardeners also tend to retain the dead stalks and seedheads of perennials for the frost – if the frost ever comes – to transform into a tableau of glistening silver, and for wind to play its 'wintery music' upon.

Not everyone admires this chilly aesthetic. Shelley, for example, didn't think of the winter wind as music but as a mirthless laugh 'upon the land / All cloudlessly and cold'. Indeed, for every person who becomes 'unspeakably cheerful' at the sight of holly, there is another who thinks of the frost as the absolute end of the show: ' 'Tis done!' For the latter group, winter is simply a time of death – a word which Edmund Spenser rhymes with yet more wind, the season's 'baleful breath'.

The difference between the two views might be summed up by comparing two novelist-gardeners – Elizabeth von Arnim, at the end of the nineteenth century, and Jamaica Kincaid, a hundred years later. Von Arnim thought that 'to go into the garden in its snowed-up state is like going into a bath of purity'; Kincaid looked out at the snow and concluded 'my garden does not exist'.

Kincaid is the supreme critic of *hiverophilia*; she finds it tiresome, even 'wilful', to admire leafless trees and clumps of frosted sedum heads. 'When my turn comes to make the world, as surely it will,' she writes, 'December, January, and February shall be allotted ten hours each.' It is in winter that Kincaid, a long-term resident of Vermont, starts dreaming of her native West Indies, 'a place that is the opposite of the one I'm in now'. She's not alone. The journey south (real or imaginary) in search of sun, colour and blossom is one that many northerners take. Vincent van Gogh and D.H. Lawrence, for example, were enchanted by the early flowering of the Mediterranean **almond**. Today, most almonds grow in California, where, Karl Shapiro notes, a winter day usually feels 'like the interior of a florist shop'.

Those unable to get to Antigua, Sicily or California make do with a greenhouse. Thanks to glass and steel, marvelled George Simcox, 'When the summer time is done / And the winter is begun / There are flowers still that do not die.' Simcox was writing in the 1860s at the height of a moral battle between different forms of winter garden. A few years earlier, William Cobbett had proposed indoor gardening as a moral 'diversion' for the upper classes: 'How much better, during a long and dreary winter, for daughters, and even sons, to assist, or attend, their mothers in a green-house, than to be seated with her at cards, or in the blubberings over a stupid novel.' But when greenhouses became cheaper and therefore more available to the middle-classes, a backlash ensued. Nailing his colours firmly to the Senecan-Addisonian mast, the novelist and Anglican clergyman Charles Kingsley declared his preference for a winter garden of ferns and evergreens growing contentedly under God's 'dome of soft dappled grey and yellow clouds', rather than a greenhouse filled with tender exotics like the South African pelargonium (**geranium**). In God's 'cathedral', he declared, 'if there be no saints, there are likewise no priestcraft and no idols'. Kingsley's mantra that nature is 'enough for me' again casts the glasshouse devotee as unnaturally greedy and, in this case, Catholic to boot.

But winter doesn't last for ever. Before long, the days start to lengthen and the flowers return. Which will be the first of the new year? A **snowdrop** or a crocus, a dwarf iris or the winter jasmine? Few flowers are more welcome than those that come in the lean months.

Violet

When the clouds lie low and grey, and it is hard to remember what sunshine feels like, the inhabitants of cold places turn gratefully to unseasonal offerings. Other chapters have already considered the carnation, rose and lily, some of the most popular all-year-rounders in the floral repertoire today. The 'shrinking violet', with its drooping head concealed among a profusion of leaves, might seem worlds away from these assertive long-stemmed beauties, but a hundred years ago, the sweet purple *Viola odorata* was the archetypal out of season flower and, therefore, a sign of true luxury. Even as late as 1941, Dennis and Adair could base a song about 'winter in Manhattan' on the miraculous power of 'Violets for Your Furs'. When Frank Sinatra croons 'vio-letts', the miniature blossoms can't help but perform 'a little simple magic', bringing a touch of April promise into dead December and making it possible to fall in love.

The oldest historical records from the Mediterranean and south west Asia all feature violets as an ingredient in the making of medicines, sweets, sherbets, garlands – and of myths, often about death and rebirth, or the metamorphosis of one life form into another. The Romans, for example, commemorated the dead with several spring flowers thought to share the purply-red colour of blood, such as crocuses, anemones and hyacinths, but only violets (signalling the start of spring) and roses (signalling its end) inspired special days – *dies violationis* or *rosationis* – devoted to the floral adornment of graves. When, in *Hamlet*, Laertes looks at Ophelia's grave, it is with the hope that violets will soon 'spring' from

A fashionable girl with violets pinned to her furs appears on the cover of an early twentieth-century lingerie box produced by Muse in Atlanta, Georgia.

her 'fair and unpolluted flesh'; John Keats 'joyed to hear' how violets spread across graves and, facing his own death, reputedly told his friend Joseph Severn that he already felt them 'growing over him.' (See also **Daisy**.) But resurrection could be political too. The Italian Parma violet was said to be a great favourite of Napoleon, and when he was banished to Elba in 1814, his supporters assured each other that, just like the flowers of spring, Corporal Violette would return. Jean Dominique Étienne Canu's etching 'Violettes du 20 Mars 1815' refers to the day when Napoleon re-emerged in Paris. Hidden among the petals and foliage, we can pick out the silhouette of his distinctive bicorn hat, on the right marked (1), along with the profiles of his wife Marie Louise (2) and their son (3).

The violet's long association with death meant it also became a flower of remembrance, or rather, argues Catherine Maxwell, of 'forgetting followed by recollection'. This particular quality, however, had less to do with funerary practices than with the way its fragrance works. One of the unusual features of ionone, the compound that gives the flower its distinctive scent, is

Jean Dominique Étienne Canu's puzzle print, 'Violettes du 20 Mars 1815'.

that it 'quickly tires and desensitizes the nose, temporarily turning off the olfactory receptors so that the odour of violets seems to disappear, only to reappear a while later.' Violets are often described as breathing or even singing their fragrance, creating a vivid synaesthesia that is hard to resist. D.H. Lawrence once crossly declared that, unlike arguments and pencils, life, love and flowers had no 'point' – 'a bunch of violets is a bunch of violets' – but that was after a lifetime of his own violet-scented recollections. In 1910, after his mother died, Lawrence salvaged a couple of violets from the wreath his fiancé Louie Burrows had sent to Nottingham, and later, sitting on the train, 'miserable' about his 'matouchka', he 'kept catching their scent all the way down to London'. Happier memories are provoked by Lady Chatterley when she chooses a half-empty bottle of 'Coty's Wood-violet perfume' to nestle among her lover's shirts. But in both instances the violet is surely making a 'point'.

Picking violets on the Côte d'Azur in the early twentieth century.

Violets had been cultivated for the labour-intensive French perfume industry, and bunches sold for buttonholes or corsages for much of the nineteenth century, but the fashion for *winter* violets was a *fin de siècle* development. Like many trends, it was the result of a coalescence of factors. In 1893, after two German scientists identified ionone as the source of the violet's scent, and pointed out that it could be more cheaply extracted from orris (the root of *Iris germanica* and *Iris pallida*) or even created in a laboratory, the market for violets diminished considerably. At the same time, the ever-increasing speed and efficiency of railway travel meant that more and more people were 'wintering' on the 'sun-warmed shores' of the Côte d'Azur, establishing a taste for *les fleurs du midi* as far away as Vienna and Moscow. Violets were sent far and wide, but the delicate flowers were often past their best by the time they arrived. And so, eventually, more northern countries began to cultivate violets for the winter market – although glass protection was needed. In Britain, the Great Western Railway regularly carried flowers from the small, largely frost-free meadows or 'quillets' of Devon and Cornwall to London's Covent Garden during a season that extended from October to May.

The taste for buttonholes and corsages led to the cultivation of varieties of violet that were not only highly fragranced but also had longer stems and larger or double flowers. The fragrant and profuse Neapolitan or Parma violet – introduced into France from Italy in the eighteenth century – was particularly popular. But it was not easy to breed every desirable quality into one plant. Growers liked a variety called 'Governor Herrick' because it was relatively trouble-free, and had long stems and large flowers. Its scent, however, was unimpressive, and rumour has it that tissue-wrapped bunches were sometimes sprayed with perfume before being loaded on the overnight 'flower express'.

By 1900, violets had become essential to many aspects of bourgeois life. Breath was freshened with violet-scented cachous, cakes decorated with candied petals (they are still made by Candiflor in Toulouse and currently sell at €85 per kilo), and wrists and handkerchiefs sweetened with the latest bottled scent. There was no shortage of choice: Lundborg's *Vio-Violet* (1895), Coty's *La Violette Pourpre* (1906), Mülhens and Kropff's *Rhine Violets* (1910) and, for those wanting a more complex concoction involving synthetic as well as natural ingredients, Guerlain's *L'Heure Bleue* (1912) – the scent, perhaps, of the ambiguous 'violet hour' in T.S. Eliot's *The Waste Land*. Dorian Gray wore 'a large buttonhole of Parma violets', while his creator, Oscar Wilde, determined to erase 'the stain and soil of prison life', asked a friend to bring a bottle of Floris's *Canterbury Wood Violets* to Reading jail.

But the greatest luxury was the flowers themselves. In a humorous poem from 1894 a man offers a bunch to his wife or girlfriend for her 'natal-day cheer', only to begrudgingly inform her that he paid a dollar for just twelve small flowers:

> Here are violets *dear,*
> Dearest flow'rs of the year.

A dollar for twelve is certainly much too dear for Alice Adams, the eponymous heroine of Booth Tarkington's 1921 Pulitzer-Prize-winning satire of social climbing. The novel's first crisis occurs when Alice is invited to a dance and worries how she'll be able to afford a corsage or bouquet. Things initially look up when she realises that it's April and that there are violets in her back garden. But although she manages to find twenty-two ('a bright omen' since that's her age), it's far too few. And so Alice must take a streetcar to a park on the outskirts of the city and spend a long rainy day picking and picking (what country folk called 'violeting') until she amasses three hundred tiny blooms. By nine o'clock that evening, 'there were two triumphant bouquets of violets, each with the stems wrapped in tin-foil shrouded by a bow of purple chiffon; and one bouquet she wore at her waist and the other she carried in her hand.' Triumph at the violet hour? Not quite. For when Alice gets to the party, she soon feels 'betrayed' by her 'rustic' bouquet; in the warm air, the violets quickly wilt and droop. As she looks for a discrete way to dispose of the unappealing clump, the rich girls walk by carrying 'lusty, big purple things', direct from the florist.

The violet lent itself well to stories of class divide, stories that generally contrasted those who wore the winter blooms with those who sold them. The starting point for George Bernard Shaw's play *Pygmalion* (1914) is the moment when Freddy Eynsford Hill, 'a young man of twenty, in evening dress, very wet around the ankles', crashes into a Covent Garden flower girl called Eliza Doolittle, knocking her basket out of her hands. 'Theres menners f'yer!' she says, 'Te-oo banches o voylets trod into the mad.' Eliza's Cockney vowels so excite Henry Higgins, an eavesdropping professor of phonetics, that he picks the Cockney 'voylet' out of the mud and promptly sets about transforming her into a very different kind of flower.

One of many postcards featuring Marie Studholme who toured British music halls performing sketches. In this one, from 1906, she appears as a flower seller called 'Sweet Violets'.

Lack of such social mobility is the problem identified in 'To His Daughter', by E. (Edith) Nesbit. Best known today for works such as *Five Children and It* (1902) and *The Railway Children* (1906), Nesbit was also a political activist and the author of *Ballads and Lyrics of Socialism*, published by the Fabian Society in 1908. (See **Snowdrop**.) One such lyric, 'To His Daughter', starts off with an indulgent father going to Ludgate Hill in London to buy his beloved daughter some December violets, for all the usual reasons.

> They whispered of the rain-wet moss,
> The budding briars, the April days,
> The pageant of the woodland ways,
> All the pleasant plots and plays
> That you and I remember.

While the spring violet – 'like a key' which 'turns noiselessly in memory's wards' – evokes years gone by, the winter flower also transports the wearer into another season. But for Nesbit's nascent socialist, more immediate recollections soon crowd out this pleasant familial scene. For the man can't help but remember that very afternoon and 'her who sold the violets – mean, / Poor, broken, desolate, unclean'. Given half a chance, he tells his daughter, that 'ruined slave' – a phrase that hints at the conventional association of flower sellers with prostitution – might have been 'a Queen like you, my darling'.

By the turn of the century, the violet's modern makeover was complete. No longer a floral 'veil'd nun' of the woods favoured by the 'meek' and impoverished (as Thomas Hood styled it), the flower had been transformed into a luxury commodity fit for affluent city queens. Those modern queens took many forms, from the fashionable Gibson girls who pinned violets on their furs to the lesbian poets who looked to 'violet-robed' Sappho for inspiration and the Suffragette members of the Women's Social and Political Union (WSPU), who often represented their colours – green, purple and white – with violets and lilies of the valley. *Votes for Women*, the WSPU newspaper, carried numerous advertisements for 'pretty and becoming' dresses that combined those colours, such as a white serge with a toque 'trimmed with purple flowers and green foliage' (for just four guineas), and even for 'a ladies' violet farm', run by Misses Allen and Brown, at Henfield Common in Sussex. Legend had it that an emphasis on violet (rather than simply purple) produced the 'secret' code of 'GWV', 'Give Women the Vote'. This seems unlikely since the WSPU wanted its supporters to openly declare their allegiance. Rather it is probably a vestige of the seemingly clandestine language of flowers: the white lily signifying purity, the purple violet hope and steadfastness, and the accompanying greenery freedom. More importantly, the WSPU was determined that its members should not become 'identified in the mind of the onlooker' with 'that extremely unpleasant person, "a frump"', but rather 'with colour, gay sound, movement, beauty'. At all times, it was said, they should sound 'the feminine note'. And so when the WSPU organised a two-week-long 'Women's Exhibition' at the Princes' Skating Rink, Knightsbridge in May 1909, the aim was not simply to raise funds but also to reinforce the message that suffrage was compatible with a traditional femininity of cakes, embroidery, paintings, china, hats, frocks and flowers. And yet the political message was not forgotten. Amid all the flowers at the Knightsbridge exhibition was a replica prison cell – with a guide explaining what happened to women in jail – and a model voting booth into which Christabel Pankhurst, lavishly bedecked with flowers of all kinds, symbolically deposited a ballot paper.

It would, however, be another nine years before British women got the vote and, as time went on, the attention-grabbing protests undertaken by suffragettes became more militant if no less flowery. In October 1909, Jane Brailsford went to prison after approaching a barricade in Newcastle with what Sylvia Pankhurst described as 'an innocent looking bouquet of chrysanthemums', only to reveal 'an axe which she raised and let fall with one dull thud'. And in February 1913, a group of suffragettes conducted a guerrilla raid on three of the orchid houses at Kew Gardens: they smashed some windows and, reported the *Times*, 'wreaked havoc among the rare and beautiful orchids' before leaving a note declaring that 'orchids could be destroyed but not women's honour'. (Perhaps coincidentally, orchids derive their name from *orchis*, the Greek for testicle.)

One final violet-scented queen of the period was the kind who sought psychoanalysis with Sigmund Freud. Indeed, Freud noted that it was precisely because the violet, and its symbolism, was so 'popular' that it tended to appear in 'the naïve dreams of healthy people'. While the dreams of neurotics were obscure (and therefore fascinating to interpret), those of the healthy were unambiguous, predictable and likely to draw on everyday sources like the Victorian language of flowers. One of Freud's case studies featured a 'somewhat prudish and reserved' woman whose wedding had been temporarily postponed. She described a dream she had had about feeling happy while arranging 'the centre of a table with flowers for a birthday'. This was an interpretative doddle for the *maestro*: the floral centre-piece represented her genitals, and the birthday was that of her future child.

But there was more. After further prompting, she told Freud that she had used 'expensive' lilies of the valley, carnations and violets in her arrangement. Again, that was easy. Using the conventional language of flowers, Freud read lilies as the valuable commodity of female chastity (the 'frequent female symbol' of the valley added an extra dimension), carnations as pink male carnality ('not a very remote association', he conceded, even before his patient explained that her fiancé often offered these 'in great numbers') and . . . well, with violets it became a bit more interesting. Conventionally, violets translated into 'modesty' or 'innocence' in the floral dictionaries, although some reserved those qualities for white flowers, drawing on classical associations of the purple violet with erotic pleasure. Cicero, for example, talked of 'beds of roses and violets', and today's Valentine cards still rhyme 'violets are blue' with 'I love you'. Freud, however, was not concerned with the colour but the word 'violet' in which he thought he could trace 'a secret meaning' based on its 'chance similarity' to the word 'violent'. The fact that the words have quite distinct etymological roots didn't matter; what interested him were the mind's self-generated puns, slippages and associations. And so finally his patient's dream was not quite so 'naïve' or 'healthy' after all, but indicated her anxiety about the cost of 'defloration' and possibly also revealed 'a masochistic trait in the character'.

John William Godward, *Violets, Sweet Violets*, 1906.

One would think that every practising psychotherapist would know of this dream, but it seems not. The plot of the 1992 thriller *Final Analysis* depends on the ignorance of Dr Isaac Barr (Richard Gere). For weeks, his patient Diana Baylor (Uma Thurman) has been telling him about her recurrent dream of arranging lilies, carnations – and 'violence'. 'Violence?' he queries. 'I said violates!' she replies angrily, 'I said violets . . . Violets . . . They're just flowers. I once did floral arranging. Does everything have to be about sex?' Barr doesn't recognise that Diane is playing him for a fool (or maybe subconsciously telling him that she's playing him for a fool?) until he stumbles into a lecture on *The Interpretation of Dreams*. If only he had taken a flower arranging class, he would have realised that tastes had changed: no one in the 1990s would have dreamed of using violets in a table centre-piece.

Geranium

By which I mean *Pelargonium*.

The confusion between the two genera began in the seventeenth century when the first tender shrubs from the southern African Cape were brought to Europe. Like the hardy perennial geraniums that Europeans already knew, these plants had five-petalled flowers and seedpods which look a bit like a crane's elongated head and beak. Because of this resemblance, the new arrivals came to be known as Cape Cranesbills.

In 1732, the botanist Johann Jacob Dillenius argued that the African plants should be acknowledged as belonging to a separate genus. As he pointed out, the flowers of each were very different. The European geranium's flowers are regular, in most cases consisting of five identical petals, and up to 15 pollen-producing stamens. The Cape plants have irregular flowers – the two upper petals differing from the lower three in size, shape and markings – with a nectar spur and far fewer pollen-producing stamens. Dillenius argued that since *Geranium* derives from the Greek word for crane, the new genus could take the Greek for stork – *Pelargonium*. Linnaeus, however, did not think that the genera were distinct, and by the time the taxonomy was properly sorted out, few gardeners were willing to give up the name they'd gotten used to. Although this chapter is about pelargoniums, and one in particular, the common red *P. x hortorum,* I'll stick with the word most people use – geranium.

Geranium

Today nearly all of our geraniums are bred to be disposable. They're cheap, summer plants that get chucked on the compost heap in September when we replace them with cyclamens and winter-flowering pansies. People never used to be so blasé. Only a few hundred years ago, geraniums were rare and exotic, the prized possessions of wealthy collectors who built expensive glasshouses to protect them from the rain and frost. Outside, the winter did its worst; inside, the southern hemisphere plants, thinking it was summer, burst into bloom.

'I doe believe I may modestly affirme,' wrote John Aubrey, 'that there is now, 1691, ten times as much gardening about London as there was Anno 1660; and wee have been, since that time, much improved in forreign plants'. And that was only the start. As imperial adventure and botanical exploration gathered momentum, the old physic gardens turned into showrooms for colonial flora and many grand private gardens established equally impressive collections.

By 1699, Mary Capell Somerset, Duchess of Beaufort, had acquired 750 species, which she housed in extensive glasshouses and, even more luxuriously, in a 100-foot 'stove' (a glasshouse heated by underground ovens). She also prepared a twelve-folio volume of dried specimens (now in London's Natural History Museum) and commissioned the painter Everard Kick (Latinised as Kickius) to document her collection in a florilegium (literally, a gathering of flowers). The earliest visual representations of plants had been by, and for, apothecaries, who were interested in their medical properties. While Kick's watercolours retain something of this older informative style (the plants are drawn to scale and uprooted), his emphasis is as much on the plant's decorative, or unusual, qualities. Novelty rather than utility was the order of the day. (See **Snowdrop** for an example of Kick's work.)

Florilegia were intended for private consumption, to provide a permanent and portable garden record of a particular collection, but a commercial market for luxury flower books was also emerging. In 1730 Mary Somerset was one of a select group of aristocratic subscribers to what is thought to be the first illustrated nursery catalogue. *The Twelve Months of Flowers* was produced by Robert Furber, 'Gardiner, at Kensington', to showcase a stock of 400 different species and cultivated varieties.

Furber's book provides striking evidence of the transformation that foreign introductions had made in British gardens over the past hundred years, especially when it came to the winter months. In 1616, when Jean Franeau published a winter-garden book, *Jardin d'hyver, ou Cabinet des fleurs*, it was as an antidote to the 'sad season', the time when 'Nature has taken back her flowers from us'. *Jardin d'hyver* is filled with illustrations of spring and summer flowers, and the accompanying poems are all, appropriately, elegies. But there are no sad seasons in *The Twelve Months*. The whole point of Furber's book was to advertise the fact that his Kensington nursery could provide flowers all through the year. Each hand-coloured print depicts a sumptuous bouquet keyed to a list of plants that would flower that particular month. The December selection is as lavish as any, and includes an early mention of a variegated or

An engraving representing 'December', by Henry Fletcher after the painting by Pieter Casteels, in Robert Furber's *The Twelve Months of Flowers*, 1730. A scarlet geranium is at the centre.

'strip'd-leav'd geranium' and, in central position, the already iconic 'scarlet geranium'.

For eighteenth-century women, flowers were never merely decorative. The study of plants was often placed at the heart of debates about the value (and, for some, the dangers) of women's education. On the one hand, botany was presented as the perfect subject for mothers to teach their children. It was considered easier than zoology, with the added advantage that, unlike animals, plants do not bleed. On the other hand, Linnaeus's proposal that plants be classified according to the number of their (male) stamens and (female) pistils emphasised the primacy of plant sexuality. In the course of a full-scale attack on 'unsex'd females', the clergyman poet Richard Polwhele, accused 'botanizing girls' of exchanging 'the blush of modesty for the bronze of impudence'.

Geraniums were particularly risqué, largely by virtue of what William Cowper, in his poem *The Task* (1785), called the 'crimson honours' of the most popular varieties, and perhaps also because of the (seemingly) suggestive way in which their petals overlapped. According to Robert Rabelais (pseud.), the sexiest women have 'pouting and geranium'd lips'.

The personification of the geranium was not, however, confined to the 'bliss botanic'. Scientists like Erasmus Darwin, the grandfather of Charles, became interested in the kinds of sentient behaviour that he thought connected flora, fauna and, conceivably, human beings. The subject was much debated. It was a little too much to claim 'absolute sense' for plants, argued the Philadelphia plantsman John Bartram, 'yet they have such facilities as came so near it that we wanted a proper epithet or explanation.' At the very least, a belief in the 'analogy of their organisation with ours', as Thomas Jefferson put it, opened up new ways of interacting with your houseplants.

Jefferson and his geraniums had a particularly sociable relationship. He first encountered them while ambassador to France in the 1780s and later enjoyed propagating specimens from cuttings, both at his Virginia home of Monticello and at the White House. As Jefferson's Presidency came to an end, his friend Margaret Bayard Smith wrote asking for a cutting of a particularly fine specimen 'which I understood you cultivated with your own hands': 'If you do not take it home with you, I entreat you to leave it with me. I cannot tell you how inexpressively precious it will be to my heart.' How could he resist? Jefferson sent the plant to Mrs Smith, apologising that it was 'in very bad condition, having been neglected latterly', but expressing confidence that, under her 'nourishing hand', it would soon recover. 'If plants have sensibility,' he added, 'it cannot be but proudly sensible of [your] fostering attentions.'

Jefferson and Smith were not the only ones who believed that an attachment to a geranium was 'healthful' for both plant and person. In terms that recall contemporary talk of holistic exercise, botanising was widely promoted as providing physical exercise, fresh air and mental stimulation. Who had time to dwell on personal problems, asked Rousseau, when 'sweet scents, bright colours, and the most elegant of shapes seem to vie for the right to seize our attention'? Plants had become therapeutic in a new way: it was no longer necessary to ingest them or apply them as poultices; it was enough to spend time in their company. Floral interaction was particularly recommended as providing solace for widows (such as the Duchess of Beaufort), invalids, and homesick presidents. Paying attention to a plant, Rousseau said, 'relaxes, amuses, and distracts the mind, and lifts the feeling of pain.'

The writer Charlotte Smith, who suffered from chronic rheumatism and depression, passionately believed that plants could 'soothe' a 'wounded mind'. More than that, she believed that botany was an antidote to the 'mawkish indolence', 'inanity' and 'torpid ignorance' that might render a woman 'burthensome to herself and uninteresting to others'. When bad weather threatened to keep women indoors (and therefore burthensome), the glasshouse came into its own. After all, as William Cowper, one of Smith's favourite poets, had famously declared, 'who loves a garden, loves a green-house too'. Never mind if 'the winds whistle and snows descend'; in the glasshouse, the most tender blooms could stay 'warm and snug'.

A coloured lithograph of the 'Forcing Garden in Winter', from Humphry Repton's *Fragments on the Theory and Practice of Landscape Gardening*, 1816.

Glasshouses with transparent roofs first appeared at the end of the eighteenth century, largely as a response to the light requirements of plants like geraniums. Heating systems also became more sophisticated, producing the warm dry air that Cape species required. The micro-climate these buildings created was very different from the steam or hot-water heated glasshouses that were developed later to house ferns and orchids. When people talk about a hot-house atmosphere it's usually these humid places they have in mind. Think of Philip Marlowe, desperately mopping his brow in the 'thick, wet, steamy' aquarium of an orchid house in Raymond Chandler's *The Big Sleep*. The earlier greenhouses were warm but airy, and the image they conveyed was one of winter health rather than year-round decadence.

Good health was the ambition of both the plants and their devotees. In 1804, Charlotte Smith even wrote an ode 'To a Geranium which Flowered during the Winter', thanking the plant whose 'cheerful hue' had punctured her 'wintry gloom' (what we would call Seasonal Affective Disorder). Flowers that could offer such relief, she said, were 'like friends in adverse fortune true'.

Fanny Price, the heroine of Jane Austen's third novel, *Mansfield Park* (1814), would likely concur. Dependent on the charity of her uncle and aunt, Fanny has only one, unheated, room to call her own – the former schoolroom which, we realise, is also a kind of glasshouse. When the atmosphere downstairs becomes unpleasant – and it often does – Fanny retreats to this room to 'visit' the plants, hoping that 'by giving air to her geraniums she might inhale a breeze of mental strength herself'. The connection between them is compelling. Both have been uprooted and transplanted from other places – the geraniums from South Africa, Fanny from lower-middle-class life in Portsmouth – in the expectation that they will flourish (decoratively) in the enriched soil of Mansfield Park.

Smith describes a similar process in 'To a Geranium'. She imagines her plant growing 'unheeded and unvalued' in 'Afric's arid lands', before its lucky escape to England, where its 'marbled' leaves and 'pencill'd' flowers can be properly appreciated. This is classic colonial rhetoric: the Empire might provide the raw material but it is European culture that gives it value. It's little wonder, Smith thinks, that her 'naturalised' geranium blooms so profusely in the winter greenhouse, for it does so 'in gratitude'.

The problem with Fanny Price (as far as her relatives, the Bertrams, are concerned) is that it takes her so long to bloom in gratitude. Only at the end of the novel do they decide she's 'worth looking at'. By then, she has grown 'two inches, at least' and her complexion is finally 'tinged with a blush'. Like a satisfied plant-hunter, Sir Thomas Bertram concludes that Fanny's 'transplantation to Mansfield' has been a success.

By the early nineteenth century, the cossetted exotics described by Smith and Austen were already something of a rarity and, by the 1850s, the geranium had a new image altogether. Or rather two new images: as a disposable summer bedding plant and as a long-term indoor companion for far less privileged women. Both incarnations relied on geraniums becoming cheap and widely available. That happened when further developments in glasshouse technology – the invention of cast iron and then plate glass – made it possible to propagate and house large numbers of plants. New railway networks enabled wide distribution and therefore encouraged mass production.

The bedding system, the practice of planting out glasshouse-reared plants during the summer, was both a consequence and a celebration of those changes. Bedding was labour-intensive, but it was labour, as much as flora, that was on conspicuous display in urban front gardens, municipally run cemeteries, public botanical gardens and parks (many of which were established in the mid-nineteenth century). During the summer of 1859, for example, it was estimated that between 30,000 and 40,000 bedding plants were planted out in London's Hyde Park.

The work of bedding had many facets. It was not simply that frost-tender plants had to be nurtured for eight months before anyone saw them. It was not even that the plants had to be of the same kind, or at least the same height, and had to flower at the same time. Nor that they were to be planted so close together as to cover the beds by mid-July. Nor even that every autumn everything had to be dug up and every spring a whole new flower garden created. The labour intensified during the season itself, since gardeners were required to maintain continual vigilance on every aspect of the display. Dead leaves and faded blooms had to be removed as soon as they appeared and stray shoots that spoiled the regularity of the look had to be cut off. Bedding, arranged in ribbons, circles, crescents, comma and kidney shapes, made a clear statement that, as Humphry Repton put it, the garden belongs to 'art rather than to nature'. Geraniums – often praised as 'obedient and plastic things' – were a perfect raw material.

For many, the bedding system came to represent all that was wrong with industrialisation more generally. How could nature's creatures be treated like 'mere masses of colour', asked the garden writer Forbes Watson, rather than as 'an assemblage of living beings'? Often, these kind of statements were hard to distinguish from simple snobbery about the 'gaudy glitter' that appealed to the 'lower elements of our taste': 'it is the savage who is caught by the gayest colours,' declared Andrew Murray of the Royal Horticultural Society, 'and a liking for them and personal ornament is a remnant of primitive barbarism.' Sophisticated tastes, it seemed, ran to naturalistic plantings of pastel-coloured hardy perennials.

But some geraniums remained acceptable. At the same time as large scarlet beds came to symbolise the ugly uniformity of industrial mass culture, the single straggly potted specimen was co-opted for a brave last stand against that culture's encroachment.

Ralph Hedley, *Blinking in the Sun*, 1881.

The geranium in its pot became a compelling symbol of home, and particularly of the Victorian ideal of home, the country cottage. Like the cat with which it was often pictured, the scarlet bloom in the window suggested that what lay within was cosy and cheerful, 'clean and bright'. Even its soft leaves were 'good-natured', enthused Leigh Hunt; the 'very feel' exudes 'household warmth' like 'clothing and comfort'. While summer bedding plants were thrown away after a single season, a relationship with the potted geranium could last for years, and through cuttings, even extend across generations. 'Look at a Scarlet Geranium,' instructed Forbes Watson, 'as you sometimes see it in a greenhouse, with its long woody stems continuing from year to year; it may be somewhat untidy but it can make you love it.'

It would be exaggerating to say that Victorian literature is filled with love letters to geraniums – but not all that much. Confined to the sick room, Amy March in *Little Women* relies on her 'pet geranium' for company, while the motherless protagonist of *Jenny's Geranium* confides her thoughts and feelings to her plant, which responds 'in an eloquent language all its own'. In the real world too, emotions ran high. The Rev. Samuel Hadden Parkes, who distributed plants to the poor of Bloomsbury, recorded the gratitude of a widow to whom he had given a pot: 'I did not believe before that I should care for anything again in this world like I have cared for that geranium. Indeed, sir, I've almost got to love it as if it could speak.' On discovering her beloved plant 'dry, sapless, withered', Charlotte S.M. Barnes was even moved to reproachful elegy:

> Why art thou dead? No watchful care
> Was spared to save thee; night and day
> I strove to shield thee from decay.
> But all in vain. Thy bloom is fled –
> Thy leaves have fallen – thou art dead!

Not everyone loved a geranium of course. For some Victorians, it was always too common, too commercial, too red. William Morris thought it achieved the near-impossible feat of demonstrating that 'even flowers can be thoroughly ugly'. Oscar Wilde, contemplating an afterlife as a flower, worried that he wouldn't come back as his favourite pre-Raphaelite lily; 'perhaps for my sins,' he joshed, 'I shall be made a red geranium!!' – a plant, that is, with 'no soul'.

Geraniums in front of the
Lenin Memorial Museum
at the Smolny Institute,
St Petersburg.

Mario Bogoni's 1915 poster
for Ente Nazionale Italiano
per il Turismo.

Today, most of us approach the flowers from a less passionate perspective than either Barnes or Morris. In fact we rather take them for granted. Walk down any street in Birmingham, Berne, Brisbane, Bombay or Berkeley, CA, and you'll see a geranium or two: trailing from a window box, or nestling among the petunias in a pub hanging basket; straining for sunlight behind an office blind, or glowing like a beacon on the seafront or at the local museum. We know we're meant to be admiring the view or the great man's statue, but it's hard to take our eyes off the bright red geraniums.

Snowdrop

That's one word for it.

There are many others: snowflake, snow bell, snow violet, dew drop, dingle-dangle, shame-faced maiden. . . . Botanically, the common snowdrop combines Greek, *Galanthus*, and Latin, *nivalis*, to conjure up the milk flower of the snow. In Britain, the snowdrop flowers in January and February; in Romania, its arrival is celebrated on 1 March; the Russian composer Tchaikovsky, in a series of twelve seasonal piano pieces, made it the emblem of April. In Denmark, it's called *vintergæk*, winter's fool, and, traditionally, the teasing flower is sent in a secret letter to one's beloved at Easter.

There's lots of time for whimsy in the winter, and for close attention to detail. Many an hour can pass just mulling over the arrangement of the flower's six petal-like segments (known as tepals) – three larger ones on the outside and three smaller ones inside. Walter de la Mare was reminded of the Holy Trinity, while Colette mused that 'if a bee had three wings, it would be a snowdrop . . . Or rather, if a snowdrop had but two wings, would it be a bee?'

Some of the flower's names (such as the French *perce-neige*, snow-piercer) refer to its strenuous upward push into the light. Thinking of snowdrops in this way leads to thoughts of bravery, soldiers, spears and helmets – at least in late nineteenth-century writing for children. The British artist Walter Crane presents them as 'white-crested' soldiers marching against King Frost, an image that Edith Nesbit picks up in a poem about the 'little armies' that lead 'the fight for the Summer'. When the silvery shoots of snowdrops emerge, she says, 'the winter's rout' is all but guaranteed.

Snowdrops in Walter Crane's *Flora's Feast: A Masque of Flowers*, 1889.

Both Crane and Nesbit were members of the Fabian Society, which believes that socialism can be achieved through attrition and indirection rather than the frontal assaults of revolutionary action; the society's name derives from the 'Fabian strategy' developed by Fabius Cunctator against Hannibal's forces. The Fabian emblems are a wolf in sheep's clothing and a tortoise that moves slowly but then 'strikes hard'. Crane's snowdrops, however, although properly helmeted, seem a little rasher in their approach, for they are determined to be 'first upon the scene'. In this, they more closely resemble the white-hatted police corps of both the US army and the British Royal Air Force, known as Snowdrops.

It's unusual to think of small, white flowers in masculine, far less military, terms. Ted Hughes couldn't quite make that leap – his snowdrop is a girl whose 'pale head' is not a helmet but simply 'heavy as metal'. The snowdrop's pendulous flower – a smart way of keeping its pollen dry in bad weather – is most often read as an expression of feminine bashfulness. 'I see thee bend / Thy forehead, as if fearful to offend,' coaxed Wordsworth. But perhaps the flower should be thought of as gender neutral. The English name 'snow drop' (as it was originally written) comes from the German *Schneetropfen*, the pearl drop that fashionable women and men wore in the sixteenth and seventeenth centuries, dangling from a necklace or brooch, or as an earring. The *Schneetropf* was popular with Vermeer's 'Girl with a Pearl Earring', but also with Walter Raleigh.

Most of the flower's English names – Fair Maid of February, White Lady, Purification Flower, Mary's Taper – are distinctly feminine, for they signal an association with the Virgin Mary. More specifically, the snowdrop is the flower of Candlemas, the purification ritual that, in accordance with Jewish law, Mary undertook on 2 February, 40 days after the birth of her child. The feast also links Christianity to older festivals, such as Roman Lupercalia (15 February), that celebrated the start of spring – at least in the Mediterranean. Further north, the farmers' almanacs looked for an indication of what was to come:

> If Candlemas Day be dry and fair
> The half o' winter's to come and mair;
> If Candlemas Day be wet and foul,
> The half o' winter's gone at Yule.

In any case, by mid-February, snowdrops should be plentiful in churchyards throughout Britain. Great colonies are still found at the sites of many former monasteries and abbeys, and it seems likely that they were brought there from Italy by monks. There is no written or visual record of snowdrops in Britain before the sixteenth century, and it wasn't until the 1770s that they were found growing wild.

Candlemas was the day on which, to celebrate the 'light' that was Christ, families brought their candles to church to be blessed. For the rest of the year these candles were used for private devotion and protection, for example one might be burned at a bedside when someone was sick. Given the name Mary's Taper, the snowdrop thus became a symbol of a symbol. In a poem about the death of his four-year-old brother Christopher, Seamus Heaney recalls that both candles and snowdrops 'soothed the bedside'.

The link with Candlemas is one reason why the snowdrop has been characterised as the embodiment of the Christian feminine virtues of purity and cleanliness, although these characteristics are shared by other white flowers such as the lily. For nineteenth-century Evangelicals, it was not enough to encounter the flower's religious and moral lessons in church; they had to be disseminated as widely as possible to the people who needed them most. The snowdrop therefore made many appearances in books and magazines, mainly addressed to children. In one story, published by the American Sunday School Union, a six-year-old is taught to be patient during the cold winter and grateful for the flower that, eventually, emerges as 'proof of the faithfulness of thy Maker'. In another tale, a child shows off her snowdrop, until she learns that it is better not to make an 'unwise display' of fortune; in another, a dying girl reassures her brother that, like the snowdrop, she'll return 'pure and white

A pivotal moment in the evangelical novel *The Snowdrops, or Life from the Dead*, 1876.

and holy'. Several stories are told from the point of view of the snowdrop itself. In one, 'a lesson for grumbling boys and girls', a 'discontented' flower discovers a purpose in life when she's potted up and placed on the windowsill of a sick child's bedroom. 'I am so glad I was of some use,' she whispers when the child recovers, 'I will never complain again because I cannot be what God never meant me to be.'

It sometimes seemed as if there were more snowdrops doing moral work indoors than flowering outside. In 1823, when Edgar Taylor first translated the Grimm story 'Schneewittchen' into English, he changed its title from 'Snow White' to 'Snow-Drop', while *The Snowdrop* was the title of Canada's first children's magazine (it ran from 1847 to 1853). At the end of the century, working-class girls in Sheffield (and then all over the north of England) were encouraged to join 'Snowdrop Bands', social clubs intended to warn them off pre-marital sex, 'immodest conduct', and 'the reading of foolish and bad books'. It's likely that the latter included poems like 'The Kiss', once attributed to Robert Burns, which tenderly described the 'dearest tie of young connections' as 'Love's first snow-drop, virgin kiss.' But rather than kissing, the Snowdrop Band girls were encouraged to attend 'brown' suppers, at which they planted bulbs, and 'white' ones, to celebrate the flowers coming into bloom.

The snowdrop also features in the idea of Mary as the New Eve. If the original Eve was blamed for having brought death into the world, the New Eve is said to be brought back to life in the form of Jesus. Applied to flowers, and the rituals of the calendar year, this idea identifies Eve with winter darkness and Mary with spring light. The snowdrop links the two seasons and the two women. A popular legend has it that when Adam and Eve were banished from Eden it began to snow. An angel appeared, caught a snowflake and breathed upon it, turning it into a snowdrop, a promise that 'sun and summer soon shall be'. In another version, it wasn't a snowflake that was transfigured but one of Eve's tears – providing yet another name for the snowdrop.

Many of these associations feed into *Adam Bede* (1859), George Eliot's first and most straightforwardly allegorical novel. The eponymous protagonist's mother Lisbeth is 'clean as a snowdrop' in her white linen cap, but more importantly, the flower is allied with the heroine Dinah Morris, who gives up work in the cotton mills of Snowfield to become a Methodist lay preacher. (Dinah also wears a white 'quaker cap' and has a face of 'uniform transparent whiteness'.) At first, the novel seems a little sceptical about the sober asceticism of the snowdrop. When Dinah expresses her love for the bleak county of Stonyshire over prosperous Loamshire, Lisbeth is quick to challenge her romanticisation of austerity: 'that's very well for ye to talk, as looks welly like the snowdrop flowers as ha' lived for days an' days when I'n gathered 'em, wi' nothin' but a drop o' water an' a peep o' daylight; but th' hungry folks as ha' better leave th' hungry country.' As the novel progresses, however, the critique largely falls away and Lisbeth comes to see Dinah as an 'angel' who radiates purity and gentleness like 'a newly gathered snowdrop'. The novel's original readers, well-versed in floral signals, would not have been surprised when this New Eve marries Adam Bede, and settles down to raise a family in Edenic Loamshire.

Thinking of snowy whiteness as the colour of purity and goodness usually relies on making black the colour of sin and evil. This was a code that African Americans understood all too well. During the campaign to abolish slavery, they were often admonished, for example, by the free black orator and essayist Maria Stewart, to 'Prove to the world that . . . Though black your skins as shades of night, / Your hearts are pure, your souls are white.'

The end of slavery, and the establishment of a system of racial segregation reliant on a 'color line', only intensified these preoccupations. Paul Laurence Dunbar is best known for an 1895 poem about the pressure put on African Americans to 'wear the mask' that would show white people what they wanted to see. Even more devastating is 'The Paradox' (1899), his vision of what it feels like to live a life of contradictions, trying to be all things at once. How can a tree produce bud, blossom, and 'late-falling leaf', all at the same time? How can a man's fingers be 'swart' (swarthy) as clay, but his hands white 'as the snowdrop'? If the displacement of the snowdrop's symbolism from morality to race seems far-fetched, consider what a book published just four years later, in 1903 – the American *Encyclopedia of Superstitions, Folklore, and the Occult Sciences of the World* – has to say about the flower: 1. that 'the snowdrop will ensure purity of thought to the wearer'; and 2. that 'if a girl eats the first snowdrop she finds in the spring, she will not get tanned in the summer'.

Devotees speak of the snowdrop in extravagant terms. Even the usually cynical Karel Čapek was moved to declare that 'no victorious palm, or tree of knowledge, or laurel of glory, is more beautiful than this white and fragile cup on a pale stem waving in the raw wind.' The Victorians were the first really devoted snowdrop fanciers, particularly after new species were brought back to Britain from the battlefields of the Crimea, but in recent years the passion has returned. There are only twenty species of *Galanthus*, but hundreds of cultivars to examine and enjoy; in 2012, the word 'galanthophile' was finally added to the Oxford English Dictionary. Like eighteenth-century auricula enthusiasts, galanthophiles construct 'theatres' to display their treasures dramatically against a black backdrop, and meet regularly to discuss the intricacies of leaf shape, petal size, flower posture, and, most of all, the positioning of the green markings that attract and guide pollinators. The mood at their meetings, notes Helen Yemm, is one of 'genteel frenzy', and considerable sums of money can sometimes change hands. In 2015, a bulb of *G. plicatus* 'Golden Fleece' reached £1,390 on an eBay auction.

But the snowdrop is not without its critics. The plant collector Reginald Farrer thought it 'an icy, inhuman, bloodless flower' that, instead of promising spring, 'crystallised winter': the very sight of a snowdrop, he said, sent him rushing to the fireside to warm up. Planted on graves during the nineteenth century, the snowdrop also gained a reputation as 'Death's Flower'. Charlotte Latham, recording some West Sussex superstitions in 1868, noted that many people 'dreaded' the flower because 'it looked for all the world like a corpse in its shroud'. More widely, it was considered unlucky to bring snowdrops – or sometimes even a single snowdrop – indoors or when visiting a sick person. These ideas are in such direct contradiction to the Candlemas associations that Richard Mabey thinks they might have anti-Catholic roots. A rather different connotation lies behind the use of 'snowdrops' in Moscow slang to refer to the bodies of those who die on the streets in winter (whether of natural causes or not) 'emerging only in the thaw' – at least that's the premise of a novel by A.D. Miller.

The snowdrop can also put you *in* the grave or at least make you very unwell. The whole plant is toxic and the bulb particularly so. If ingested, it can cause stomach cramps, diarrhoea, nausea, dizziness and vomiting. It is surprising therefore to read that in 1956, when a group of US airmen were sent to live on an uninhabited island in Lough Erne as a survival test, they ate little but snowdrop stew for nine days. 'On their return,' reported the *Illustrated London News*, 'they were medically examined and showed no appreciable ill-effects.'

Proceeding more cautiously, plant biochemists have spent much of the last fifty years exploring the chemical composition of the snowdrop and considering its potential medical and agricultural uses.

Agricultural biotechnology has long been interested in lectins, a group of proteins that are thought to have evolved in plants to deter predators from eating them. If the plants themselves could repel predators, the argument went, then the use of insecticides could be reduced. In the early 1990s, geneticists began to experiment by cloning the gene for snowdrop lectin, *Galanthus nivalis* agglutinin (GNA), and inserting it into crops like wheat, rice and potatoes. Snowdrop lectin had been found to work well as an insecticide against aphids, beetles and moths, and produced no ill effects in mammals. The next step was to see whether crops that had been genetically engineered with GNA were also safe. Controversy arose in 1998 when the biologist Arpad Pusztai announced on TV that the GNA-modified potatoes he'd been studying were harmful to rats and that if he had a choice he would 'certainly not' eat them. Pusztai became a hero to anti-genetic-modification campaigners and a pariah to scientists who found his experiments flawed and inconclusive. Today, many different crops are genetically modified with the GNA gene.

The other significant snowdrop derivative – an alkaloid called galantamine – has a less controversial history. In 1951, the Russian pharmacologist Mikhail

Mashkovsky observed that villagers in the Ural Mountains rubbed ground-up flowers of *G. woronowii* (Green Snowdrop) onto their foreheads as a headache cure, and also gave decoctions of the plant to children afflicted with polio. Astonished to see the children recover without any paralysis, Mashkovsky and his colleagues spent the next few years isolating the active compound, galantamine, and experimenting with its role in neurotransmission. Galantamine was officially approved for use as a drug in Bulgaria in 1958. This was at the height of the Cold War, and the compound was not known beyond Eastern Europe until the 1980s when it was discovered by researchers searching for new treatments for Alzheimer's disease. Today it is widely used as an effective symptomatic treatment for the earlier stages of the disease.

Another offshoot of galantamine research has been a possible solution to the age-old problem of identifying the 'magic herb' that Homer calls 'moly'. Hermes offers the 'potent' plant to Odysseus to protect him from the 'wicked' drug that Circe had already given to his crew 'to wipe from their memories any thought of home'. There's been much speculation about what Aegean plant Circe might have used. The best guess seems to be atropine-containing *Datura stramonium*, which causes delusions and pronounced amnesia by blocking a particular neurotransmitter in the brain. In 1981, as knowledge of galantamine was coming to light, Andreas Plaitakis and Roger Duvoisin took the stage at the World Congress of Neurology to propose that moly sounded a lot like a snowdrop, and that, if it were a snowdrop, the *Odyssey* would be 'the oldest recorded use of an anticholinesterase to reverse central anticholinergic intoxication'. It's pure coincidence, however, that the datura and its antidote, the snowdrop, are placed side by side in a watercolour that Everard Kick included in the Duchess of Beaufort's florilegium.

Datura stramonium at the centre, with *Galanthus nivalis* 'Flore Pleno' on the left and *Saxifraga paniculata* syn. *Aizoon* on the right. Everard Kick (Kickius), 1703–5.

Almond

At a certain point in the winter, the point when it feels as if it will never end, even the garden snowdrops begin to lose their charm. It's then that the shivering northerner heads south in search of more congenial snow – in the form of pink-tinged showers of almond blossom.

The great winter longing for the south is a well-worn theme. Today it's not too expensive to fly from Glasgow to Tenerife or from Moscow to Phuket. In the past, however, only the wealthy could afford to up sticks and spend the winter elsewhere. In the late eighteenth century, it became fashionable for the British, and later the Russian, aristocracy to spend several months on the French and Italian Rivieras. Initially the journey was medically sanctioned – 'heliotherapy' (restorative sunbathing) could ease tubercular lungs – but no one really needed an excuse to visit such a beautiful place. And by the mid-nineteenth century, when the arrival of railways and hotels made the Riviera more accessible, artists, writers and other members of the middle class gradually joined in. It wasn't until the 1920s that the Côte d'Azur established itself as primarily a summer destination.

The idea of a 'winter life' with flowers was very attractive, and many expatriates, most famously Lawrence Johnston at Serre de la Madone, Menton, and Baroness Béatrice de Rothschild at Villa Ephrussi, Cap Ferrat, relished the chance to grow plants that would struggle back home. Preceding both was Thomas Hanbury, now best known as the man who donated Wisley to the

Royal Horticultural Society. In 1867, feeling thoroughly 'disgusted with the cold and gloom of a long English winter', Hanbury bought a rundown palazzo on the Ligurian coast, and created a spectacular garden, La Mortola. One of his great New Year pleasures was to record everything that was in flower at that time, and then send the list to the *Gardeners' Chronicle* 'as evidence of the possibilities of horticulture on the Riviera during the winter months'. Hanbury had enough nous to realise that his readers might feel just a little bit jealous. 'Is it,' he asked, 'a benevolent act to publish a list of over 500 species of plants blossoming in the open air at a place thirty hours distant by rail, to be read by those compelled to endure the full rigour of a northern winter?' The *Chronicle* made some attempts to encourage its British readers to emulate Hanbury's achievement in their suburban greenhouses, but it had to concede that 'do what we may, we cannot have the continuous Riviera sunshine.'

John Russell, *Armandiers et ruines, Sicile*, 1887.

In Tuscany, the weather was even better – 'pink houses, pink almond, pink peach and purply apricot, pink asphodels', rhapsodised D.H. Lawrence, and in Sicily, even the end of February could be 'suddenly very hot', making the almond blossom fall 'like pink snow, in the touch of the smallest breeze'. (In Britain, where everything happened much later, the poet Edwin Arnold described almond blossom as 'April's gift to April's bees'.)

Lawrence had thought about Mediterranean almond blossoms for a long time before he got to see any. In 1909, at which point he had never been abroad, he wrote a poem comparing the spring violets that hid under his local hedge to those southern blossoms of 'abandonment'. It was no coincidence, he argued, that 'the happy lands', Provence, Japan and Italy, were 'under the almond tree'. Lawrence's own happy encounter with almond groves finally arrived in 1920, when he and his wife Frieda rented a house in the hills above Taormina on the north-east coast of Sicily. It was close to where the Australian Impressionist John Peter Russell had painted *en plein air* in the 1880s. Close inspection of Russell's *Armandiers et ruines* reveals a petal stuck in the paint.

The weather did not, however, always oblige the sun pilgrims. In February 1888, Russell's friend Vincent van Gogh arrived in Provence to find real snow had turned the countryside white 'like the winter landscapes of the Japanese'. Van Gogh, like many of his generation, was obsessed with Japan. (See **Chrysanthemum**.) He went to the south of France hoping to find a subject matter that would prove amenable to the pared-down, flattened style he admired in Japanese woodcuts. And, beyond that, he wanted to emulate what he saw as the ability of the Japanese to 'live in nature as though they themselves were flowers'. Part of becoming 'more and more' Japanese meant paying attention to the flowers that the peasants grew in the fields and orchards rather than seeking out unusual specimens in gardens like La Mortola. In fact, both of van Gogh's signature plants had exotic origins – the sunflower came from

Vincent van Gogh, *Sprig of Flowering Almond in a Glass*, 1888.

Mexico, the almond from the mountains of western Asia. Once again, long residency had bestowed a native aura upon immigrants.

Little more than a week after van Gogh arrived in Arles, he wrote to his brother Theo to tell him that, while the hard frost and snow continued, he'd managed to paint two 'little studies of a branch of an almond tree that's already in flower despite everything'. The Japanese influence is apparent in the closely cropped simplicity of the arrangement: the straight line of the table edge is reinforced by a red line on the wall and, working against this pattern, a twiggy diagonal of pinkish blossom crosses an otherwise blank space. The European still life is not usually an optimistic genre; in presenting *nature morte*, it evokes life's brevity. But this painting is full of joyful expectation. For a start, the very idea of a sprig is a reminder that greater things exist. Moreover, the pink promise in the blossoms seems to move up the painting into the line on the wall and then into van Gogh's underlined red signature. It's an expression of all that he hoped would come from living in Provence.

Two years later van Gogh painted *Almond Blossoms*, his most famous homage to the tree, and to hope. It was painted outside and gives the sense of looking up at 'big branches against a sky-blue [*bleu-celeste*] background'. Van Gogh began work on it in February 1890, as soon as he heard about the birth of Theo's son, who had been named Vincent in his honour. *Almond Blossoms* was a gift for the baby and van Gogh wanted it to hang over his crib. After working on the painting for about a month, he confided to Theo that he thought it 'perhaps the best, the most patiently worked thing' he had ever done, for it had been undertaken with a Japanese-like 'calm' and 'firmness of touch'. But this buoyant and confident mood was not to last. Van Gogh's devastating breakdowns were becoming more frequent. After finishing *Almond Blossoms*, he felt 'done for like a brute' and, in July 1890, he committed suicide.

Van Gogh did not, of course, only paint almond blossom. In April 1888 alone, he moved rapidly between peach, apricot, apple, pear and plum orchards, creating a 'frenzy of impastos'. It was necessary to work fast, he said, because 'the whole show' could end up 'on the ground at any moment'. Van Gogh clearly felt that when we look at blossom, we see trees 'rejoicing' and, as Pliny had put it, 'rivalling each other with the varied hues of their colouring.' But the almond is different. While the others take part in the unstoppable procession of buds we call spring, the February blossoms of the almond provide no more than a taste of what's to come. They're an *amuse bouche* before the feast.

The association of almonds and prophecy was first made in the Old Testament book of Jeremiah, where it's reinforced by Hebrew wordplay between *shaqed*, an almond tree, and *shoqed*, a verb meaning to be watchful; the association confirms God's commitment to Jeremiah's role as an almond-branch-holding prophet. Many poems and paintings put a sprig of almond blossom into a protagonist's hand to suggest powers of domestic prophecy. In one anonymous Victorian magazine poem for example, a husband recalls some kind of crisis in which he was 'heart-sick of labour' and 'tired of life' until, that is, his wife appeared with an 'almond-spray' in her hand to issue reassuring 'words of hope' about their future happiness. Needless to say, she proved right.

Although priests and poets get a lot of mileage out of the almond's early flowering, few ask *why* this particular fruit tree breaks its dormancy before close relatives such as the peach. For fruit growers who live in fear of an unexpected late frost, it's a vital question and one that geneticists are trying to answer, in the hope that nature might be persuaded to slow down. Myth-makers, by contrast, have never been short of an explanation.

Consider the story of Phyllis and her absent lover Demophoon. Despairing that Demophoon will ever return, Phyllis hangs herself and is transformed into a leafless wintery almond tree (*phylla* in Greek). When the penitent Demophoon finally shows up and sees what has happened, he embraces the tree in sorrow. In some versions, the tree then comes into leaf; in others, more concerned with botanical accuracy, it bursts lovingly into bloom. In both cases, the lovers are reconciled.

The Victorians loved the story. Edward Burne-Jones, feeling guilty about the way he'd treated his mistress Maria Zambaco, painted the scene twice; the second attempt (in which he disguises her identity a bit better) is entitled

Edward Burne-Jones, *The Tree of Forgiveness*, 1882.

The Tree of Forgiveness (1882). In neither version, however, does Demophoon seem very pleased to see Phyllis. Rather than focusing on the woman's emergence from deadly captivity or, as the title might lead us to expect, her forgiveness, Burne-Jones's attention is all on the poor man recoiling from his arboreal stalker. The London *Times* thought it 'repellent in the extreme', but Henry James admired its 'fresh and moist-looking' blossoms.

A chaste, Christian version of the tale – involving siblings instead of lovers – did the rounds of the expatriate community of the Côte d'Azur. One winter, reported *Riviera Nature Notes*, St Patrick went to study at the monastery of Lérins on the Île Saint-Honorat, promising to return to his sister on the mainland when the fruit trees began to flower. But the winter was long, and (despite being in Cannes) the sister grew impatient. She pleaded with all the trees to hurry, but 'one feared the frost, another shunned the biting breath of the mistral, while a third was unwilling to be conspicuous by flowering when all the other trees were bare.' Only the compassionate almond agreed to open its buds. A spray was duly sent over to the island, St Patrick returned to the mainland, and the tree, 'proud of the sister's gratitude and of the saint's approving smile, has ever since that time flowered earlier than any other flower.'

The almond's capacity to reconcile and renew also appealed to D.H. Lawrence, although he preferred to emphasise its 'primitive' and 'pagan' associations with Persephone returning from the underworld or with the phoenix rising up from the flames. In the gnarled and knotted trees that he saw from his Taormina terrace, Lawrence found a symbol that could connect 'far-off Mediterranean mornings' to the modern world and, in doing so, express his own hope for twentieth-century renewal. One of the protagonists of his wartime novel *Women in Love* had confidently asserted that 'no flowers grow upon busy machinery'; in the 'ancient southern earth' of Sicily, however, the boundary seemed less absolute. The twisted branches of the almond tree in winter resemble ironwork (as if they, like Lawrence, have been transplanted from industrial Nottingham) but here, he discovers, 'even iron can put forth':

This is the iron age,
But let us take heart
Seeing iron break and bud,
Seeing rusty iron puff with clouds of blossom.

In Sicily, then, even iron is alive and acutely sensitive to its environment. In another poem, the bare branches of trees are transfigured first into 'old, twisted implements' and then into 'some strange magnetic apparatus', the fine 'steel tips' of which pick up electrical messages emanating, 'in some secret code', from Mount Etna.

Lawrence's quest for sunshine and flowers did not end in Sicily. He found many other plants to admire in Sri Lanka, Australia, Mexico and New Mexico. But he never forgot the almond trees and, in 1930, a few months before his death at the age of 44, he returned to the subject. Now his mind was on the Midrash legend that the coccyx was the body's 'almond bone' from which, after death, a new body could emerge 'like almond blossom in January'. 'Have you not seen, in the wild winter sun of the southern Mediterranean, in January and February, the rebirth of the almond tree, all standing in clouds of glory?' he asked: 'Ah yes! Ah yes! Would I might see it again!'

Lawrence was right to see the almond tree as a link to ancient civilisations. The tree that's mainly grown today, *Prunus dulcis* or the sweet almond, seems to have been selected from millennia-old wild species that grew on rocky hillsides of Armenia, Turkey and Azerbaijan. It's not clear exactly when and where domestication took place, but archeobotanists in Syria found the charred pieces of an 11,000-year-old storage structure containing fragments of *P. dulcis*. Other evidence is textual. We know that the almond was grown in Palestine and Israel before it reached Egypt because, in Genesis, when Jacob sends his sons to Egypt to trade 'some of the choice fruits of the land', he includes almonds and pistachios. The tree becomes even more precious in the story of Jeremiah, as we've seen, and that of Aaron's rod, which 'budded, and brought forth buds, and bloomed blossoms, and yielded almonds' in a single night. These signs finally reach fruition in the almond-branched menorah created by Moses, which is now the emblem of the State of Israel.

In Palestinian culture, the olive tree remains a pre-eminent symbol, but the almond does not lag far behind. In 2008, the poet Mahmoud Darwish slyly compared the difficulty in capturing the elusive qualities of the almond blossom with the struggle for political recognition for Palestine: only if a writer succeeded in the describing the blossom, he said, would everyone say 'these are the words of our national anthem'.

All the positive associations I've discussed so far relate to the sweet almond. As a ritual food, it signals health, happiness and luck, the renewal of life and fertility, especially when sweetened further with a sugary coating. That's why sugared almonds are distributed at weddings in many different cultures; in Greece unmarried girls sometimes place them under their pillows in order to dream of their future husbands. The scent of bitter almonds has very different connotations. It evokes death, murder (especially in Agatha Christie's novels) and, for Dr Juvenal Urbino in Gabriel García Márquez's *Love in the Time of Cholera*, the sorrows of unrequited love. The scent of bitter almonds is, of course, the scent of cyanide.

All almonds contain the cyanide precursor, amygdalin. Only trace amounts are found in sweet varieties, however; bitter varieties (and the kernels of related fruits like apricots) contain up to fifty times more. Just seven or eight bitter almonds can kill a child. This extreme toxicity is the reason why, in 1995, the US Food and Drug Administration finally restricted sales of the nut – except to food manufacturers who, in making products such as marzipan, amaretti biscuits or Amaretto liqueur, know how to eliminate the toxin. The risk of cyanide poisoning is also why the FDA clamped down on the distribution of amygdalin 'supplements' (often sold as if it's a vitamin, B17) which had been heavily promoted as a 'natural' treatment for cancer. But the ruling is difficult to enforce in this internet age. The scientific consensus that amygdalin is 'a highly toxic product that has not shown any effect on treating cancer' is dismissed as a conspiracy of vested interests. And quacks continue to sell hope in the shape of bitter almonds and ground-up apricot kernels.

Today 82 per cent of the world's almonds grow in the Central Valley of California – 18,000 square miles, bounded by mountains on all sides, consisting of the Sacramento Valley in the north and the drier San Joaquin Valley in the south. When John Muir visited in the 1890s, he found 'one smooth, flowery, lake-bed of fertile soil'. It took a while for almonds to find their way there. The Spanish first introduced the nut into Mexico, and then tried to grow it in the missions they established along the coast from San Diego to San Francisco. The damp and humid conditions did not suit the trees, however, and interest in almonds faded. It was a case of finding a place that was cool enough in the winter and warm enough in summer, where there were not many late frosts and sufficient water. The Central Valley fitted the bill and in the early twentieth century almonds began to be cultivated alongside many other nuts, fruits and vegetables. In the 1920s, almond farming occupied around 20,000 acres of land; by 2017, the number had risen to 1 million acres, mostly in the southern half of the San Joaquin Valley. Most of this expansion has taken place over the last twenty years, due partly to a concerted campaign to promote the almond as 'nutritionally, the best single food a person could eat', and partly to increased purchasing power in China and India. Today the almond is California's most valuable agricultural export.

The creation of the new orchards coincided with years of severe drought, however, and the almond found itself at the heart of debates about the ecological implications of 'factories in the fields'. Almond production consumes about 10 per cent of California's water supply – largely because of the necessity to keep irrigating, whatever the weather. (Fields that are usually devoted to lettuce or melon, on the other hand, can be left fallow.) Although growers claim to have developed new methods of conserving and capturing water, critics point out that the real solution is to plant fewer trees.

Another ongoing concern is pollination. In the 1950s, there were enough bee colonies in the Central Valley to pollinate all the almond blossoms. But the rapid growth in demand – the accepted ratio is two hives per acre, so that's

2 million hives – and the loss of bees to colony collapse disorder meant that a lot of bees have to be trucked in from Oregon, Washington, Arizona and even Florida.

Beekeepers are ambivalent about the almond boom. On the one hand, rental prices continue to rise (in 2000, it was around $50 per hive; in 2019, $200). Moreover, while every other crop pollination, such as melons, blueberries and alfalfa, reduces the health of bee colonies, the almond season leaves them fatter and stronger. On the other hand, concentrating so many bees in one place encourages the spread of mites and viruses and, when the brief season is over, the bees quickly go 'from feast to famine'. As Joe Traynor, a California bee broker, recently said, 'if almond trees bloomed all year long, rather than only 2 or 3 weeks, life would be sweet indeed for both bees and beekeepers'. Instead their lives, like all things related to the almond, are distinctly bittersweet.

Literary Seeds and Sources

GATHERING FLOWERS

Aesop's Fables, trans. Laura Gibbs (Oxford: Oxford University Press, 2002)

Bacon, Francis, 'Of Gardens', in *The Essays*, ed. John Pitcher (Harmondsworth: Penguin, 1985)

Baudelaire, Charles, 'Une charogne' ('A Carcass'), in *The Flowers of Evil: Parallel Text*, trans. James McGowan (Oxford: Oxford University Press, 1993)

Brooks, Gwendolyn, 'The Second Sermon on the Warpland', in *The Essential Gwendolyn Brooks* (New York: Library of America, 2005)

Buchmann, Stephen, *The Reason for Flowers: Their History, Culture, Biology, and How They Change Our Lives* (New York: Scribner, 2015)

Coates, Alice M., *Flowers and their Histories* (London: Adam & Charles Black, 1956)

Dickens, Charles, *Hard Times* (Harmondsworth: Penguin, 1995)

Dickinson, Emily, 'Did the Harebell loose her girdle', in *Emily Dickinson's Poems: As She Preserved Them*, ed. Christanne Miller (Princeton: Princeton University Press, 2006)

Dove, Rita, 'Evening Primrose', in *Black Nature: Four Centuries of African American Nature Poetry*, ed. Camille T. Dungy (Athens: University of Georgia Press, 2009)

Dowling, Laura, *Floral Diplomacy at the White House* (Oostkamp: Stichting Kunstboek, 2017)

Emerson, Ralph Waldo, 'Gifts', in *Essays and Lectures* (New York: Library of America, 1983)

Folkard, Richard, *Plant-Lore, Legends, and Lyrics* (London: Sampson Low, Marston, Searle, & Rivington, 1884)

Goody, Jack, *The Culture of Flowers* (Cambridge: Cambridge University Press, 1983)

Guéguen, Nicolas, Sébastien Meineri and Jordy Stefan, '"Say It with Flowers" . . . To Female Drivers: Hitchhikers Holding a Bunch of Flowers and Driver Behavior', *North American Journal of Psychology* 14, no. 3 (2012), 623–28

Haviland-Jones, Jeannette, Holly Hale Rosario, Patricia Wilson and Terry R McGuire, 'An Environmental Approach to Positive Emotion: Flowers', *Evolutionary Psychology* 3, no. 1 (2005), 104–32

Herrick, Robert, 'To the Virgins, to make much of Time', in *Robert Herrick*, ed. Stephen Romer (London: Faber, 2010)

Heywood, V.H., R.K. Brummitt, A. Culham and O. Seberg, *The Flowering Plant Families of the World* (New York: Firefly, 2007)

Hoyles, Martin, *The Story of Gardening* (London: Journeyman Press, 1991)

— *Bread and Roses: Gardening Books from 1560–1960* (London: Pluto, 1991)

Inwards, Richard, *Weather Lore: A Collection of Proverbs, Sayings, and Rules Concerning the Weather* (Cambridge: Cambridge University Press, 2015)

Johnson, Louisa, *Every Lady Her Own Flower Gardener* (New Haven: S. Babcock, 1839)

Kaur, Rupi, 'Sunflowers', in *The Sun and Her Flowers* (New York: Simon & Schuster, 2017)

Knapp, Sandra, *Flora: An Artistic Voyage through the World of Plants* (London: Natural History Museum/Scripta, 2003)

Lawrence, D.H., 'Nottingham and the Mining Countryside', in *Late Essays and Articles*, ed. James T. Boulton (Cambridge: Cambridge University Press, 2004)

— 'The Shades of Spring', in *Complete Poems* (Harmondsworth: Penguin, 1994)

— *Women in Love* (Cambridge: Cambridge University Press, 1987)

Mabey, Richard, *Flora Brittanica* (London: Sinclair-Stevenson, 1996)

— *The Cabaret of Plants: Botany and the Imagination* (London: Profile Books, 2015)

Mahood, M.M., *The Poet as Botanist* (Cambridge: Cambridge University Press, 2008)

Marrs, Suzanne, *One Writer's Imagination: The Fiction of Eudora Welty* (Baton Rouge: Louisiana State University Press, 2002)

McKay, Claude, 'Joy in the Woods', in *Complete Poems*, ed. William J. Maxwell (Urbana: University of Illinois Press, 2004)

McKay, George, *Radical Gardening: Politics, Idealism and Rebellion in the Garden* (London: Frances Lincoln, 2011)

Moore, Marianne, 'Roses Only', in *New Collected Poems*, ed. Heather Cass White (London: Faber, 2017)

Muir, John, 'My First Summer in the Sierra', in *Nature Writings* (New York: Library of America, 1997)

Nevins, Allan, *John D. Rockefeller: The Heroic Age of American Enterprise*, vol. 2 (New York: Charles Scribners' Sons, 1940)

Plants of the World Online, www.plantsoftheworldonline.org

Potter, Jennifer, *Seven Flowers and How They Shaped Our World* (London: Atlantic Books, 2013)

Ruskin, John, *The Brantwood Diary*, ed. Helen Gill Viljoen (New Haven and London: Yale University Press, 1971)

Schuyler, James, 'February', in *Collected Poems* (New York: Farrar, Straus and Giroux, 1993)

Seaton, Beverley, *The Language of Flowers: A History* (Charlottesville: University Press of Virginia, 1995)

Seidel, Frederick, 'Prayer', in *Poems, 1959–2009* (New York: Farrar, Straus and Giroux, 2009)

Shakespeare, William, *Macbeth*, in *The Complete Works*, ed. Peter Alexander (London: Collins, 1951)

Stewart, Amy, *Flower Confidential: The Good, the Bad, and the Beautiful in the Business of Flowers* (New York: Algonquin Books, 2008)

Stowe, Harriet Beecher, *Uncle Tom's Cabin* (Oxford: Oxford University Press, 2008)

Todd, Helen M., 'Getting Out the Vote: An Account of a Week's Automobile Campaign by Women Suffragists', *American Magazine*, September 1911

Veblen, Thorstein, *The Theory of the Leisure Class* (Oxford: Oxford University Press, 2007)

Vickery, Roy, *Vickery's Folk Flora* (London: Weidenfeld & Nicolson, 2019)

Walcott, Derek, 'Isla Incognita', in *Caribbean Literature and the Environment*, eds. Elizabeth M. DeLoughrey, Renée K. Gosson and George B. Handley (Charlottesville: University of Virginia Press, 2005)

Walker, Alice, 'In Search of Our Mothers' Gardens', in *In Search of Our Mothers' Gardens* (London: The Women's Press, 1984)

— 'Revolutionary Petunias', in *Revolutionary Petunias and Other Poems* (New York: Harcourt Brace, 1982)

Ward, Bobby J., *A Contemplation Upon Flowers: Garden Plants in Myth and Literature* (Portland: Timber Press, 1999)

Watson, Bruce, *Bread and Roses: Mills, Migrants, and the Struggle for the American Dream* (New York: Viking, 2005)

Watts, D.C., *Elseviers Dictionary of Plant Lore* (Amsterdam: Elsevier, 2007)

Way, Twigs, *The Wartime Garden* (Oxford: Shire, 2015)

Willes, Margaret, *The Gardens of the British Working Class* (New Haven and London: Yale University Press, 2014)

Woolf, Virginia, 'Sketch of the Past' (1939), in *Moments of Being: Autobiographical Writings*, ed. Jeanne Schulkind (London: Pimlico, 2002)

Wright, Richard, *12 Million Black Voices* (1941) (New York: Basic Books, 2008)

SPRING

Barker, Elspeth, *O Caledonia* (London: Penguin, 1992)

Durkheim, Émile, *Suicide: A Study in Sociology* (1897), trans. John A. Spaulding and George Simpson, ed. George Simpson (London: Routledge and Kegan Paul, 1952)

Gershwin, George (music) and Ira Gershwin (lyrics), ' 'S Wonderful' (1927)

Hardy, Thomas, *Far from the Madding Crowd* (Oxford: Oxford University Press, 2002)

Hawthorne, Nathaniel, 'Buds and Bird Voices', in *Tales and Sketches* (New York: Library of America, 1982)

Hopkins, Gerard Manley, 'Spring', in *The Major Works* (Oxford: Oxford University Press, 1986)

Housman, A.E., *A Shropshire Lad and Other Poems* (London: Penguin, 2010)

Hughes, Langston, 'Earth Song' in *The Complete Poems*, eds. Arnold Rampersad and David Roessel (New York: Vintage, 1994)

Landesman, Frances (lyrics) and Tommy Jr. Worf (music), 'Spring Can Really Hang You Up the Most' (1955)

Lawrence, D.H., *Lady Chatterley's Lover* (London: Penguin, 2006)

Ovid, *Metamorphoses*, trans. A.D. Melville (Oxford: Oxford University Press, 1986)

Shelley, Percy Bysshe, 'Adonais', in *The Complete Poems* (New York: Modern Library, 1997)

'A Small Request', trans. Velecheru Narayana Rao and David Shulman, in *Indian Love Poems*, ed. Meena Alexander (London: Everyman, 2005)

Smith, Ali, *Spring* (London: Hamish Hamilton, 2019)

Snodgrass, W.D., 'April Inventory', in *Not for Specialists: New and Selected Poems* (Rochester: BOA Editions, 2006)

Thoreau, Henry David, *The Journal, 1837–1861*, ed. Damion Searls (New York: New York Review of Books, 2009)

DAISY

de Beauvoir, Simone, *Brigette Bardot and the Lolita Syndrome* (London: Four Square, 1962)

Bevis, John, *The Keartons: Inventing Nature Photography* (Axminster: Uniformbooks, 2016)

Burns, Robert, 'To a Mountain-Daisy', in *Flora Poetica: The Chatto Book of Botanical Verse,* ed. Sarah Maguire (London: Chatto & Windus, 2003)

Carroll, Lewis, *Alice in Wonderland* and *Through the Looking Glass* (London: Penguin, 1998)

Clare, John, 'To an April Daisy', in *The Early Poems of John Clare, 1804–1822*, volume 1, eds. Eric Robinson and David Powell (Oxford: Oxford University Press, 1989)

Eliot, George, *The Mill on the Floss* (Oxford: Oxford University Press, 1996)

Fitzgerald, F. Scott, *The Great Gatsby* (London: Penguin, 1984)

Griffiths, Brent, 'Clinton Campaign Evokes "Daisy Girl" to attack Trump on Nuclear Weapons', *Politico*, 31 October, 2016, www.politico.com

Horton, Robert, *Frankenstein* (New York: Columbia University Press, 2004)

Hunt, Leigh, *The Descent of Liberty: A Mask* (London: Gale, Curtis & Fenner, 1815)

Kearton, Richard, *Wild Nature's Ways*, with photographs by Richard and Cherry Kearton (London: Cassell, 1903)

Kell, Katherine T., 'The Folklore of the Daisy', *The Journal of American Folklore* 69, no. 274 (Oct-Dec 1956), 368–76

Kent, Elizabeth, *Flora Domestica, or the Portable Flower-Garden* (Cambridge: Cambridge University Press, 2017)

Kerouac, Jack, 'Pull My Daisy', in *Scattered Poems* (San Francisco: City Lights Books, 1971)

Kieman, Frances, *Seeing Mary Plain: A Life of Mary McCarthy* (New York: Norton, 2000)

Lawrence, D.H., 'Piccadilly Circus at Night: Street Walkers', in *Complete Poems* (Harmondsworth: Penguin, 1994)

Mabey, Richard, *Flora Brittanica* (London: Sinclair-Stevenson, 1996)

de Machaut, Guillaume, '*Le Dit de la Marguerite*' and '*Le Dit de la Fleur de Lis et de la Marguerite*', in *Chaucer's Dream Poetry: Sources and Analogues*, ed. and trans. B.A. Windeatt (Woodbridge: D.S. Brewer 1982)

Mann, Robert, *Daisy Petals and Mushroom Clouds: LBJ, Barry Goldwater, and the Ad That Changed American Politics* (Baton Rouge: Louisiana State University Press, 2011)

McCarthy, Mary, *The Group* (London: Virago, 2009)

Rousseau, Jean-Jacques, *Letters on the Elements of Botany, Addressed to a Lady*, trans. Thomas Martyn (Cambridge: Cambridge University Press, 2017)

Stott, Annette, 'Floral Femininity: A Pictorial Definition', *American Art* 6, no. 2 (Spring 1992), 60–77

Wordsworth, William, 'To the Daisy' and 'To the Same Flower', in *The Major Works*, ed. Stephen Gill (Oxford: Oxford University Press, 2000)

DAFFODIL

Attar, Samar, *Borrowed Imagination: The British Romantic Poets and Their Arabic-Islamic Sources* (Lanham: Lexington Books, 2014)

Brend, Barbara, *Perspectives on Persian Painting* (London: Routledge Curzon, 2003)

Chelkowski, Peter, *Mirror of the Invisible World: Tales from the Khamseh of Nizami* (New York: Metropolitan Museum of Art, 1975)

Danticat, Edwidge, *Breath, Eyes, Memory* (London: Abacus, 1994)

Forbes, Duncan, 'Ode from the Dīwān of Khākānī', in *A Grammar of the Persian Language: To Which is Added, a Selection of Easy Extracts for Reading, Together with a Copious Vocabulary* (London: W.H. Allen, 1869)

Hafez, 'Ode 44', trans. Richard Le Gallienne, in *Persian Poems*, ed. Peter Washington (London: Everyman, 2000)

Herrick, Robert, 'To Daffodils', in *Robert Herrick*, ed. Stephen Romer (London: Faber, 2010)

Homer, 'Hymn 2: To Demeter', in *The Homeric Hymns*, trans. Michael Crudden (Oxford: Oxford University Press, 2001)

Howard, Thad M., *Bulbs for Warm Climates* (Austin: University of Texas, 2002)

Jones, William, *A Grammar of the Persian Language* (London: W. and J. Richardson, 1771)

Kincaid, Jamaica, 'Garden Inspired by William Wordsworth's Dances with Daffodils', *Architectural Digest*, April 2007, www.architecturaldigest.com

— *Lucy* (New York: Farrar, Straus and Giroux, 2002)

— 'What Joseph Banks Wrought', in *My Garden (Book)* (London: Vintage, 2000)

Mabey, Richard, *Flora Britannica* (London: Sinclair-Stevenson, 1996)

Naipaul, V.S., *A House for Mr. Biswas* (London: Picador, 2002)

— 'Jasmine', in *The Overcrowded Barracoon* (Harmondsworth: Penguin, 1976)

Ovid, *Metamorphoses*, trans. A.D. Melville (Oxford: Oxford University Press, 1986)

Rhys, Jean, 'The Day They Burned the Books', in *Tigers are Better-Looking* (Harmondsworth: Penguin, 1972)

Schimmel, Annemarie, *The Two-Colored Brocade: The Imagery of Persian Poetry* (Chapel Hill: University of North Carolina Press, 1992)

Shakespeare, William, *The Winter's Tale*, in *The Complete Works*, ed. Peter Alexander (London: Collins, 1951)

Spenser, Edmund, 'Aprill', in *The Shepheardes Calender*, in *The Shorter Poems*, ed. Richard A. McCabe (London: Penguin, 1999)

Thackston, W.M., 'Mughal Gardens in Persian Poetry', in *Mughal Gardens*, eds. James L. Westcoat Jr and Joachim Wolschke-Bulhman (Washington: Dumbarton Oaks, 1996)

Walcott, Derek, 'The Muse of History', in *What the Twilight Says* (New York: Farrar, Straus and Giroux, 1998)

Woof, Robert (ed.), *William Wordsworth: The Critical Heritage, Vol. 1: 1793–1820* (London: Routledge, 2001)

Wordsworth, Dorothy and William Wordsworth, *Home at Grasmere* (Harmondsworth: Penguin, 1978)

Wordsworth, William, 'I wandered lonely as a Cloud', in *The Major Works* (Oxford: Oxford University Press, 2000)

Wu, Duncan, *Wordsworth's Reading, 1770–1799* (Cambridge: Cambridge University Press, 1993)

Yoshikawa, Saeko, *William Wordsworth and the Invention of Tourism, 1820–1900* (Farnham: Ashgate, 2014)

Zonneveld, B.J.M., 'The Systematic Value of Nuclear DNA Content for All Species of Narcissus L. (Amaryllidaceae)', *Plant Systematics and Evolution* 275, no. 1 (2008), 109–32

LILY

Allen, S.R., 'Easter Lilies', in *Pictures and Poems of Arkansas*, eds. Bernie Babcock and O.C. Ludwig (Little Rock: Sketchbook, 1906)

Barrett, William Alexander, *Flowers and Festivals: Or Directions for the Floral Decoration of Churches* (London: J.G.F. & J. Rivington, 1868)

'The Belfast Agreement', see item 5 under 'Rights, Safeguards, and Equality of Opportunity: Economic, Social and Cultural Issues', www.gov.uk/government/publications

'Bloom for the Somme!', The Orange Order, 26 February, 2016, www.grandorangelodge.co.uk

Bos, Fred, '*Lilium bulbiferum* L. subsp. *croceum* (Chaix) arcang., the orange lily, a special plant of lowland NW Europe', *Floriculture and Ornamental Biotechnology* 6 (December 2012), 54–56

Bottome, Margaret, 'Easter Lilies', *Christian Advocate*, 20 March, 1893

'California', *The Churchman*, 18 May, 1878

Clancy, Paddy, 'Orange Order plan to sell orange lily bulbs in Battle of Boyne soil', *The Irish Times*, 28 June, 2007

'Display of Lilies in Parliament Buildings', transcript of debate, 10 April, 2001, Northern Ireland Assembly Archive, www.archive.niassembly.gov.uk

Faber, Frederick William, 'The Cherwell Water Lily', in *The Cherwell Water Lily and Other Poems* (London: J.G.F. & J. Rivington, 1840)

Fenton, Siobhán, 'As Northern Ireland's flag debate rages on, could a new neutral design be the answer?', *New Statesman*, 4 August, 2015

Friend, Hilderic, *Flowers and Flower-Lore* (London: W. Swan Sonnenshein, 1884)

'A Glossary of Terms Relating to the Conflict', Conflict Archive on the Internet (CAIN), University of Ulster, www.cain.ulster.ac.uk/othelem/glossary

Hale, Anne G., 'Easter Flowers', *The Villa Gardener*, April 1876

Hayward, H. Richard, *Ulster Songs and Ballads of the Town and Country* (London: Duckworth, 1925)

Higgins, Roisin, '"The Irish Republic was proclaimed by poster": the politics of commemorating the Easter Rising', in *Remembering 1916*, eds. Richard S. Grayson and Fearghal McGarry (Cambridge: Cambridge University Press, 2016)

Hirn, Yrjo, *The Sacred Shrine: A Study of the Poetry and Art of the Catholic Church* (Boston: Beacon Press, 1912)

Johnston, Niall, 'The Northern Ireland Assembly: A New Beginning?', *The Journal of Legislative Studies* 8, no. 1 (2002), 1–9

Loftus, Belinda, *Mirrors: Orange and Green* (Dundrum: Picture Press, 1994)

'Louisville, KY', in *The American Florist*, 1 May, 1887

Lynes, Barbara Buhler, *Georgia O'Keeffe and the Calla Lily in American Art, 1860–1940* (London and New Haven: Yale University Press, 2002)

McKay, Claude, 'The Easter Flower', in *Complete Poems*, ed. William J. Maxwell (Urbana: University of Illinois Press, 2004)

Morris, Ewan, *Our Own Devices: National Symbols and Political Conflict in Twentieth-Century Ireland* (Dublin: Irish Academic Press, 2005)

'New York', *The American Florist*, 1 March, 1887

Perry, Leonard, 'Easter Lilies', Department of Plant Sciences, University of Vermont, www.pss. uvm.edu/ppp/articles/eastlily

Sackville-West, Vita, *Vita Sackville-West's Garden Book*, ed. Philippa Nicolson (London: Book Club Associates, 1974)

Schmidt, Leigh Eric, *Consumer Rites: The Buying and Selling of American Holidays* (Princeton: Princeton University Press, 1995)

Souhami, Diana, *Gluck: Her Biography* (London: Quercus, 2013)

'Stormont Lilies Row Raises Head Again', BBC News Online, 1 March, 2002

Tomkins, Calvin, 'Georgia O'Keeffe's Vision', *The New Yorker*, 4 March, 1974

CARNATION

Antolini, Katherine Lane, *Memorializing Motherhood: Anna Jarvis and the Struggle for Control of Mother's Day* (Morgantown: West Virginia University Press, 2014)

Beckson, Karl, 'Oscar Wilde and the Green Carnation', *English Literature in Transition (1880–1920)* 43, no. 4 (2000), 387–97

— *Arthur Symons: A Life* (Oxford: Clarendon Press, 1987)

Bradley, Richard, *New Improvements of Planting and Gardening: Both Philosophical and Practical* (London: A. Bettesworth, J.& J. Pemberton, J.& P. Knapton, D. Brown, 1739)

'Carnations $1 Each for Mother's Day', *New York Times*, 9 May, 1921

Cather, Willa, 'Paul's Case: A Study in Temperament', in *The Short Stories of Willa Cather*, ed. Hermione Lee (London: Virago, 1989)

Coward, Noel, 'We All Wore a Green Carnation', in *Bitter-Sweet*, in *Plays: Two* (London: Methuen, 1979)

Darwin, Erasmus, 'The Loves of the Plants', the second part of *The Botanic Garden: A Poem, in two parts* (London: J. Johnson, 1791)

Duthie, Ruth, *Florists' Flowers and Societies* (Aylesbury: Shire, 1988)

Ellmann, Richard, *Oscar Wilde* (New York: Vintage, 1988)

Foner, Philip S., *American Labor Songs of the Nineteenth Century* (Urbana: University of Illinois Press, 1975)

Hobsbawm, Eric, 'Birth of a Holiday: The First of May', in *Uncommon People: Resistance, and Jazz* (London: Abacus, 1999)

Howells, William Dean, *Life in Letters,* vol. 1, ed. Mildred Howells (New York: Doubleday, Doran, 1928)

Janes, Dominic, *Oscar Wilde Prefigured: Queer Fashioning and British Caricature, 1750–1900* (Chicago: University of Chicago Press, 2016)

Kastan, David Scott, *On Color* (London and New Haven: Yale University Press, 2018)

'Keep Mother's Day Without Flowers', *New York Times*, 2 May, 1920

Leverson, Ada, 'The First Last Night', in *Oscar Wilde: Interviews and Recollections*, vol. 2, ed. E.H. Mikhail (Basingstoke: Macmillan, 1979)

Linnaeus, *The Elements of Botany*, trans. Hugh Rose (London: T. Cadell & M. Hingeston, 1775)

Liu, Shu and Linda M. Meyer, 'Carnations and the Floriculture Industry: Documenting the Cultivation and Marketing of Flowers in Colorado', *Journal of Archival Organization* 6, nos. 1–2 (2008), 6–23

'Making More of Mother's Day', *Florists' Review*, 22 April, 1920

Mansfield, Katherine, 'Carnation', in *The Collected Stories* (London: Penguin, 2001)

McKenna, Neil, *The Secret Life of Oscar Wilde* (New York: Basic Books, 2005)

McWhorter, Diane, 'The Bum Who Fathered Mother's Day', *New York Times*, 8 May, 1994

Menkes, Suzy, 'Pistil Packin'', *New York Times Magazine*, 7 November, 2004

'Mother's Day', *New York Times*, 7 May, 1922

'Mother's Day, Theme in Pulpits of the City', *New York Times*, 15 May, 1922

Nash, Elizabeth, 'Shy Rebel Puts Carnations into Portugal's Revolution', *The Independent*, 26 April, 1999

Ostrom, Lizzie, *Perfume: A Century of Scents* (London: Hutchinson, 2015)

Parker, Geoffrey, *Global Crisis: War, Climate Change and Catastrophe in the Seventeenth Century* (London and New Haven: Yale University Press, 2013)

Pastoureau, Michel, *Red: The History of a Color*, trans. Jody Gladding (Princeton: Princeton University Press, 2017)

'Retail Store Management', *Florists' Review*, 15 April, 1920

Sex and the City, HBO, series 6, episode 6, 'Hop, Skip and a Week', first aired 27 July, 2003

Shakespeare, William, *The Winter's Tale*, in *The Complete Works*, ed. Peter Alexander (London: Collins, 1951)

Soboleva, N.A., 'From the History of Soviet Political Symbolism', *Russian Studies in History* 47, no. 2, 59–91

Stafford, Fiona, 'Gillyflowers', in *The Brief Life of Flowers* (London: John Murray, 2018)

Storey, Margaret M., *Loyalty and Loss: Alabama's Unionists in the Civil War and Reconstruction* (Baton Rouge: Louisiana University Press, 2004)

Symons, Arthur, *The Symbolist Movement in Literature* (Manchester: Carcanet, 2014)

Unowsky, Daniel L., *The Pomp and Politics of Patriotism: Imperial Celebrations in Habsburg Austria, 1848–1914* (West Lafayette: Purdue University Press, 2005)

Utley, Getje, *Picasso: The Communist Years* (London and New Haven: Yale University Press, 2000)

Varela, Raquel, *A People's History of the Portuguese Revolution*, trans. Sean Purdy (London: Pluto, 2019)

Way, Twigs, *Carnation* (London: Reaktion, 2016)

'Which Trends Offer Opportunities on the European Cut Flowers and Foliage Market?', CBI, May 2017, www.cbi.eu

Wilde, Oscar, 'Phrases and Philosophies for the Use of the Young', in *The Artist as Critic: Critical Writings* (New York: Random House, 1970)

— *The Complete Letters of Oscar Wilde*, eds. Merline Holland and Rupert Hart-Davis (London: Fourth Estate, 2000)

SUMMER

Arkell, Reginald, *Old Herbaceous: A Novel of the Garden* (New York: Modern Library, 2003)

Boas, Franz, 'Poetry and Music of Some North American Tribes', *Science*, 22 April, 1887, 383–5

Bosanquet, Theodora, *Henry James at Work*, ed. Lyall H. Powers (Ann Arbor: University of Michigan Press, 2006)

Clare, John, *The Midsummer Cushion*, eds. Kelsey Thornton and Anne Tibble (Manchester: Carcanet, 1990)

Keats, John, 'To Autumn', in *The Complete Poems*, ed. Miriam Allott (London: Longman, 1970)

Lawrence, D.H., *Lady Chatterley's Lover* (London: Penguin, 2006)

— *Women in Love* (Cambridge: Cambridge University Press, 1987)

Pendleton, S.L., G.H. Miller, N. Lifton, et al., 'Rapidly receding Arctic Canada glaciers revealing landscapes continuously ice-covered for more than 40,000 years', *Nature Communication* 10, no. 445 (2019), online

Stewart, Amy, *Flower Confidential: The Good, the Bad, and the Beautiful in the Business of Flowers* (New York: Algonquin Books, 2008)

Thoreau, Henry David, *The Journal, 1837–1861*, ed. Damion Searls (New York: New York Review of Books, 2009)

— 'The Soul's Season', in *Collected Essays and Poems* (New York: Library of America, 2001)

Ton, Peter, *Cotton and Climate Change: Impacts and Options to Mitigate and Adapt* (Geneva: International Trade Centre, 2011)

Wharton, Edith, *A Backward Glance* (London: Everyman, 1993)

ROSE

Bataille, Georges, 'The Big Toe' and 'The Language of Flowers', in *Visions of Excess: Selected Writings, 1927–1939*, trans. Allan Stoekl, with Carl R. Lovitt and Donald M. Leslie Jr., ed. Allan Stoekl (Minneapolis: University of Minnesota Press, 1985)

Blake, William, 'The Sick Rose', in *Songs of Experience*, in *Blake's Poetry and Designs*, eds. Mary Lynn Johnson and John E. Grant (New York: Norton, 1979)

Bridgman, Richard, *Gertrude Stein in Pieces* (New York: Oxford University Press, 1970)

'Bring Roses', *The Urban Dictionary*, theurbandictionary.com

Collins, Lauren, 'Fragrant Harvest', *The New Yorker*, 19 March, 2018

Dalzell, Tom and Terry Victor (eds), *The New Partridge Dictionary of Slang and Unconventional English* (London: Routledge, 2013)

Dionysius the Sophist, 'You with the Roses', in *The Greek Anthology, Volume 1: Books 1–5*, trans. W.R. Paton, revised Michael A. Tueller (Cambridge: Harvard University Press, 2014)

Freedman, Ralph, *Life of a Poet: Rainer Maria Rilke* (New York: Farrar, Straus and Giroux, 1995)

Gass, William, *Reading Rilke: Reflections on the Problems of Translation* (New York: Knopf, 1999)

Genet, Jean, *Querelle of Brest*, trans. Gregory Steatham (London: Faber, 2019)

— *Miracle of the Rose,* trans. Bernard Frechtman (New York: Grove Press, 1966)

Goethe, Johannes, 'Heidenröslein', in *Selected Verse*, trans. David Luke (Harmondsworth: Penguin 1964)

Hardy, Thomas, *Jude the Obscure* (Oxford: Oxford University Press, 2020)

Herrick, Robert, 'To the Virgins, to make much of Time', in *Robert Herrick*, ed. Stephen Romer (London: Faber, 2010)

Lawrence, D.H., 'The Shadow in the Rose Garden', in *The Complete Short Stories*, vol. 1 (Harmondsworth: Penguin, 1976)

de Lorris, Guillaume and Jean de Meun, *The Romance of the Rose*, trans. Frances Horgan (Oxford: Oxford University Press, 1994)

Ovid, *Fasti*, trans. Anne and Peter Wiseman (Oxford: Oxford University Press, 2013)

Paletta, Damian, 'In rose beds, money blooms', *Washington Post*, 10 February, 2018

Pollan, Michael, 'Into the Rose Garden', in *Second Nature* (London: Bloomsbury, 1996)

Richards, Jeffrey, *Sex, Dissidence and Damnation: Minority Groups in the Middle Ages* (London: Routledge, 1991)

Sackville-West, Vita, *Even More for Your Garden* (London: Frances Lincoln, 2004)

Schimmel, Annemarie, *And Muhammad is His Messenger: The Veneration of the Prophet in Islamic Poetry* (Chapel Hill: University of North Carolina Press, 1985)

Shakespeare, William, Sonnet 35, in *Complete Sonnets and Poems*, ed. Colin Burrow (Oxford: Oxford University Press, 2002)

Sharp, Jane, *The Midwives Book: or the Whole Art of Midwifery Discovered* (1671) (Oxford: Oxford University Press, 1999)

'Should You Bring Her Flowers on the First Date?', *The Art of Charm*, www.theartofcharm.com

Spenser, Edmund, *The Faerie Queene* (London: Penguin, 1987)

Stein, Gertrude, *Four in America* (London and New Haven: Yale University Press, 1947)

— 'Poetry and Grammar', in *Look at Me Now and Here I Am: Writings and Lectures, 1909–1945*, ed. Patricia Meyerowitz (London: Penguin, 1984)

Stern, Jesse, 'What Every Man Should Know About Flowers and How to Exploit It for Personal Gain', *Primer*, 2011, www.primermagazine.com

Swift, Jonathan, 'Strephon and Chloe', in *The Poems of Jonathan Swift*, volume 2, ed. Harold Williams (Oxford: Oxford University Press, 1958)

Tennyson, Alfred Lord, *Maud: A Monodrama*, in *Tennyson: A Selected Edition*, ed. Christopher Ricks (London: Longman, 1989)

Thomas, Graham Stuart, *The Graham Stuart Thomas Rose Book* (London: John Murray, 1994)

'Tips for Navigating the First Date', *Esquire*, 6 June, 2016

Wang, Chen-ho, *Rose, Rose, I Love You*, trans. Howard Goldblatt (New York: Columbia University Press, 1998)

Williams, Gordon, *Shakespeare's Sexual Language: A Glossary* (London: Continuum, 1997)

Williams, William Carlos, 'The Rose', in *Collected Poems I: 1909–1939*, eds. A. Walton Litz and Christopher MacGowan (Manchester: Carcanet, 2018)

Woolf, Virginia, 'How It Strikes a Contemporary' and 'On Being Ill', in *The Crowded Dance of Modern Life*, ed. Rachel Bowlby (London: Penguin, 1993)

— *Mrs Dalloway* (London: Penguin, 1992)

LOTUS

Barthlott, Wilhelm and Christoph Neinhuis, 'Purity of the Sacred Lotus, or Escape from Contamination in Biological Surfaces', *Planta* 202, no. 1 (1997), 1–8

Bertol, Elisabetta, Vittorio Fineschi, et al., '*Nymphaea* Cults in Ancient Egypt and the New World: A Lesson in Empirical Pharmacology', *Journal of the Royal Society of Medicine* 97, no. 2 (2004), 84–5

Conrad, Joseph, *Heart of Darkness* (Oxford: Oxford University Press, 1990)

Conze, Edward (ed.), *Buddhist Texts through the Ages* (New York: Harper and Row, 1964)

Dodd, George, *The History of the Indian Revolt and of the Expeditions to Persia, China, and Japan, 1856–1858* (London: W. and R. Chambers, 1859)

The Egyptian Book of the Dead, trans. E.A. Wallis Budge (London: Penguin, 2008)

Eliot, T.S., 'Burnt Norton', in *Four Quartets*, in *The Complete Poems and Plays of T.S. Eliot* (London: Faber, 1969)

Goodyear, W.H., *The Grammar of the Lotus* (London: Low, 1891)

Griffiths, Mark, *The Lotus Quest: In Search of the Sacred Flower* (London: Chatto & Windus, 2009)

Haksar, A.N.D. (ed. and trans.), *Subhashitavali: An Anthology of Comic, Erotic and Other Verse* (London: Penguin, 2007)

Herodotus, *The Histories*, trans. Robin Waterfield (Oxford: Oxford University Press, 1998)

Homer, *The Odyssey*, trans. Emily Wilson (New York: Norton, 2017)

Jerrold, Douglas, 'The Lotus Eaters of Downing Street', *Punch, or the London Charivari* 13 (October 1847)

Joyce, James, *Ulysses: The 1922 Text* (Oxford: Oxford University Press, 1993)

Nanakaiyar, Kaccipettu, 'What She Said', trans. A.K. Ramanujan, in *Indian Love Poems*, ed. Meena Alexander (London: Everyman, 2005)

Poems of Life and Love in Ancient India: Hāla's Sattasaī, trans. Peter Khoroche and Herman Tieken (Albany: State University of New York University Press, 2009)

Tennyson, Alfred Lord, 'The Lotos-Eaters', in *Tennyson: A Selected Edition*, ed. Christopher Ricks (London: Longman, 1989)

Theophrastus, *Enquiry into Plants, Volume 1: Books 1–5*, trans. Arthur Hort (Cambridge: Harvard University Press, 1916)

Thomson, Mowbray, *The Story of Cawnpore* (London: R. Bentley, 1859)

Thoreau, Henry David, *The Journal, 1837–1861*, ed. Damion Searls (New York: New York Review Books, 2009)

— 'Slavery in Massachusetts', in *Political Writings*, ed. Nancy L. Rosenblum (Cambridge: Cambridge University Press, 1996)

Yanovsky, Elias, *Food Plants of the North American Indians* (Washington: U.S. Department of Agriculture, 1936)

COTTON

Beckert, Sven, *Empire of Cotton: A New History of Global Capitalism* (London: Penguin, 2014)

Breward, Christopher, *The Culture of Fashion* (Manchester: Manchester University Press, 1995)

Herodotus, *The Histories*, trans. Robin Waterfield (Oxford: Oxford University Press, 1998)

Hughes, Langston, 'Share-Croppers', in *The Complete Poems*, eds. Arnold Rampersad and David Roessel (New York: Vintage, 1994)

Hughs, S.E., T.D. Valco and J.R. Williford, '100 Years of Cotton Production, Harvesting, and Ginning Systems Engineering: 1907–2007', *Transactions of the ASABE* 51, no. 4, 1187–98

Kincaid, Jamaica, 'The Glasshouse', in *My Garden (Book)* (London: Viking, 2000)

Lewington, Anna, *Plants for People* (London: Natural History Museum, 1990)

Mandeville, John, *Book of Marvels and Travels*, trans. Anthony Bale (Oxford: Oxford University Press, 2012)

Northup, Solomon, *Twelve Years a Slave*, in *I Was Born a Slave: An Anthology of Classic Slave Narratives, vol. 2: 1849–1866*, ed. Yuval Taylor (Edinburgh: Payback Press, 1999)

Patton, Charley, 'Mississippi Bo Weevil Blues', in *Complete Recorded Works in Chronological Order*, Volume 1 (Document Records, 1990)

Pauly, Philip J., *Fruits and Plains: The Horticultural Transformation of America* (Cambridge: Harvard University Press, 2007)

Riello, Georgio, *Cotton: The Fabric That Made the Modern World* (Cambridge: Cambridge University Press, 2013)

Rothermund, Dietmar, *An Economic History of India: From Pre-Colonial Times to 1986* (London: Croom Helm, 1988)

Smith, Chloe Wigston, '"Callico Madams": Servants, Consumption and the Calico Crisis', *Eighteenth-Century Life* 31, no. 2 (Spring 2007), 29–55

Smith, Wayne C. (ed), *Cotton: Origin, History, Technology and Production* (New York: John Wiley and Sons, 1999)

Stephen, Alexander M., *Hopi Journal*, ed. Elsie Clews Parsons (New York: Columbia University Press, 1936)

Toomer, Jean, 'November Cotton Flower', in *Cane* (New York: Penguin, 2019)

Turpin, Edna, *Cotton* (New York: American Book Company, 1924)

Whittier, John Greenleaf, 'The Peace Autumn', in *Anti-Slavery: Songs of Labor and Reform* (New York: Houghton, Mifflin, 1888)

Wright, Richard, *12 Million Black Voices* (New York: Basic Books, 2008)

Wyke, Terry, with Harry Cocks, *Public Sculpture of Greater Manchester* (Liverpool: Liverpool University Press, 2004)

Yafa, Stephen, *Cotton: The Biography of a Revolutionary Fiber* (New York: Viking, 2005)

SUNFLOWER

Atamian, H.S., N.M. Creux, E.A. Brown, et al., 'Circadian Regulation of Sunflower Heliotropism, Floral Orientation, and Pollinator Visits', *Science*, 5 August, 2006, 587–90

Blackman, Benjamin K., Moira Scascitelli, et al., 'Sunflower Domestication Alleles Support Single Domestication Centre in Eastern North America', *Proceedings of the National Academy of Sciences of the United States of America* 108, no. 34 (2011), 14360–14365

Byron, Lord, *Don Juan*, in *The Major Works* (Oxford: Oxford University Press, 2000)

Cather, Willa, *My Antonia* (Oxford: Oxford University Press, 2006)

Cooney, Catherine M., 'Sunflowers Remove Radionuclides from Water in Ongoing Phytoremediation Field Tests', *Environmental Science and Technology* 30, no. 5 (1996), 194A

Cowley, Abraham, *Six Books of Plants* (1689), Electronic Text Center, University of Virginia Library, www.cowley.lib.virginia.edu

Debaeke, Philippe, Pierre Cadadebaig, et al., 'Sunflower Crop and Climate Change', *Oilseeds and Fats, Crops and Lipids* 24, no. 1 (2017), online

Donghuan, Xu, 'Xu Jiang's Sunflowers Are Symbol of a Lost Generation', *South China Morning Post*, 18 October, 2014

Druick, Douglas W., *Van Gogh and Gauguin: The Studio of the South* (London: Thames & Hudson, 2001)

Fengyuan, Ji, *Linguistic Engineering: Language and Politics in Mao's China* (Honolulu: University of Hawai'i Press, 2004)

Finnegan, Margaret, *Selling Suffrage: Consumer Culture and Votes for Women* (New York: Columbia University Press, 1999)

Gauguin, Paul, *Intimate Journals*, trans. Van Wyck Brooks (New York: Crown, 1936)

Gerard, John, *The Herbal, or General History of Plants*, The Complete 1633 Edition, as revised and enlarged by Thomas Johnson (New York: Dover, 2015)

Ginsberg, Allan, 'Sunflower Sutra', in *Collected Poems, 1947–1997* (London: Penguin, 2006)

'Global Trends in Sunflower Production', 9 March, 2019, www.nuseed.com

Greenwell, Dora, 'The Sun-flower', in *Poems* (London: Walter Scott, 1889)

Harris, Stephen A., *Sunflowers* (London: Reaktion, 2018)

Heiser, Charles B., 'The Sunflower among the North American Indians', *Proceedings of the American Philosophical Society* 95, no. 4 (1951), 432–48

Kaur, Rupi, 'The Sun and Her Flowers', in *The Sun and Her Flowers* (New York: Simon & Schuster, 2017)

Mancoff, Debra N., *Sunflowers* (Chicago: Art Institute of Chicago, 2001)

Marsh, Peter, 'China Noses Ahead as Top Goods Producer', *Financial Times*, 13 March 2011

McPherson, Alan, *State Botanical Symbols* (Bloomington: AuthorHouse, 2013)

Murphy, Bernadette, *Van Gogh's Ear: The True Story* (London: Chatto & Windus, 2016)

Ovid, *Metamorphoses*, trans. A.D. Melville (Oxford: Oxford University Press, 1986)

Pappalardo, Joe, *Sunflowers, The Secret History: The Unauthorized Biography of the World's Most Beloved Weed* (Woodstock: Overlook Press, 2008)

Peacock, John, *The Look of Van Dyck: The Self-Portrait with a Sunflower and the Vision of the Painter* (London: Routledge, 2006)

Perlez, Jane, 'Sunflower Seeds Replace Ukraine's Old Missile Sites', *New York Times*, 5 June, 1996

Pollan, Michael, 'Consider the Castor Bean', in *My Favourite Plant*, ed. Jamaica Kincaid (London: Vintage, 1999)

Swinton, Jonathan, Erinma Ochu and The MSI Turing's Sunflower Consortium, 'Novel Fibonacci and non-Fibonacci Structure in the Sunflower: Results of a Citizen Science Experiment', Royal Society Open Science, 1 May, 2016, www.royalsocietypublishing.org

Takenaka, Chisato, 'Effects on Agricultural Products and Wild Plants', in *Environmental Contamination from the Fukushima Nuclear Disaster* (Cambridge: Cambridge University Press, 2019)

Van Gogh, Vincent, *The Letters*, eds. Leo Jansen, Hans Luijten and Nienke Bakker, vangoghletters.org

Waters, Frank, *Book of the Hopi* (New York: Viking, 1963)

Wilde, Oscar, 'Impressions', in *Complete Poetry*, ed. Isobel Murray (Oxford: Oxford University Press, 1997)

Wilson, Gilbert L., *Buffalo Bird Woman's Garden: Agriculture of the Hidatsa Indians* (1917) (St Paul: Minnesota Historical Society Press, 1987)

AUTUMN

Baudelaire, Charles, '*Chant d'automne*' ('Autumn Song'), in *The Flowers of Evil: Parallel Text*, trans. James McGowan (Oxford: Oxford University Press, 1993)

Blake, William, 'To Autumn', in *Blake's Poetry and Designs*, eds. Mary Lynn Johnson and John E. Grant (New York: Norton, 1979)

Čapek, Karl, *The Gardener's Year*, trans. M. and R. Weatherall (London: George Allen & Unwin, 1931)

Dickinson, Emily, 'A Field of Stubble – lying sere', 'Apparently with no surprise', and 'God made a little Gentian', in *Emily Dickinson's Poems: As She Preserved Them*, ed. Christanne Miller (Princeton: Princeton University Press, 2006)

Donne, John, 'The Autumnal', in *The Complete English Poems*, ed. A.J. Smith (Harmondsworth: Penguin, 1971)

Farr, Judith, *The Gardens of Emily Dickinson* (Cambridge: Harvard University Press, 2009)

Hopkins, Gerard Manley, 'Spring and Fall: to a Young Child', in *The Major Works* (Oxford: Oxford University Press, 1986)

Hughes, Ted, 'The Seven Sorrows', in *Season Songs* (London: Faber, 1985)

Keats, John, 'To Autumn', in *The Complete Poems*, ed. Miriam Allott (London: Longman, 1970)

Moore, Thomas, 'The Last Rose of Summer', in *Irish Melodies*, ed. J.W. Glover (Dublin: James Duffy, 1859)

Pushkin, Alexander, 'Autumn (A Fragment)', in *Selected Lyric Poetry*, trans. James E. Falen (Evanston: Northwestern University Press, 2009)

Rossetti, Christina, 'October', in *The Months: A Pageant*, in *The Complete Poems* (London: Penguin, 2001)

Ruskin, John, *Praeterita* (London: Rupert Hart-Davis, 1949)

al-Shabbi, Abu al-Qasim, 'The Will of Life', trans. Naomi Shihab Nye and Lena Jayyusi, in *Arabic Poems: A Bilingual Edition*, ed. Marlé Hammond (London: Everyman, 2014)

Sweeting, Adam, *Beneath the Second Sun: A Cultural History of Indian Summer* (Hanover: University Press of New England, 2003)

Wilder, Louise Beebe, *The Fragrant Garden* (New York: Dover, 1974)

SAFFRON

Alsayied, Nouf Fakieh, José Antonio Fernández, et al., 'Diversity and Relationships of *Crocus sativus* and Its Relatives Analysed by Inter-retroelement Amplified Polymorphism (IRAP)', *Annals of Botany* 116, no. 3 (2015), 359–368

Culpeper, Nicholas, *Culpeper's Complete Herbal* (London: W. Foulsham, 1950)

Dalby, Andrew, *Dangerous Tastes: The Story of Spices* (Berkeley: University of California Press, 2000)

Deepak, Sharanya, 'This Land is Meant Only for Saffron. Without It, It Means Nothing', *The Eater*, 13 February, 2019, www.eater.com

Evelyn, John, *The Diary*, ed. Guy de Bédoyère (Woodbridge: Boydell Press, 1995)

Fernie, W.T., *Herbal Simples, Approved for Modern Uses of Cure* (Bristol: John Wright, 1897)

Fisher, Celia, *The Medieval Flower Book* (London: British Library, 2013)

Flavin, Susan, *Consumption and Culture in Sixteenth-Century Ireland: Saffron, Stockings and Silk* (Woodbridge: Boydell Press, 2014)

Fluch, Silvia, Karin Hohl, et al. '*Crocus sativus* L.: Molecular Evidence on Its Clonal Origin', *Acta Horticulture* 850 (2010), 41–46

Freedman, Paul, *Out of the East: Spices and the Medieval Imagination* (London and New Haven: Yale University Press, 2008)

Graber, Cynthia and Nicola Twilley, 'The Spice That Hooked Medieval Nuns', *The Atlantic*, 23 January, 2018

Hakluyt, Richard, 'Remembrances for a Factor', in *The Principal Navigations, Voyages, Traffiques and Discoveries of the English Nation*, volume 5 (Cambridge: Cambridge University Press, 2014)

Hammond, Peter, *Food and Feast in Medieval England* (Stroud: Sutton, 1993)

Hayward, Maria, *Rich Apparel: Clothing and the Law in Henry VIII's England* (Farnham: Ashgate, 2009)

Herbert, Ian, 'Gangs Make a Fortune from the Ancient Art of Adulterating Saffron', *The Independent*, 8 April, 2000

Holmes, Clare Patricia, *Economic Activity in Saffron Walden between the Sixteenth and Eighteenth Centuries (with particular reference to the crocus industry)* (s.l.: C.P. Holmes, 1988)

Jones, Anne Rosalind and Peter Stallybrass, *Renaissance Clothing and the Materials of Memory* (Cambridge: Cambridge University Press, 2000)

Joyce, James, *Finnegans Wake* (Oxford: Oxford University Press, 2012)

— *Letters*, volume 1, ed. Stuart Gilbert (London: Faber, 1957)

— *Ulysses: The 1922 Text* (Oxford: Oxford University Press, 1993)

Joyce, P.W., *A Social History of Ancient Ireland*, volume 2 (London: Longmans, Green, 1903)

Kiani, Sajad, Saeid Minaei, et al., 'Integration of Computer Vision and Electronic Nose as Non-destructive Systems for Saffron Adulteration Detection', *Computers and Electronics in Agriculture* 141 (September 2017), 46–53

Klemetillä, Hannele, *The Medieval Kitchen* (London: Reaktion, 2012)

Muffet, Thomas, 'Theater of Insects', in Edward Topsell, *The History of Four-footed Beasts, Serpents and Insects* (London: G. Sawbridge, 1658)

Nemati, Zahra, Dört Harpke, et al., 'Saffron (*Crocus sativus*) is an Autotriploid in Attica (Greece) from Wild *Crocus cartwrightianus*', *Molecular Phylogenetics and Evolution*, 136 (July 2019), 14–20

Parashar, Parmanand, *Kashmir: The Paradise of Asia* (New Delhi: Sarup and Sons, 2004)

Parker, Rowland, *The Common Stream: 200 Years of the English Village* (Chicago: Academy Chicago Publishers, 1994)

Pegge, Samuel, *The Forme of Cury: A Roll of Ancient English Cookery* (London: J. Nichols, 1780)

Pereira, Jonathan, *The Elements of Materia Medica and Therapeutics*, Volume 2: Part 1 (Cambridge: Cambridge University Press, 2014)

Pliny the Elder, *Natural History*, Volume 6: Books 20–23, trans. W.H.S. Jones (Cambridge: Harvard University Press, 1951)

The Proceedings of the Old Bailey, 1674–1913, www.oldbaileyonline.org

Raffield, Paul, 'Reformation, Regulation and the Image: Sumptuary Legislation and the Subject of Law', *Law and Critique* 13, no. 2 (2002), 127–55

Schier, Volker, 'Probing the Mystery of the Use of Saffron in Medieval Nunneries', *Senses and Society* 5, no. 1 (2010), 57–72

Schleif, Corine and Volker Schier, *Katerina's Windows: Donation and Devotion, Art and Music, as Heard and Seen Through the Writings of a Birgittine Nun* (University Park: Penn State Press, 2009)

Shafiee, Mojtaba, Soheil Arekhi, et al., 'Saffron in the Treatment of Depression, Anxiety and Other Medical Disorders', *Journal of Affective Disorders* 227 (2018), 330–37

Shakespeare, William, *The Winter's Tale*, in *The Complete Works*, ed. Peter Alexander (London: Collins, 1951)

Spenser, Edmund, *A View of the State of Ireland* (Oxford: Blackwell, 1997)

Theophrastus, *Enquiry into Plants*, Volume 2: Books 6-9, trans. Arthur Hort (Cambridge: Harvard University Press, 1926)

Thompson, Daniel V., *The Materials of Medieval Painting* (London: G. Allen and Unwin, 1936)

Weiss, E.A., *Spice Crops* (Wallingford: CABI Publishing, 2002)

Willard, Pat, *Saffron: The Vagabond Life of the World's Most Seductive Spice* (Boston: Beacon Press, 2001)

Yeats, William Butler, 'The Wanderings of Usheen [Oisin]', in *When You Are Old: Early Poems, Plays, and Fairy Tales*, ed. Robert Doggett (London: Penguin, 2015)

CHRYSANTHEMUM

Abe, Naoko, *'Cherry' Ingram: The Englishman who Saved Japan's Blossoms* (London: Chatto & Windus, 2019)

Alonso, Harriet Hyman, *Peace as a Women's Issue: A History of the US Movement for World Peace and Women's Rights* (Syracuse: Syracuse University Press, 1993)

'Behind the Image: Protesting the Vietnam War with a Flower', Magnum Photos, www.magnumphotos.com

Bergreen, Laurence, *Capone: The Man and the Era* (New York: Simon & Schuster, 1994)

Dumas, Ann, 'Monet's Garden at Giverny', in *Painting the Modern Garden* (London: Royal Academy of Arts, 2015)

Fish, Margery, *We Made a Garden* (London: W.H. & L. Collingridge, 1956)

Ginsberg, Allen, 'Demonstration or Spectacle as Example, As Communication or How to Make a March/Spectacle' (November 1965), in *Deliberate Prose: Selected Essays, 1952–1995*, ed. Bill Morgan (London: HarperCollins, 2000)

Haggard, H. Rider, *A Gardener's Year* (Cambridge: Cambridge University Press, 2012)

Iorizzo, Luciano, *Al Capone: A Biography* (Westport: Greenwood, 2003)

Jezer, Marty, *Abbie Hoffman: American Rebel* (New Brunswick: Rutgers University Press, 1992)

Keefe, Rose, *Guns and Roses: The Untold Story of Dean O'Banion* (Nashville: Cumberland House, 2003)

Liming, Wei, *Chinese Festivals* (Cambridge: Cambridge University Press, 2011)

Lloyd, Jenna M. 'War is Not Healthy for Children and Other Living Things', *Environment and Planning D: Society and Space* 27, no. 3 (2009), 403–24

Marc Riboud: 60 ans de photographie (Paris: Flammarion, 2014)

Mouse, John, *Monet: Nature into Art* (London and New Haven: Yale University Press, 1986)

Nelson, Susan E. 'Revisiting the Eastern Fence: Tao Qian's Chrysanthemums', *The Art Bulletin* 83, no. 3 (2001), 437–60

Ohnuki-Tierney, Emiko, *Flowers That Kill: Communicative Opacity in Political Spaces* (Stanford: University of Stanford Press, 2015)

— *Kamikaze, Cherry Blossoms, and Nationalisms* (Chicago: University of Chicago Press, 2002)

Okakura, Kakuzō, *The Book of Tea* (London: Penguin, 2016)

Proust, Marcel, *In the Shadow of Young Girls in Flower*, trans. James Grieve (London: Penguin, 2002)

Radnor, Abigail, 'That's Me in the Picture: Jan Rose Kasmir at an Anti-Vietnam-War Rally at the Pentagon, in 1967', *The Guardian*, 7 November, 2014

Silva, Horacio, 'Karma Chameleon', *New York Times Magazine*, 9 October, 2017

Spaargaren, Jaap J., *Origin and Spreading of the Cultivated Chrysanthemum, and World Market Analysis of Cut Flowers* (Aalsmeer: J.J. Spaargarden, 2015)

Taylor, Judith M., *An Abundance of Flowers: More Great Flower Breeders of the Past* (Athens: Swallow Press, 2018)

Tian, Xiaofei, *Tao Yuanming and Manuscript Culture: The Record of a Dusty Table* (Seattle: University of Washington Press, 2005)

Willsdon, Clare A.P., *In the Gardens of Impressionism* (London: Thames & Hudson, 2004)

— 'Making the Modern Garden', in *Painting the Modern Garden* (London: Royal Academy of Arts, 2015)

MARIGOLD

Bye, Robert and Edelmira Linares, 'Creating the Illusion of the Countryside: Frida Kahlo's Post-Revolutionary Mexican Suburban Domestic Garden', in *Frida Kahlo's Garden*, eds. Adrian Zavala, Mia D'Avanza and Joanna L. Groake (New York: New York Botanical Garden, 2015)

Chadha, Kumkum, *The Marigold Story: Indira Gandhi and Others* (Chennai: Tranquebar, 2019)

Curry, Helen Anne, *Evolution Made to Order: Plant Breeding and Technological Innovation in Twentieth-Century America* (Chicago: University of Chicago Press, 2016)

Doctor, Vikram, 'This Lok Sabha Election, Mega Garlands Made from Apple, Almond and Raisins Are in Vogue', *The Economic Times*, 20 April, 2019

Elferink, J.G.R. and J.A. Flores Frafán, 'Yauhtli and Cempoalxochitl: The Sacred Marigolds, *Tagetes* Species in Aztec Medicine and Religion', CIESAS, Mexico, Academia.edu, n.d.

Heyden, Doris, 'Symbolism of Ceramics from the Templo Mayor', in *The Aztec Templo Mayor*, ed. Elizabeth Hill Boone (Washington D.C.: Dumbarton Oaks, 1987)

Jekyll, Gertrude, *Colour Schemes for the Flower Gardens* (London: Francis Lincoln, 1988)

Knutson, Lawrence L., 'It's Official: Rose to be Official National Flower', Associated Press, 24 September, 1986, www.apnews.com

Kraft, Ken, *Garden to Order: The Story of Mr Burpee's Seeds and How They Grow* (New York: Doubleday, 1963)

Lahiri, Jhumpa, *The Namesake* (New York: Houghton Mifflin, 2003)

Lomnitz, Claudio, *Death and the Idea of Mexico* (New York: Zone Books, 2005)

Mackaman, Frank H., 'Promoting the Marigold as National Floral Emblem', The Dirksen Congressional Center, August 2011, www.direksencenterprojects.org

Myers, Helen, *Music of Hindu Trinidad: Songs from the Indian Diaspora* (Chicago: University of Chicago Press, 1998)

Robinson, William, *The English Flower Garden* (London: Bloomsbury, 1998)

Siegel, R.K., P.R. Collings and J.L. Díaz, 'On the Use of *Tagetes lucida* and *Nicotioana rustica* as a Huichol Smoking Mixture: The Aztec "Yauhtli" with Suggestive Hallucinogenic Effects', *Economic Botany* 31, no. 1 (1977), 16–23

'Still Searching', *Nevada Daily Mail*, 24 September, 1972

Taylor, Judith M., *Visions of Loveliness: Great Flower Breeders of the Past* (Athens: Swallow Press, 2014)

'A True Drama: The Effect of Alice Vonk on Pure White Marigolds', *People*, 15 September, 1975

Wyndham, John, *The Day of the Triffids* (London: Penguin, 2008)

Zindel, Paul, *The Effect of Gamma Rays on Man-in-the-Moon Marigolds* (New York: HarperTrophy, 2005)

POPPY

Ahmed, Sofia, 'No, I won't wear the "Poppy Hijab" to prove I'm not a Muslim extremist', *The Independent*, 4 November, 2015

Allen, Chris, 'The Poppy Hijab Is Just Islamophobia with a Floral Motif', *New Statesman*, 3 November, 2014

Baum, L. Frank, *The New Wizard of Oz*, with pictures by W.W. Denslow (Indianapolis: Bobs-Merrill Company, 1903)

Clare, John, 'May', in *The Shepherd's Calendar*, eds. Eric Robinson, Geoffrey Summerfield and David Powell (Oxford: Oxford University Press, 1964)

Conan Doyle, Arthur, 'The Man with the Twisted Lip' (1891), in *The Complete Sherlock Holmes* (Harmondsworth: Penguin, 1981)

Colette, 'Poppy', in *Flowers and Fruit*, trans. Matthew Ward and ed. Robert Phelps (London: Secker & Warburg, 1986)

Courtwright, Daniel T., *Dark Paradise: Opiate Addiction in America Before 1940*, enlarged ed. (Cambridge: Harvard University Press, 2001)

Crabbe, George, *The Village*, in *Tales, 1812 and Other Selected Poems*, ed. Howard Mills (Cambridge: Cambridge University Press, 1967)

Douglas, Alfred, 'Two Loves', *The Chameleon* 1, no. 1 (1894)

Homer, *The Iliad*, trans. Robert Fagles (London: Penguin, 1990)

Hopkins, Gerard Manley, 'The Woodlark', in *The Major Works* (Oxford: Oxford University Press, 1986)

Johnson, Heather Anne, *Madame Guérin*, poppyladymadameguerin.wordpress.com/

Lack, Andrew, *Poppy* (London: Reaktion, 2017)

Lawrence, D.H., 'Study of Thomas Hardy', in *Study of Thomas Hardy and Other Essays* (Cambridge: Cambridge University Press, 1985)

Longley, Michael, 'Poppies', in *The Ghost Orchid* (London: Jonathan Cape, 1995)

Mabey, Richard, *Weeds: The Story of Outlaw Plants* (London: Profile Books, 2010)

Ohnuki-Tierney, Emiko, *Kamikaze, Cherry Blossoms, and Nationalisms: The Militarization of Aesthetics in Japanese History* (Chicago: Chicago University Press, 2002)

Okakura, Kakuzō, *The Book of Tea* (London: Penguin, 2016)

Plath, Sylvia, 'Poppies in July', in *The Collected Poems*, ed. Ted Hughes (New York: HarperPerennial, 2008)

Ruskin, John, *Proserpina. A Study of Wayside Flowers*, vol. 1 (Orpington: George Allen, 1879)

Seward, Anna, 'Sonnet LXXI: To the Poppy', in *British Women Poets of the Romantic Era: An Anthology*, ed. Paula R. Feldman (Baltimore: Johns Hopkins University Press, 1997)

The Song of Roland and Other Poems of Charlemagne, trans. Simon Gaunt and Karen Pratt (Oxford: Oxford University Press, 2016)

'What is the U.S. Opioid Epidemic?', U.S. Department of Health and Human Services, www. hhs.gov/opiods/about-the-epidemic

Wolf, Eric, *Envisioning Power: Ideologies of Dominance and Crisis* (Berkeley: University of California Press, 1999)

WINTER

Addison, Joseph, *The Spectator* no. 477, 6 September, 1712, in *The Genius of the Place: The English Landscape Garden, 1620–1820*, eds. John Dixon Hunt and Peter Willis (Cambridge: MIT Press, 1988)

Bacon, Francis, 'Of Gardens', in *The Essays*, ed. John Pitcher (Harmondsworth: Penguin, 1985)

'Climate Change Indicators: Length of Growing Season', US Environmental Protection Agency, August 2016, www.epa.gov/climate-indicators

Cobbett, William, *The English Gardener* (Oxford: Oxford University Press, 1980)

Coleridge, Samuel Taylor, 'Frost at Midnight', in *The Complete Poems* (London: Penguin, 1997)

Kincaid, Jamaica, 'Winter' and 'Spring', in *My Garden (Book)* (London: Vintage, 2000)

Kingsley, Charles, 'My Winter Garden', in *Prose Idylls, New and Old* (London: Macmillan, 1873)

Martial, 'Garlands of Roses', in *Epigrams, with Parallel Latin Text*, trans. Gideon Nisbet (Oxford: Oxford University, 2015)

Sackville, Thomas, Earl of Dorset, 'Winter', in *The Four Seasons*, ed. J.D. McLatchy (London: Everyman, 2008)

Seneca, *Letters from a Stoic*, ed. and trans. Robin Campbell (Harmondsworth: Penguin, 1969)

Shakespeare, William, *Love's Labour's Lost* (1597), in *The Complete Works*, ed. Peter Alexander (London: Collins, 1951)

Shapiro, Karl, 'California Winter', in *Selected Poems*, ed. John Updike (New York: Library of America, 2003)

Sheldon, Ernie, 'Bring Me a Rose', on *Never Underestimate the Power of The Womenfolk* by The Womenfolk (RCA, 1964)

Shelley, Percy Bysshe, 'The Zucca', in *The Complete Poems* (New York: Modern Library, 1997)

Simcox, George Augustus, 'Hothouse Flowers', in *Poems and Romances* (London: Strahan and Co., 1869)

Spenser, Edmund, 'December', in *The Shepheardes Calender*, in *The Shorter Poems*, ed. Richard A. McCabe (London: Penguin, 1999)

Thompson, James, 'Winter. A Poem', in *The Seasons*, ed. James Sanbrooke (Oxford: Oxford University Press, 1981)

von Arnim, Elizabeth, *Elizabeth and Her German Garden* (London: Virago, 1985)

VIOLET

Atkinson, Diane, *Purple, White and Green: Suffragettes in London, 1906–1914* (London: Museum of London, 1992)

Barnard, Edward W., 'Winter Violets', *Puck*, 28 March, 1894

Cicero, *Tusculan Disputations*, trans. J.E. King (Cambridge: Harvard University Press, 1927)

Coombs, Roy E., *Violets: The History and Cultivation of Scented Violets* (London: Croom Helm, 1981)

Crawford, Elizabeth, 'Sussex Violets And "Votes For Women"', *Woman and Her Sphere*, 3 March, 2017, www.womanandhersphere.com/suffrage-stories

Eliot, T.S., *The Waste Land*, in *The Complete Poems and Plays of T.S. Eliot* (London: Faber, 1969)

The Flower Fields, BBC Radio 4 Extra, October 2012

Freud, Sigmund, 'The Question of Symbolism in the Dreams of Normal Persons' (1914), addition to chapter 6 of *The Interpretation of Dreams* (1900), trans. James Strachey (Harmondsworth: Penguin, 1976)

Hamilton, Cecily, *Life Errant* (London: Dent, 1935)

Hood, Thomas, 'The Plea of the Midsummer Fairies', in *The Plea of the Midsummer Fairies, and Other Poems* (London: Longman, Rees, Orme, Brown and Green, 1827)

Kastan, David Scott, *On Color* (London and New Haven: Yale University Press, 2018)

Lawrence, D.H., 'Do Women Change?', in *Late Essays and Articles*, ed. James T. Boulton (Cambridge: Cambridge University Press, 2004)

— *Lady Chatterley's Lover* (London: Penguin, 2006)

— *The Letters*, Volume 1, 1901–1913, ed. James T. Boulton (Cambridge: Cambridge University Press, 1979)

Maxwell, Catherine, *Scents and Sensibility: Perfume in Victorian Literary Culture* (Oxford: Oxford University Press, 2017)

Mee, Arthur, *Cornwall: England's Farthest South* (London: Hodder and Stoughton, 1937)

Miller, Patricia Cox, *The Corporeal Imagination: Signifying the Holy in Late Ancient Christianity* (Philadelphia: University of Pennsylvania Press, 2009)

Mitford, Mary Russell, *Our Village* (Harmondsworth: Penguin, 1987)

Nesbit, Edith, 'To His Daughter', in *Ballads and Lyrics of Socialism, 1883–1908* (London: Fabian Society, 1908)

— 'Winter Violets', in *Leaves of Life* (London: Longmans, Green, 1888)

Pankhurst, Christabel, 'The Political Importance of the Colours', *Votes for Women*, 7 May, 1909

Pankhurst, E. Sylvia, *The Suffragette: The History of the Women's Militant Suffrage Movement, 1905–1910* (London: Sturgis & Walton, 1911)

Sappho, *A New Translation of the Complete Works*, trans. Diane J. Rayor (Cambridge: Cambridge University Press, 2014)

Shakespeare, William, *Hamlet*, in *The Complete Works*, ed. Peter Alexander (London: Collins, 1951)

Sharp, William, *The Life and Letters of Joseph Severn* (London: Sampson, Low, Marston & Co., 1892)

Shaw, George Bernard, *Pygmalion* (London: Penguin, 2003)

'The Suffragette and the Dress Problem', *Votes for Women*, 30 July, 1908

Tarkington, Booth, *Alice Adams*, in *Novels and Stories* (New York: Library of America, 2019)

Toynbee, J.C., *Death and Burial in the Roman World* (Baltimore: Johns Hopkins University Press, 1996)

de Vilmorin, Henry L., *Flowers of the French Riviera* (London: Spottiswoode and Co., 1898)

'Where Dresses in the Colours Can Be Bought', *Votes for Women*, 23 April, 1909

Wilde, Oscar, *A Picture of Dorian Gray* (Oxford: Oxford University Press, 2006)

— *The Complete Letters*, eds. Merline Holland and Rupert Hart-Davis (London: Fourth Estate, 2000)

GERANIUM

Alcott, Louisa May, *Little Women* (Oxford: Oxford University Press, 2008)

Anonymous, *Jenny's Geranium; or, the Prize Flower of a London Court* (London: S.W. Partridge, 1869)

Aubrey, John, *Aubrey's Natural History of Wiltshire*, ed. John Britton (Newton Abbott: David and Charles, 1969)

Austen, Jane, *Mansfield Park* (Harmondsworth: Penguin, 1984)

Barnes, Charlotte S.M., 'The Dead Geranium', *The Churchman's Magazine* 8 (1845), p. 7

Blunt, William and William T. Stearn, *The Art of Botanical Illustration*, revised ed. (Woodbridge: Antique Collectors Club, 1994)

Boddy, Kasia, *Geranium* (London: Reaktion, 2013)

Chandler, Raymond, *The Big Sleep* (London: Penguin, 2005)

Cottesloe, Gloria, and Doris Hunt, *The Duchess of Beaufort's Flowers* (Exeter: Webb and Bower, 1983)

Cowper, William, *The Task* (London: James Nisbet, 1855)

Darwin, Erasmus, 'The Loves of the Plants', the second part of *The Botanic Garden: A Poem, in Two Parts* (London: J. Johnson, 1791)

Elliot, Brent, *Victorian Gardens* (Portland: Timber Press, 1986)

Ellmann, Richard, *Oscar Wilde* (New York: Vintage, 1988)

George, Samantha, *Botany, Sexuality and Women's Writing, 1760–1830* (Manchester: Manchester University Press, 2007)

Harvey, John, *Early Gardening Catalogues* (London: Phillimore, 1972)

Hunt, Leigh, 'A Flower for Your Window', in *Selected Essays* (London: Dent, 1947)

Jefferson, Thomas, *Thomas Jefferson's Garden Book, 1776–1824*, ed. Edwin Morris Betts (Philadelphia: American Philosophic Society, 1944)

Morris, William, 'Making the Best of It', in *Hopes and Fears for Art* (Bristol: Thoemmes Press, 1994)

Parkes, Revd Samuel Hadden, *Window Gardens for the People, and Clean and Tidy Rooms; Being an Experiment to Improve the Lives of the London Poor* (London: S.W. Partridge, 1864)

Polwhele, Richard, *The Unsex'd Females* (1798), in *Revolutions in Romantic Literature: An Anthology of Print Culture, 1780–1832*, ed. Paul Keen (Toronto: Broadview Press, 2004)

Rabelais, Robert, *A Nineteenth Century, and Familiar History of the Lives, Loves, and Misfortunes of Abeillard and Heloisa* (London: Bumpus, 1819)

Repton, Humphry, *The Landscape Gardening and Landscape Architecture of the Late Humphry Repton*, ed. J.C. Loudon (London: Longman, 1840)

Rousseau, Jean-Jacques, *Reveries of the Solitary Walker*, trans. Russell Goulbourne (Oxford: Oxford University Press, 2011)

Saunders, Gill, *Picturing Plants* (Berkeley: University of California Press, 1995)

Slaughter, Thomas P., *The Natures of John and William Bartram* (New York: Knopf, 1996)

Smith, Charlotte, 'To a geranium which flowered during the winter' and 'To the goddess of botany', in *The Poems*, ed. Stuart Curran (Oxford: Oxford University Press, 1993)

Smith, Margaret Bayard, *The First Forty Years of Washington Society* (New York: Scribner's, 1906)

Watson, Forbes, *Flowers and Gardens* (London: Strahan and Co., 1872)

Webb, William J., *The Pelargonium Family* (London: Croom Helm, 1984)

Woods, Mary and Arete Swartz Warren, *Glass Houses: A History of Greenhouses, Orangeries, and Conservatories* (New York: Rizzoli, 1988)

SNOWDROP

Bartley, Paula, *Prostitution: Prevention and Reform, 1860–1914* (London: Routledge, 2000)

Čapek, Karel, *The Gardener's Year*, trans. M. and R. Weatherall (London: George Allen & Unwin, 1931)

Colette, 'Snowdrop', in *Flowers and Fruit*, trans. Matthew Ward and ed. Robert Phelps (London: Secker & Warburg, 1986)

Crane, Walter, *Flora's Feast: A Masque of Flowers* (London: Cassell, 1889)

Daniels, Cora Linn Morrison and Charles McClellan Stevens, *Encyclopaedia of Superstitions, Folklore, and the Occult Science of the World*, vol. 2 (Milwaukee: J.H. Yewdale, 1903)

De la Mare, Walter, 'A Snowdrop', in *A Snowdrop* (London: Faber, 1929)

'The Discontented Snowdrop: A Lesson for Grumbling Boys and Girls', *Juvenile Instructor and Companion*, May 1871, 123–25

Dunbar, Paul Laurence, 'The Paradox', in *The Collected Poetry*, ed. Joanne M. Braxton (Charlottesville: University of Virginia Press, 1993)

Eliot, George, *Adam Bede* (London: Penguin, 1985)

Ewan, Stanley and Arpad Pusztai, 'Effects of Diets Containing Genetically Modified Potatoes Expressing *Galanthus nivalis* Lectin on Rat Small Intestine', *Lancet* 354, 16 October, 1999, 1353–4

Farrer, Reginald, *In a Yorkshire Garden* (London: Edward Arnold, 1909)

Harland, Gail, *Snowdrop* (London: Reaktion, 2016)

Heaney, Seamus, 'Mid-Term Break', in *Opened Ground: Selected Poems 1966–1996* (New York: Farrar, Straus and Giroux, 1998)

Heinrich, Michael and H. Lee Toah, 'Galanthamine from snowdrop – The development of a modern drug against Alzheimer's disease from local Caucasian knowledge', *Journal of Ethnopharmacology* 92, nos. 2/3 (2004), 147–62

Hughes, Ted, 'Snowdrop', in *Lupercal* (London: Faber, 1960)

Latham, Charlotte, 'Some West Sussex Superstitions Lingering in 1868', *The Folk-Lore Record* 1 (1878), 1–67

Mabey, Richard, *Flora Brittanica* (London: Sinclair-Stevenson, 1996)

Miller, A.D., *Snowdrops* (London: Atlantic Books, 2010)

Muire, Edward, *Ritual in Early Modern Europe* (Cambridge: Cambridge University Press, 2005)

Nesbit, Edith, 'The Champion', in *Many Voices* (London: Hutchinson, 1922)

Plaitakis, Andreas and Roger Duvoisin, 'Homer's Moly Identified as *Galanthus nivalis* L.: Physiologic Antidote to Stramonium Poisoning', *Clinical Neuropharmacology* 6, no. 1 (1983), 1–5

'Prophetic Days', *Chambers's Journal*, 11 October, 1873, 655–56

Randerson, James, 'Arpad Pusztai: Biological Divide', *The Guardian*, 15 January, 2008

The Snow Drop (Philadelphia: American Sunday School Union, 1909)

'The Snowdrop', in *The Juvenile Miscellany of Facts and Fiction*, volume 1 (London: Houlston & Stoneman, 1844)

The Snowdrop, or Life from the Dead (London: S.W. Partridge, n.d.)

Stewart, Maria, 'Religion and the Pure Principles of Morality', in *Words of Fire: An Anthology of African-American Feminist Thought*, ed. Beverley Guy-Sheftall (New Press: New York, 1995)

'Volunteer Castaways: U.S. Airmen, Based in Britain, on a Survival Test', *Illustrated London News*, 12 May, 1956

Wordsworth, William, 'To a Snowdrop', in *The Major Works*, ed. Stephen Gill (Oxford: Oxford University Press, 2000)

Yemm, Helen, 'Why We All Love Snowdrops So Much', *The Telegraph*, 10 February, 2016

ALMOND

'Almond-Blossom', *All the Year Round*, 3 April, 1886

Arnold, Edwin, 'Almond Blossom', in *Griselda: A Tragedy and Other Poems* (London: David Bogue, 1855)

[Casey, George C. E.], *Riviera Nature Notes* (Manchester: Labour Press, 1898)

Darwish, Mahmoud, 'To Describe an Almond Blossom', in *Almond Blossoms and Beyond*, trans. Mohammad Shaheen (Northampton: Interlink Books, 2009)

Edwards, Thornton B., 'The Sugared Almond Modern Greek Rites of Passage', *Folklore* 107 (1996), 49–56

García Marquéz, Gabriel, *Love in the Time of Cholera*, trans. Edith Grossman (London: Penguin, 1989)

'The Grosvenor Gallery', *The Times*, 8 May, 1882

Hamblin, James, 'The Dark Side of Almond Use', *The Atlantic*, 28 August, 2014

Hanbury, Thomas, 'Plants on the Riviera', *Gardeners' Chronicle*, 20 February, 1886

James, Henry, 'London Pictures, 1882', in *The Painter's Eye: Notes and Essays on the Pictorial Arts*, ed. John L. Sweeney (Madison: University of Wisconsin Press, 1989)

Lawrence, D.H., 'Flowery Tuscany', in *Sketches of Etruscan Places and Other Essays*, ed. Simonetta De Fillipis (Cambridge: Cambridge University Press, 1992)

— 'Letter from Town: The Almond Tree', 'Almond Blossom', 'Bare Almond-Trees', and 'Sicilian Cyclamens', in *Complete Poems* (Harmondsworth: Penguin, 1994)

— 'Sun', in *The Woman Who Rode Away and Other Stories* (London: Penguin, 1997)

— *Women in Love* (Cambridge: Cambridge University Press, 1987)

Lerner, Irving J., 'Laetrile: A Lesson in Cancer Quackery', *CA – A Cancer Journal for Clinicians* 31, no. 2 (1981), 91–5

Muir, John, *The Mountains of California* (London: Penguin, 2008)

Pliny the Elder, *Natural History*, Volume 4: Books 12–16, trans. H. Rackham (Cambridge: Harvard University Press, 1945)

Reichman, Edward and Fred Rosner, 'The Bone Called Luz', *Journal of the History of Medicine and Allied Sciences* 51 (1996), 52–61

Sánchez-Perez, Raquel, Jorge Del Cueto, et al., 'Recent Advancements to Study Flowering Time in Almond and Other Prunus Species', *Frontiers in Plant Science* 5, no. 334 (2014) online

Sewell, Philip, 'Winter-Flowering Plants at La Mortola', *Gardeners' Chronicle*, 15 March, 1890

'Sir Thomas Hanbury', *The Times*, 12 March, 1907

Traynor, Joe, 'A History of Almond Pollination in California', *Bee World* 94, no. 3 (2017), 69–79

van Gogh, Vincent, *The Letters*, eds. Leo Jansen, Hans Luijten and Nienke Bakker, vangoghletters.org

Weinberg, H. Barbara, *American Impressionism and Realism* (New York: Metropolitan Museum of Art, 2009)

Willcox, George, Sandra Fornite and Linda Herveux, 'Early Holocene Cultivation before Domestication in Northern Syria', *Vegetation History and Archeobotany* 17, no. 3 (2008), 313–25

Illustration Credits

'Woman in a wide dress, garland in her hands', *c.* 1910–20, hand-coloured watercolour on paper, 295 x 249 mm. Rijksmuseum, Amsterdam. — p. xi

Jacques-Laurent Agasse, *Studies of Flowers*, 1848, oil on canvas. 489 x 833 mm. Yale Center for British Art, Paul Mellon Collection. — p. xiii

Hendrick Goltzius, *A Young Man with Flowers in His Hand*, 1582, engraving on paper, 258 x 138 mm. Rijksmuseum, Amsterdam. — p. xiii

Anya Gallaccio, *Red on Green*, 2012, 10, 000 red roses laid in a field upon the gallery floor, dimensions variable. © Anya Gallaccio. All rights reserved, DACS/Artimage 2019. — p. xiv

Guy Spencer, cartoon featuring John D. Rockefeller Jr and an American Rose, *The Commoner*, April 21, 1905, p. 1. — p. xix

Eyebright and a human eye illustrating the 'doctrine of signatures', coloured ink drawing, *c.* 1923, after a woodcut by Giambattista della Porta in *Phytognomonica*, 1588. CC BY, Wellcome Collection. — p. 8

Photograph of the Daisy Chain at Vassar College, 1910. Author's collection. — p. 10

Cover of the first US edition of Mary McCarthy *The Group*, New York: Harcourt, Brace, 1963. Author's collection. — p. 11

Still from 'Peace, Little Girl', also known as 'Daisy Girl', advertisement for Lyndon B. Johnson's 1964 Presidential Campaign. Lyndon B. Johnson Library, University of Texas, Austin. — p. 12

Gari Melchers, *Red Hussar, c.* 1912–15, oil on canvas, 120.6 x 100.9 cm. Gari Melchers Home and Studio, University of Mary Washington. — p. 14

Cover of promotional booklet for *En effeuillant la marguerite*, movie dir. Marc Allégret, 1956. Author's collection. — p. 16

Photograph of an ornamental tray. Royal Falcon Ware, J.H. Weatherby & Sons, Hanley, Staffordshire. Author's collection. — p. 21

Shaikh Zada, detail of 'Bahram Gur in the White Palace on Friday', p. 23
Folio 235 from a *Khamsa (Quintet)* of the poet Nizami, 1524–25, Herat
in present-day Afghanistan. Metropolitan Museum of Art, New York.

Zhao Mengjian, detail of handscroll, ink on paper, China, mid-thirteenth- p. 23
century, handroll image 33.2 x 374 cm; overall with mounting
34.1 x 993.6 cm. Metropolitan Museum of Art, New York.

Early twentieth-century Easter card. Author's collection. p. 30

Early twentieth-century Easter card. Author's collection. p. 31

Charles Walter Stetson, *An Easter Offering*, 1896, oil on canvas, p. 32
101.9cm x 127.6cm. Spencer Museum of Art, University of Kansas.
Museum purchase 1982.0051.

Diego Rivera, *The Flower Seller (Girl with Lilies)*, 1941, oil on p. 33
Masonite, 121.9 x 121.9 cm. Norton Simon Museum, Gift of Mr Cary
Grant. © Banco de México Diego Rivera Frida Kahlo Museums Trust,
México, D.F./ DACS 2019.

Georgia O'Keeffe, *Yellow Calla,* 1926, oil on fibreboard, 22.9 x 32.4 cm. p. 34
Smithsonian American Art Museum, Washington DC.

Keith Ruffles, photograph of a mural featuring a lily pin, Béal Feirste, p. 36
Belfast, 2010.

Jan Davidsz. de Heem, *Cartouche with a Portrait of Prince William III* p. 37
of Orange, mid-1660s, oil on canvas, 132 x 108 cm. Musée des
Beaux-Arts, Lyon.

Alexander Marshal, *Florilegium*, L. CV. Royal Collection Trust / © Her p. 40
Majesty Queen Elizabeth II 2019 (RCIN 924390).

Arno Mohr, poster for the Socialist Unity Party of Germany, advertising p. 47
May Day, 1946. Author's collection.

A Soviet postcard from the 1980s. Author's collection. p. 48

25 Abril 1974, poster based on a lithograph by Sergio Guimarães, p. 49
Portugal, 1974. Author's collection.

Mother's Day Card, 1914. Author's collection. p. 52

Miniature of the lover tending the rose, from *Le Roman de la Rose*, p. 60
Harley ms 4425, f. 284 v, Bruges, *c.* 1490–1500, British Library.

Two lovers, or a man with a courtesan, holding roses within an oval frame, p. 62
watercolour drawing, Kalighat, no date. CC BY, Wellcome Collection.

Illustration of woman in utero, from Jane Sharp, *The Midwives Book: or* p. 63
the Whole Art of Midwifery Discovered, 1671. CC BY, Wellcome Collection.

'Sah ein Knab' . . . mach's Mit'. Bundeszentrale für gesundheitliche p. 66
Aufklärung, Cologne, 1990s, lithograph printed in colour, after Marcel
Kolvenbach and Guido Meyer, 59.5 x 42 cm. CC BY, Wellcome Collection.

Jean Cocteau, poster of Vaslav Nijinsky in *Le Spectre de la Rose* for the Ballets   p. 69
Russes, 1913, colour lithograph, printing ink on paper, 189 x 129 cm.
© ADAGP/DACS/Comité Cocteau, Paris 2019/Victoria & Albert
Museum, London.

Screenshot from *Un Chant d'Amour* dir. Jean Genet, 1950.   p. 70

Adam Eastland, photograph of Roman mosaic featuring Nile river scene,   p. 72
from the House of the Faun, Pompeii, 120 BCE, Archaeological Museum,
Naples, photograph 2016. Alamy Stock Photo.

Lotus inlay, Faience, Egypt, New Kingdom, Amarna, 1353–1336 BCE,   p. 73
3.7 x 4.4 x 0.6 cm. Metropolitan Museum of Art, New York.

Vishnu and Lakshmi seated on a Lotus Blossom, early 1800s, Himachal   p. 76
Pradesh, Pahari, Northern India, gum tempera and gold on paper,
13.3 x 9 cm. Cleveland Museum of Art, Cleveland.

A Buddhist monk holding a lotus, wall painting (pigments on mud plaster),   p. 77
Kizil cliffs, China, sixth to seventh century, 81.3 x 37.5 cm. Metropolitan
Museum of Art, New York.

A 'Pond Lily' leaded glass and bronze table lamp, Tiffany Studios,   p. 80
New York, early twentieth century, 67.3cm high, shade diameter 45.7cm.
© Christie's Images, London/Scala, Florence.

Watercolour of *Gossypium hirsutum* from the William Roxburgh collection,   p. 84
no. 1497, Royal Botanical Gardens, Kew.

The Vegetable Lamb of Tartary, woodcut from the 1725 edition of   p. 87
The Voiage and Travaile of John Mandeville, Knight. Granger Historical
Picture Archive/Alamy Stock Photo.

Lamar Baker, *The Slave Plant*, lithograph on paper, 1939, 28.3 x 40.6 cm.   p. 89
Smithsonian American Art Museum, Washington DC.

Carol Highsmith, photograph of the boll weevil monument, Enterprise,   p. 92
Alabama, 2010. The George F. Landegger Collection of Alabama Photographs
in Carol M. Highsmith's America, Library of Congress, Prints and
Photographs Division.

Photograph of Mahatma Gandhi spinning cotton on a charkha, late 1940s.   p. 93

Vincent van Gogh, *Sunflowers*, 1887, oil on canvas, 43.2 x 61 cm.   p. 96
Metropolitan Museum of Art, New York.

Paul Gauguin, *The Painter of Sunflowers (Portrait of Vincent van Gogh)*, 1888,   p. 97
oil on canvas, 73 x 91 cm. Van Gogh Museum, Amsterdam (Vincent van
Gogh Foundation).

Roland Holst, lithograph on cover of *Tentoonstelling der nagelaten werken*   p. 98
van Vincent van Gogh, a catalogue for an exhibition of Vincent van Gogh's
work, 1892, 18.2 x 21 cm. Museum of Fine Arts, Boston.

Poster for Die Grünen, the German Green Party, *c.* 1980, 85 x 59.5 cm.   p. 100
International Institute of Social History, Amsterdam.

Illustration Credits

W.W. Denslow, illustration for L. Frank Baum's *The Wonderful Wizard of Oz*, New York, 1900. Author's collection.   p. 157

Cover of a Muse lingerie box, Atlanta, Georgia, early twentieth century. Author's Collection.   p. 166

Jean Dominique Étienne Canu, 'Violettes du 20 Mars 1815', hand-coloured etching on paper, 141 x 90 mm. British Museum, London.   p. 167

Postcard of violet-picking on the Côte d'Azur. Author's Collection.   p. 168

Postcard featuring the music hall star Marie Studholme as flower seller 'Sweet Violets'. Author's collection.   p. 171

John William Godward, *Violets, Sweet Violets*, 1906, oil on canvas, 92 cm diameter. Private Collection.   p. 175

'December', engraving by Henry Fletcher after the painting by Pieter Casteels, from Robert Furber, *The Twelve Months of Flowers*, London, 1730.   p. 178

'Forcing Garden in Winter', coloured lithograph from Humphry Repton, *Fragments on the Theory and Practice of Landscape Gardening*, London, 1816.   p. 181

Ralph Hedley, *Blinking in the Sun*, 1881, oil on canvas, 53 x 42.9 cm. Laing Art Gallery, Newcastle upon Tyne.   p. 184

Photograph of Geraniums in front of the Lenin Memorial Museum at the Smolny Institute, St Petersburg. © Edifice/The Bridgeman Art Library.   p. 186

Mario Bogoni, poster for Ente Nazionale Italiano per il Turismo, 1915. Author's collection.   p. 186

Walter Crane, 'Snowdrops', from *Flora's Feast: A Masque of Flowers*, London: Cassell, 1889. Almay Stock Photo.   p. 189

Illustration from *The Snowdrop, or Life from the Dead*, London, 1876. Author's Collection.   p. 191

Everard Kick (Kickius), *Datura stramonium* at the centre, with *Galanthus nivalis* 'Flore Pleno' on the left and *Saxifraga paniculata* syn. *Aizoon* on the right. Duchess of Beaufort Florilegium, 1703–5.   p. 197

John Russell, *Armandiers et ruines, Sicilie (Almond Trees and Ruins, Sicily)*, 1887, oil on canvas, 64.5 x 81.2 cm. Queensland Art Gallery. Purchased 1989 from the estate of Lady Trout with a special allocation from the Queensland Government.   p. 199

Vincent van Gogh, *Sprig of Flowering Almond in a Glass*, 1888, oil on canvas, 24.5 x 19.5 cm. Van Gogh Museum, Amsterdam.   p. 201

Edward Burne-Jones, *The Tree of Forgiveness*, 1882, oil on canvas, 90.5 x 106.7 cm. National Museums Liverpool.   p. 204

Acknowledgements

I'd like to thank everyone at Yale University Press who worked hard to make this book: Lucy Buchan, Philip Dyson, Percie Edgeler, Chloe Foster, Eve Leckey, Clarissa Sutherland, and many others. I'm particularly grateful to Heather McCallum for suggesting I write the book. Her sage advice, and that of Marika Lysandrou and the press's anonymous readers, made a big difference to the final outcome.

Many thanks also to the museum, gallery and picture library staff who supplied many of the images for this book, and to the Faculty of English at the University of Cambridge for helping with the costs. I'd also like to thank John David and Jonathan Gregson at the Royal Horticultural Society, who gave me the latest on the Tenby Daffodil's taxonomy.

Closer to home, I've been lucky to be able to talk about flowers with many people. Particular thanks to: Ali Smith, who was full of wonderful suggestions; Silvia Frenk Elsner, who cast a Mexican eye over the marigold; Heather Glen, who lent books and moral support; Janet Boddy, who sent wonderful photographs of India that I sadly couldn't use; and Ada Boddy, who supplied me with Russian translations and perfume, and who sang 'Czerwone maki na Monte Cassino'.

My warmest appreciation goes to my close readers: to Jane Ezersky, for endless encouragement and indispensable transatlantic edits, and to David Trotter, for every reason going.

You all deserve an enormous bouquet.

Index

Principal coverage of a topic is entered in **bold**. Locations for illustrations are entered in *italics*.